D1235062

ARE CHARTERS DIFFERENT?

PUBLIC EDUCATION, TEACHERS, AND THE CHARTER SCHOOL DEBATE

Zachary W. Oberfield

Harvard Education Press

Cambridge, Massachusetts

EDUCATION POLITICS AND POLICY SERIES

Paperback ISBN 978-1-61250-067-2
Library Edition ISBN 978-1-61250-070-2

Library of Congress Cataloging-in-Publication Data
Names: Oberfield, Zachary W., author.
Title: Are charters different? : public education, teachers, and the charter
    school debate / Zachary W. Oberfield.
Description: Cambridge, Massachusetts : Harvard Education Press, [2017] |
    Includes bibliographical references and index.
Identifiers: LCCN 2017013578| ISBN 9781682530672 (pbk.) |
    ISBN 9781682530702 (library edition)
Subjects: LCSH: Charter schools—United States. | Public schools—United
    States. | Teacher participation in administration—United States. |
    Teachers—Job satisfaction—United States. | School management and
    organization--United States. | Educational leadership—United States. |
    Education—Parent participation—United States.
Classification: LCC LB2806.36 .O24 2017 | DDC 371.01—dc23
    LC record available at https://lccn.loc.gov/2017013578

Published by Harvard Education Press,
an imprint of the Harvard Education Publishing Group

Harvard Education Press
8 Story Street
Cambridge, MA 02138

Cover Design: Wilcox Design
Cover Illustration: GraphicStock

The typefaces used in this book are Scientia and Avenir.

For Felicia, Theo, and Charlie,
whom I dearly love

CONTENTS

FOREWORD

EDUCATION POLICY used to be a relatively placid arena, but that's no longer the case. The belief that American schools are among the best in the world was severely shaken by the 1983 publication *A Nation at Risk*, and since then, gnawing frustration with mediocre and unequal educational outcomes has led many to conclude that the fundamental organization of public education needs to be reshaped. As discussion shifted from the personal ("Is my Johnny's teacher the best our school has to offer?") to the systemic ("Should we shift control of education away from locally elected school boards?"), the stakes were raised. With these higher stakes, policy debates have become sharper, more partisan, and more ideologically infused.

This new tone in policy debates has very much influenced discussions of charter schools As originally conceived, charter schools were a way to incrementally improve traditional school systems; charters would nudge urban school districts to become less rigid and less directive in their dealings with the schools they oversaw. But early on, the impetus was adopted—some would say co-opted—by those favoring a more radical shift toward market-based solutions in which competition for students among private schools, charter schools, and traditional public schools would generate the pressure to improve education. This framing of the issue around the relative merit of market-based versus government-based solutions drew the charter school issue into the vortex of larger and ongoing debates between liberals and conservatives.

Inevitably, the community of research has been affected. Elsewhere, I've written about how various interests try to spin research to convince policy makers and the public that consumer-oriented charter schools are demonstrably better than (or a demonstrable threat to) traditional systems accountable to democratic institutions and the bureaucracies they create.[1] Done well, research provides an independent and ultimately self-correcting source of information that can help citizens and policy makers navigate tough decisions. But if research comes to be seen as nothing more than another tool for building political power, there's a risk that it will lose credibility and that increasingly cynical audiences will discount its claim to objectivity.

Beneath the noise and heat of political maneuvering, however, the core enterprise of research often plugs along just as we'd wish it to, gradually improving measurements of important phenomena, probing and replicating studies to see if findings hold up in different settings, over time, and with different methodological approaches. Charter school research has seen this steady, gradual improvement as well. Compared with the decades immediately following the birth of charters, we now have better data, guiding concepts that are more commonly defined, research designs that are more sophisticated, and more confidence about what we know and do not know.[2] Better research does not mean that debates about charters, markets, and democracy have been resolved by any measure. But good data can help us distinguish evidence-based claims from assertions of values and power and thus can lead to more nuanced and sophisticated, if not necessarily less contentious, public discourse.

Are Charters Different? Public Education, Teachers, and the Debate over Charter Schools makes a genuine contribution to the emerging body of illuminating research. It's the first volume in the Education Politics and Policy series, which I will be editing for Harvard Education Press. Books in the series will differ in their substantive focus, their methodological bent, and the implications of their claims. But all of them, we hope, will share with this one an earnest effort to wrestle with important questions and favor honest analysis and interpretation over political bombast.

Several attributes account for this book's value. First, its grounding in the concept of *publicness* as a continuum immediately challenges the common but simplistic tendency to pose government and markets as either-or alternatives. Both scholars and ideologues, for different reasons, find it useful to distill what is distinct about each sector's actors, norms, and behaviors. Scholars do it because elucidating ideal types can help them focus on core attributes and their implications; ideologues because simplification makes their appeals more stirring.

In practice, though, all our collective endeavors represent mixtures of public and private incentives and behaviors. Even a classical market transaction like purchasing groceries at a market is circumscribed by government laws and regulations related to food quality, transport, and labeling and to worker hours and benefits. Similarly, a classical governmental activity like law enforcement is affected by how potential criminals calculate risks and opportunities, whether victims and witnesses decide to report crimes and testify, the costs of building and operating a prison system, and the competitive labor market for hiring police.

Framing publicness as a continuum highlights the central differences between traditional public schools, charters, and vouchers but also acknowledges important differences in how each of these sectors responds to both market and government forces. For example, there are traditional schools districts that expand parent choice and school-level decision making; charter schools that operate in a well-regulated environment and are held accountable by public authorities; and voucher schemes that are designed by legislators to promote equity and diversity.

A second strength of the book is its use of multiple datasets. Every survey that has strengths also has limits. Surveys with national coverage often lack the precision to provide state-specific estimates. Surveys that compile extensive data about respondents' backgrounds often lack information about the institutions in which the participants operate or their attitudes and actions in specific areas of interest. Zachary Oberfield brings to bear three separate surveys offering different geographic coverage, a different balance of questions, and various periods. With these multiple datasets, he can distinguish general, national patterns from narrower ones, which may be particular to the policy and educational markets in particular places, and can provide contemporary information that is so important in the context of rapid change.

A third contribution of the book is the attention to changes over time. In their rush to decide whether this or that policy initiative is workings as promised, both scholars and policy makers typically fail to take seriously the maturation of policy regimes. By *policy regime*, I mean the full array of institutions, expectations, political interests, and framing ideologies that determine the capacity and commitment with which the policy is imbued. The maturation of a policy regime refers to how policies develop over time, whether the development is positive (e.g., marked by growing knowledge and capacity) or negative (e.g., marked by waning enthusiasm or growing routinization and rigidity).

Both the charter and the traditional public school sectors have changed substantially over the past twenty-five years. A charter sector that initially comprised small, locally based, stand-alone charters has matured into one marked increasingly by large networks operating multiple schools, in multiple cities, and often in multiple states. A traditional sector dominated by the model of neighborhood-based schools and assigned attendance zones has increasingly adopted various forms of public school choice, allowing and sometimes forcing parents to shop around for the school that they believe best fits their children's needs. Both charter and traditional public school sectors have experienced intense No Child Left Behind pressure to improve student outcomes. Schools within both sectors have responded with an array of curriculum, teaching, and accountability strategies that have altered—perhaps differentially—what it means to be a teacher. Only a longitudinal perspective, such as the one that Professor Oberfield develops here, has a chance to capture such dynamics and begin to unearth their implications.

Precisely because the charter sector has been changing, the book's attention to intrasector differences—between stand-alone and networked charters, between the for-profit and nonprofit operators—constitutes a fourth valuable attribute. Almost from its beginning, the charter school movement has been animated by two contrasting visions. One was a vision of small, nonprofit, community-based providers injecting variety into an overly homogenous and bureaucratic system. The other was a vision of customer-pursuing businesses responding to demand by honing products and reducing costs in a competitive environment that would reward success with expansion and growth. Today's charter world includes both types of providers and is sustained by supporters loyal to both visions. The sector might be stronger and better by virtue of this internal diversity, but such diversity might also hide the fact that one model performs better than the other or that the competing visions are ultimately inconsistent. By considering differences in the teaching climate in both independent charters and franchised ones, and in both for-profit and nonprofit schools, *Are Charters Different?* offers a more thorough analysis of the ultimate benefits of various school approaches.

A final benefit of the book has to do with Professor Oberfield's modesty in making claims. In the higher-profile and higher-stakes environment that now characterizes education policy debates, there are seductive pressures to make overly confident assertions. The media, advocacy groups, and policy makers often signal that they have little tolerance for scholars who recommend further research. These critics paint the need-more-research stance as a timid one that lacks usefulness to those who have to make real and hard decisions and who cannot sit on their hands until all the facts are in. I understand their impatience but am inclined to throw the charge of timidity back at the critics. In asking researchers to stoke their assertions of certainty and to draw overly bold policy implications, the media, advocacy groups, and politicians are often looking for cover. They want to sidestep or deflect the pressure on them to do what their positions demand: to be discerning and to make tough decisions even though information is always incomplete, causal inferences always tentative, and consequences never ensured.

The strengths of a book, of course, largely reflect the author's own strengths. Zach Oberfield is thoughtful and deliberate, a modest scholar himself who wrestles with the evidence and presents it to readers fairly and clearly, despite the winds of political controversy that still rage around the charter school issue.

Are Charters Different? is not the last word in the long debate over charter schools. The debate, fueled by much more than the need for better information, will keep burning for quite some time even as better information is brought to bear. Nevertheless, we must still strive to sharpen our understanding of not only charter schools per se but also the broader nature of government, markets, and the public-private mash-ups that increasingly characterize the policy terrain. It's no easy task, but this book confirms that we are making progress.

Jeffrey R. Henig
Professor of Political Science and
Education at Teachers College,
Columbia University

PREFACE

PEOPLE HAVE STRONG OPINIONS about charter schools. Some see them as our best chance to shake up a failing public education system; for them, criticism of charters is retrograde and a sign of support for the status quo. To others, charter schools drain crucial resources from public schools—in the form of money, students, and attention—and are unaccountable to the public. In a way, these divergent viewpoints make sense: our politics are as divided as ever. Also, media accounts of charter schools—which tend to focus on attention-grabbing examples—suggest a bimodal distribution, consisting of remarkably successful and troubled schools.

As I studied this topic, I became more and more confused about these conflicting viewpoints: the research base is filled with mixed findings about what is happening inside these schools and what effects, if any, they're having on students. If the results from studies that compare charter and public schools are mixed, how could proponents and opponents of charter schools be so sure of their positions? A second reason for confusion came from my assessment of what we know and don't know about how charter schools are operating. A variety of studies have looked deeply inside various charter and public schools to understand how they function; these accounts offer amazing detail. However, charter schools are a famously diverse group, and because the sector has changed considerably over the years, it's hard to say whether such studies can be used to make general claims about differences and similarities between public and charter schools.

As a result, this book aims to provide a different perspective. By putting teachers center stage and looking over a sustained period, the book asks whether charter and public schools are cultivating different teaching climates. In other words, if we look at what teachers are doing and experiencing, do we see evidence that charter schools represent a new approach to public education? To answer this question, the book examines hundreds of thousands of teacher surveys—collected at different times over the past fifteen years—from all fifty states. But before getting too deep into how, who, and what this book examines, readers should know about my "priors." If most people have strong opinions about charter schools, what were my opinions as I began my research?

I was born into a left-leaning family of educators: my mother, brother, aunt, grandmother, and cousins all teach or taught at one time. It's part of our family heritage. Although some of us teach in private schools, it's a group that's strongly committed to public education. There's also a general support for teachers unions, and my aunt was the president of her local chapter of the National Education Association. In one of my earlier memories, she is preparing to lead the teachers in her district out on a strike and preparing to face time in prison as a result. I remember feeling scared but also proud that she was fighting a worthy battle.

Another set of early memories: long, weighty breakfast conversations among the adults about the difficult realities of urban public schools, poverty, and racial injustice. While I attended a public high school in a relatively privileged white area—with little serious crime and a tradition of graduation and college enrollment—the public schools in a nearby majority-minority district were the opposite in every way: these schools were known for having high levels of violence, high dropout rates, and low student achievement. At that time, poor families had few options if they didn't want to send their children to the district's public schools. To say the least, this seemed unfair.

However, today there are a handful of charter schools in this troubled district, offering parents and students options if they cannot move or find the money for a private school. It's hard for me not to feel good about that.

All of this is to say that if I have a bias, it's probably toward traditional public education. However, I'm open to reforms that might make the lives of public school students—especially students of color in poor neighborhoods—better. Whatever my feelings on the matter, I have tried to put my biases aside and conduct this analysis as neutrally as possible. In other words, I let the data steer my conclusions.

One other question may be on readers' minds at this point: why did a political scientist write a book about schools? Although I am trained as a political scientist and teach in a (terrific) political science department, I'm a student of bureaucracy and public policy. A few years ago, I wrote *Becoming Bureaucrats: Socialization at the Front Lines of Government Service,* a book that tried to understand how police officers and welfare caseworkers developed over the first two years on the job. Essentially, I wanted to know more about how government organizations (in this case, municipal agencies) shaped incoming street-level bureaucrats: to what extent did institutional characteristics affect how newcomers did their work and, in the end, how policy was made? This book asks a similar question but from a different angle. The central premise of the charter school experiment—as well as the broader privatization movement—is that an organization's publicness, that is, the extent to which it is publicly controlled, funded, and owned, strongly influences how it operates. If we accept that street-level bureaucrats make the decisions that determine how organizations function, for publicness to matter it would need to shape the experiences and behavior of these operative employees. This book seeks to determine whether it does.

Finally, readers should understand what this book can and can't do. It looks deeply into a specific question: do public and charter schools foster different teaching climates? But it cannot speak to many other aspects of the charter school debate, including concerns about how charter schools are affecting public school students and allegations about financial improprieties in charter school accounting. Consequently, the book doesn't aim to be the last word in what has been a contentious twenty-five-year debate. Rather, by looking across time and studying schools and teachers in all fifty states, it sets a more modest goal: moving one part of the debate forward. With incremental steps like this, I hope we can develop a more accurate understanding of what the charter experiment means for the future of US public education.

ONE

Teaching Climates
and Publicness

FOR MANY YEARS, advocates have argued that charter schools provide different learning opportunities for students, at least in part, by changing the status and work of teachers.[1] Ember Reichgott Junge, the Minnesota state legislator who wrote the first state charter law, noted: "For me, chartering was all about empowering teachers—giving them the authority to take leadership as professionals by spearheading and forming new chartered schools."[2] Similarly, Joe Nathan, an early supporter of charter schools, placed teachers at the heart of the case for charter schools:

> This country's public schools employ many talented, committed educators. Unfortunately, these excellent teachers are often frustrated by a system that does not value their skills. They are disappointed by an administrative bureaucracy that sometimes stifles their creativity and by parents who object to proposed reforms and do not want their children to participate. They discover that it is difficult to remove mediocre teachers from public schools. As the frustrations mount, energetic, enthusiastic teachers become bitter, burned-out teachers. . . . The charter school movement gives real power not only to parents and

1

children to choose the kind of school that makes sense for them but also to teachers to use their skills, talents, and energy. Along with this opportunity comes responsibility—the responsibility to demonstrate improved student achievement as measured by standardized tests and other assessments.[3]

By changing the "environment in which teachers work," he argued, there would be "rewards for progress with students and consequences if there is no progress."[4]

Early theorists' focus on teachers makes sense: teachers aren't all-powerful, but they occupy a central position in popular and academic theories of how schools function and students learn.[5] But their prominence isn't just theoretical. Empirical research shows a relatively strong connection between a school's teaching climate—the nature of its teaching environment—and the outcomes that students achieve.[6] If teaching climates matter, and charter schools aimed to foster teaching climates different from those found in public schools, did the experiment turn out as expected? In essence, there are three competing views.

From one perspective, charter schools have fulfilled their potential: they are relatively free of red tape and full of innovation.[7] Because they have few of the bureaucratic encumbrances that come with traditional public schools (hereafter "public schools"), teachers in charter schools can use their expertise and discretion to reach students in nuanced, tailored ways. But this view doesn't envision teachers as having unrestrained freedom. Along with the schools they teach in, teachers are accountable for student learning. That is, charter teachers, like their schools, have greater autonomy in exchange for greater accountability. In this way, they have become what Albert Shanker, an early supporter, hoped. He believed that charter schools would give teachers "the latitude to abandon things that don't work and to create a structure that more closely reflects what we know about how students engage and learn." He added a caveat, however: "This in no way means going back to the 1960s and giving every teacher and student a license to 'do their own thing' without supervision or accountability."[8]

A contrasting view depicts life inside charter schools as unregulated, mismanaged, and obsessed with high-stakes testing. From this perspective, the charter experiment went quickly off the rails as corporations and educational management organizations (EMOs) seized control of public dollars and schools.[9] Because charter schools have lower levels of unionization, they create difficult working conditions for teachers (less pay, more work), sacrifice teacher discretion for the dictates of a corporate board, and prevent teachers from using their collective voice.[10] These test-focused schools lose the forest for the trees and put unremitting pressure on teachers to meet student performance goals. Therefore, we shouldn't be surprised when we see a video of an elementary school teacher in a Brooklyn charter school screaming unreasonably at a little girl for getting an answer wrong on a math quiz.[11]

A third view emphasizes the diversity of charter schools and suggests few commonalities in teaching and learning across the charter landscape. One early tour of the sector noted "the enormous differences found among charter schools in almost every conceivable way—site, curriculum, philosophy, and ages of students, to name a few points of divergence."[12] Another observer noted that charter schools were so diverse that it would be misleading to generalize about them as if they were "one entity."[13] A more recent review makes a similar point: "It is impossible to make a generalization that applies equally to all charters" because "charters vary from state to state, and charters vary even within the same district."[14] As a result, some have argued, the charter idea is a pedagogic "empty vessel."[15] If these accounts are right—and recognizing that a school is a charter conveys little information about how it operates or what students experience—it becomes harder to justify the scholarly attention and resources (public and philanthropic) devoted to this experiment. In other words, if the charter label isn't associated with actual differences in teaching and learning, it's like arguing about differences between West Coast and East Coast schools: it's a distinction with little meaningful difference.

If teaching is central to the theory of how charter schools work —and an enormous amount of time and resources has been spent

comparing public and charter schools—how can these three perspectives coexist? One reason for the confusion is that most studies of charter schools have focused on outcomes, like student test
scores or graduation rates.[16] These studies are helpful, but because
test scores are influenced by more than just in-school influences,
the scores may reveal little about the intermediate aspects of the
theory: what teachers and students are doing and how schools are
functioning. To address this omission, in this book I take a different approach. Putting teachers at the center of the analysis, I ask,
do charter schools cultivate different teaching climates from those
found in public schools? To answer this question, I have analyzed
hundreds of thousands of teacher surveys from across the nation
over a fifteen-year period.

Clearly, this approach isn't perfect. For one thing, teachers aren't
the only perspective needed to understand teaching and learning
inside charter and public schools. Also, how schools function inside
their walls says nothing about their effects on the broader system
of public education (including questions about segregation, diverted
funding, etc.).

Nonetheless, examining teaching climates is crucial because
they are central to arguments for and against charter schools. By
comparing this aspect of life in public and charter schools—rigor-
ously and over time—the book provides clarity about why we might
or might not expect different student outcomes in the first place.
To begin the inquiry, let's scrutinize the rationale behind the case
for charter schools: advocates suggest that charter schools function
better than public schools because charters are less public. Why, at
the level of theory, might we expect that publicness matters for how
schools operate?

PUBLICNESS, ORGANIZATIONAL THEORY, AND CHARTER SCHOOLS

Like the broader privatization movement, arguments for charter
schools are rooted in expectations about the nature and performance of public organizations.[17] Specifically, critics allege that public

schools—like most other public organizations—have shortsighted leadership and layer upon layer of red tape.[18] However, differences between public and private organizations that seem obvious at first glance are often harder to discern on closer inspection.[19] For this reason, it is important to define publicness and locate public and charter schools accordingly.

For many years, scholars have described the blurred lines between state and market and public and private.[20] As a result, publicness is best understood as a continuum: Organizations that are predominantly owned, funded, and controlled by public or political authorities are classified as more public. Those predominantly owned, funded, and controlled by private authorities or economic forces are closer to the private end of the continuum.[21] Organizations with a mixture of public and private ownership, funding, and control are somewhere between these poles.

Using this framework, both charter schools and public schools have high levels of publicness. In terms of funding, both types of schools rely predominantly on public revenues; in fact, though both receive nonpublic funds, charter schools may, on average, depend more on public money than do public schools.[22] Similarly, there are few differences in ownership: both are authorized by public entities like states, school districts, or charter-granting agencies. The key difference, then, is in how the schools are controlled: charter schools are privately operated and tend to have more leeway from state and district rules and regulations than do public schools.[23] In other words, although charter schools are theoretically accountable to the public via charter-granting agencies—or to parents who choose to apply or not apply to the schools (voting with their feet)—it is more difficult for the public to influence how charter schools are managed on a day-to-day basis.

As a result, many decisions about how charter schools are run—from curricula to grades offered to decisions about personnel—are made by privately selected school leaders or boards of directors. If so, charter schools are not analogous to private or parochial schools, which are funded, owned, and operated privately. Rather, they are best understood as public-private hybrids or quasi-public entities.[24]

However we choose to label them, charter schools are less public than public schools, which are directly controlled and regulated by district and state entities.[25] If this characterization is right, why might the teaching climates of public and charter schools differ?

To answer this question, we must understand how teaching climates are formed and what effect, if any, publicness might have on them. Teaching climates—as a part of a school's general climate—are likely to be shaped by how schools are formally and informally organized, the character of the people who join them, and the decisions made by school leaders.[26] In other words, if you want to understand the influences on a school's teaching climate, you need to understand a broad array of structural factors—like where the school is located and how it is funded—as well as narrower influences like who works there. For publicness to matter inside schools, it would need to affect these drivers of teaching climate. In fact, the public-administration literature suggests that variation in publicness may affect how schools are organized, staffed, and operated.

At the most general level, public organizations are thought to be more constrained by political authority—they must answer to elected officials from varied political institutions and pay close attention to public opinion.[27] Though this constraint may be desirable from the standpoint of popular sovereignty, many have argued that this makes public organizations less responsive to change, more focused on processes than outcomes, and less efficient.[28] Because private or quasi-public organizations are less constrained by political authority and more constrained by economic authority, like making a profit or meeting a budget, they may be more nimble and efficient.[29] If these accounts are right, an organization's publicness may in fact affect how it operates. Specifically, public organizations would function differently from private organizations because of differences in management, rule environment, and employee self-selection. Let's explore each of these in turn.

Most management theories are premised on a simple expectation: the choices that leaders make, as they interact with their environments and employees, can affect how their organizations operate. In this way, managers matter.[30] Though all managers can influence how their employees and organizations perform, public managers are often considered less powerful: they are more likely than managers in private or quasi-public organizations to be given ambiguous objectives and to have to respond to multiple political leaders (e.g., a mayor and a school board).[31] Additionally, public managers must reckon with civil-service rules and high levels of union membership, both of which narrow the scope of their managerial options.[32] As a result, these managers theoretically have a more difficult time exercising leadership, punishing and rewarding employees and, in the aggregate, managing their organizations. If these general expectations apply to schools, teachers in charter schools might experience more dynamic, results-driven school leaders than those in public schools.

Second, publicness might matter because of its association with different rule environments. If public organizations are often saddled with vague or conflicting goals, they may be more focused on process and process accountability than their private counterparts, which are more focused on outcomes.[33] In public organizations, this could lead to a thickened regulatory environment and red tape: "rules, regulations, and procedures that remain in force and entail a compliance burden but do not advance the legitimate purposes the rules were intended to serve."[34] In fact, two veteran organizational theorists observe: "One of the most enduring findings in red tape research . . . is one that conforms nicely to commonsense expectations—government agencies tend to have higher levels of red tape."[35] Because they are less public, charter schools might foster teaching climates that are less bureaucratic and more encouraging of innovation than public school teaching climates.

The third pathway by which publicness might affect a school's teaching climate is self-selection. Many organizational theories suggest that there are established patterns of selection between individuals and organizations. For example, attraction-selection-attrition and person-organization fit theories argue that organizations are shaped by the attributes of the people who are attracted to, and choose to remain in, them.[36] Because of long-standing socioeconomic connections and patterns, people who think or act in a particular way may self-select into specific organizations. An organization's character and continuity may therefore depend more on employee self-selection than on organizational imprinting.[37] If so, perhaps organizations with different levels of publicness attract employees with different mind-sets.[38] For instance, we might imagine that teachers choosing charter schools—which tend to have lower salaries but may offer teachers greater autonomy—bring a different approach and set of expectations to their work than do teachers choosing public schools. In this way, self-selection could help explain why charter and public schools would foster different teaching climates.

As this discussion shows, there are theoretical reasons to expect that charter and public schools would foster different teaching climates: because they are less public, charter schools might be managed differently, have different rule environments, and attract different types of teachers. Nonetheless, there is considerable disagreement about this expectation. As described in chapter 2, some theorists argue that too much has been made of a school's publicness. Instead, they argue, a variety of other factors shape how schools function. This book takes these concerns seriously. In fact, its main point is to scrutinize this disagreement empirically by determining whether charter and public schools actually have different teaching climates.

INSIDE THE CHARTER SECTOR

As noted at the beginning of this chapter, some observers have asked whether charter schools are alike enough to be grouped categorically. This book will speak to this question by evaluating whether there are discernable differences between the teaching climates of public and charter schools. Whether there are differences or not, each chapter of the book also devotes some space to a secondary inquiry: looking inside the charter sector itself. Specifically, the book asks: what explains differences in the teaching climates of charter schools?

It answers this question by focusing on two high-profile characteristics of these schools: whether the teachers worked in schools run by EMOs and whether they worked in nonprofit or for-profit schools.[39] These factors direct our attention to organizational characteristics and motives that, on their face, would seem to have the potential to explain why some charter schools have different teaching climates than others. In addition, chapters 4, 5, and 8 look at the amount of operational flexibility granted to schools by their state's charter law (as gauged by a charter schools advocacy group, the Center for Education Reform, or CER).

Chapter 2 considers the theories driving these expectations in some depth. It asks why a school's status as a part of a franchise (run by an EMO versus operating independently) or profit status (for-profit versus nonprofit) might affect its teaching climate. It also investigates how a state's charter law—be it operationally permissive or restrictive—might affect the teaching climates in charters. By subjecting these explanations to empirical scrutiny, the book helps explain variation in teaching climates within the charter sector.

RESEARCH DESIGN

Methodologically, there are a variety of options for studying teachers and teaching climates, including ethnographies, interviews, and surveys. Each approach has its costs and benefits. This book, which seeks to determine whether there were differences in the teaching climates of charter and public schools over time and across a wide geographic space, relies chiefly on surveys. Using a wide lens is helpful because the public debate over charter schools tends to be dominated by anecdotes pointing to one or two high-flying or troubled schools.[40] The academic literature has more nuance, but a recent review of over five hundred academic publications concluded: "There is a paucity of national studies of charter schools."[41] Rather, most studies tend to focus on a handful of schools or locations. For example, in their section looking at teacher collaboration they note: "The research to date is spotty, with little conclusive evidence of widespread practices that promote increased opportunities for teacher collaboration. One limitation of the research in this area is that it tends to report on isolated case studies . . . [that] are by no means generalizable to the broader charter school population."[42] By examining hundreds of thousands of teacher surveys from three sources, one of which covers a fifteen-year period, I hope to develop a broader perspective on differences in the teaching climates of charter and public schools.

Data

The most geographically broad data that I analyze in this book are teachers' responses to the Schools and Staffing Survey (SASS), a national survey conducted by the US Department of Education's National Center for Education Statistics (NCES). Since the 1999–2000 survey, the NCES has included charter schools and teachers, along with its traditional focus on public and private schools and teachers. Because many of the questions asked on the SASS are repeated each year, the book can present a dynamic picture of how charter and public schools evolved over time. Specifically, it will compare teachers in charter and public schools in the 1999–2000, 2003–2004, 2007–2008, and 2011–2012 school years. Because the SASS has a nationally representative sampling frame, the results of this analysis can be generalized across the United States. Across these years, the survey included an average of 35,000 teachers in 7,500 schools; of this total, an average of 1,500 teachers worked in 400 charter schools.

A geographically narrower source of data comes from six statewide Teaching, Empowerment, Leading, and Learning (TELL) surveys conducted by the New Teacher Center (NTC). The NTC, a nonprofit organization devoted to improving student learning by studying school teaching and learning conditions, fielded surveys in Delaware, Colorado, Tennessee, and Maryland during the 2012–2013 school year and in North Carolina and Massachusetts during the 2013–2014 school year. In contrast with the SASS, which use a nationally representative sample, the TELL surveys examined entire populations: with some exceptions, all teachers in charter and public schools within each state had an opportunity to take the surveys. Although the survey questionnaires used in each state were not identical, many of the questions were asked in all six settings.

Consequently, the TELL data enable an in-depth comparison of a great many schools and teachers across six states. In total, the pooled dataset includes approximately 235,000 teachers in 8,500 schools; of this total, around 5,000 teachers worked in 338 charter schools.

I collected the final data—the Delaware Teachers Survey (DTS)—during the 2014–2015 school year. Like the TELL surveys, the DTS gave all teachers in charter and public schools the chance to take the survey.[43] In total, the DTS dataset included around 1,000 teachers in 180 schools; of that total, 130 teachers taught in 20 charter schools. These data are obviously the narrowest geographically, but because I designed the questionnaire, I could ask previously unasked questions to understand the differences between the teaching climates of charter and public schools. For example, the DTS included standard questions from leadership research to learn whether teachers in public and charter schools had different experiences with transformational and transactional leadership. In this way, these data permitted an exploration of parts of teaching climate that the other datasets could not. Supplementing this survey data, I conducted a handful of in-depth interviews with a subset of survey respondents. These interviews enabled me to provide some qualitative evidence to supplement the book's statistical analysis.

Of the three datasets, the SASS data had several advantages. The data (1) were nationally representative; (2) enabled a dynamic view of the charter sector; (3) could be used to study turnover (when paired with NCES's Teacher Follow-up Survey); and (4) included the most wide-ranging control variables of the three datasets. For these reasons, the book gives the most weight to the findings from the SASS analysis. The TELL and DTS data serve as useful complements by exploring aspects of the teaching climates of charter and public schools not covered on the SASS. Although the pooled TELL data include a geographically diverse array of states, and although Delaware was selected for the DTS partly because of its fairly middle-of-the-road charter law (as rated by CER), neither of these surveys was representative of all states.[44] Accordingly, the findings from the

TELL survey and the DTS, unlike those from the SASS, cannot be generalized to the rest of the nation.

Self-Selection

Previous efforts to gauge differences between charter and public schools have raised serious concerns about self-selection.[45] Because students are not randomly assigned to schools, it is not clear whether any differences in student achievement or learning are driven by in-school influences, like teaching, programing, or school leadership, or out-of-school influences, like student and family characteristics. Although this book moves away from test scores and focuses on teaching climates, self-selection may play some role in the findings reported here.

Teachers, like students, are not randomly assigned to schools but, rather, pick and choose schools according to a mixture of financial, professional, and personal factors.[46] As noted above, this choice may have a significant impact on a school's teaching climate: Wayne Hoy notes that a school's climate is "influenced by the formal organization, informal organization, *personalities of participants*, and the leadership of the school" (emphasis added).[47] However, while student self-selection does obvious harm to inferences about the effects of charter schools on student learning, the effect of teacher self-selection on inferences about teaching climates is not as concerning.

To understand why, assume for the moment that teachers who favor greater classroom flexibility self-select into charter schools and, in the surveys analyzed here, reported greater autonomy. Readers might question the legitimacy of this finding, arguing that these teachers were biased toward that view at the outset or had bought into the school's rhetoric about flexibility. In response, I would make two points. First, teachers who chose a school for flexibility might be harder judges about whether they actually have autonomy than teachers who did not. In other words, the view that self-selection biases teachers' responses ignores the possibility that their experiences could have the opposite effect: perhaps autonomy-seeking teachers make it harder to show that charter schools cultivate more autonomous classroom environments because such teachers come in with high expectations.

Second, and related to this point, the finding that charter teachers believe that they work in flexible workplaces would not undermine the inference that charter schools foster greater teacher autonomy unless these teachers were falsely reporting that they had autonomy. Although false reporting may happen, it is not unique to teachers in charter schools. In other words, survey researchers rarely know how much respondents actually do or believe what they say, but teachers in charter schools are probably no more likely to dissemble than are teachers in public schools.[48] In the absence of false reporting, self-selection would not affect the inferences drawn about teaching climate because, from the perspective of student experiences and learning, it matters little *why* teachers in charter schools report doing things differently than teachers in public schools; the key question is whether these differences actually exist.

However, student self-selection may harm efforts to discern differences between charter and public schools in a key way: students and parents play some role in shaping teaching climates. To put it simply, the experiences teachers report are likely to be tied at least partly to the students who select into their schools. This connection is important to keep in mind; but there are two reasons student self-selection does not totally defeat what this book is trying to accomplish. First, to deal with any effect that student self-selection may have on teaching climates, the book's empirical analysis includes a variety of school-level variables that measure student characteristics like race, ability, and poverty. In doing so, the analysis controls for some of the observable differences created by self-selection and enables greater confidence that any observed differences in teaching climate are due to school type (charter versus public).

Second, although students may play some role in shaping what teachers experience and do, in-school influences like how a school is organized and led are thought to play the major role. For example, Robert Kelley and colleagues argue that school administrators have the biggest effect on a school's learning environment.[49] Even though students affect a school's teaching climate, it is unlikely that they play the dominant or decisive role. For example, whether teachers believe that they are effective leaders in their schools, a topic explored in chapter 5, seems likely to be driven more by influences from administrators or school policies than by the characteristics of students.

As this example suggests, concerns about student self-selection are less worrisome in some areas that this book investigates than others: chapters gauging teachers' experiences with autonomy and accountability (chapter 4), teacher leadership and coordination (chapter 5), working conditions (chapter 6), and experiences with administrators (chapter 8) would seem to be less influenced by student self-selection. However, the book's focus on parent and community engagement (chapter 7) and student characteristics (chapter 3) are likely to be more influenced by student self-selection.

Limitations and caveats

In addition to the challenge of self-selection, this book has a few other limitations and caveats. First, teaching climates affect student learning but aren't all-powerful. Research shows that student achievement is most strongly associated with an array of factors over which schools and teachers have little control, like student socioeconomic status.[50] Thus, the book argues that teachers and the environments that they work in are important foci of study; at the same time, it acknowledges that student learning is shaped by much more than a school's teaching climate.

Second, teachers are vital stakeholders in schools and, as operative employees, offer a crucial perspective on what is happening inside them.[51] But there are a variety of other critical perspectives on how schools operate, including those experienced by parents, students, and administrators. The school climate literature recognizes that the best way to understand how a school functions is to study the perspectives and experiences of a diverse array of stakeholders.[52] This book's portrait of teaching climates is limited in that it only provides the perspectives of teachers.

Third, teaching climates, like any part of an organization's climate, consist of multiple characteristics. This book focuses on six aspects of a school's teaching climate which are prominent in the education literature and the charter school debate (outlined below). The areas covered here are expansive but incomplete. Just as there are many views about what matters in a school's climate, several important aspects of teaching are not included here. For instance, I will not address differences or similarities in the content of what is taught, instructional quality, or the socioemotional connections fostered between teachers and students. In other words, this book doesn't claim to study all aspects of a school's teaching climate; hopefully, future work can fill in the gaps left here.

Finally, and perhaps most important, the debate over charter schools raises organizational and systemic questions, but this book focuses only on organizational issues. Since organizational claims are central to arguments for and against charter school, this is an essential approach. Nonetheless, research like this can't speak to system-wide effects like segregation or defunding.[53] Readers will therefore need to take the findings presented here and determine how the organizational characteristics of charter and public schools fit with research on what effects, if any, charter schools are having on the broader public school system.

Each of the aforementioned limitations and caveats is real and should not be minimized. At the same time, all efforts to compare charter and public schools have important limitations, so they aren't fatal for what this book tries to do.[54] By providing a novel perspective on whether the rhetoric on both sides of the charter school debate matches the reality of life inside these schools, this book offers a crucial perspective for scholars, advocates, and policy makers.

CHAPTER OVERVIEW: COMPARING THE TEACHING CLIMATES OF CHARTER AND PUBLIC SCHOOLS

This book is motivated by a desire to understand whether charter and public schools function differently. The question draws from and reflects a general logic—evident in public discourse about privatization, as well in academic fields like organizational studies, public administration, and public policy—that an organization's level of publicness has a significant effect on how it functions. The book uses teachers' experiences, attitudes, and behaviors as indicators of their schools' teaching climates. My goal is to assess the extent to which public and charter schools actually have different teaching climates.

To begin the inquiry, chapter 2 revisits the theoretical question at the heart of this book: why might the publicness of a school affect its teaching climate? Many argue that publicness drives or is associated with factors that shape how schools and teachers function. If so, we would expect that charter schools, by being less public, might foster teaching climates that differ considerably from those found in public schools. However, some organizational theorists argue that too much has been made of publicness. Countering the proponents of privatization, and the conventional wisdom about government bureaucracy, these theorists imply that publicness would not likely shape how schools and teachers function. If so, perhaps we would not expect to see differences in the teaching climates of charter and public schools. Chapter 2 also discusses the theories behind the book's secondary goal: explaining the variation in teaching climates within the charter sector.

The book then moves to its empirical analysis. Chapter 3 examines the school, student, and teacher characteristics of charter and public schools from the 1999–2000 through the 2011–2012 school years. Specifically, it compares these schools in terms of their locations (urban and rural), enrollments, and student bodies. It also examines the characteristics of teachers in these different schools. By detailing where these schools were located, and the characteristics of the people inside them, this chapter starts to compare the teaching climates of charter and public schools. In addition, by showing how charter and public schools systematically differ, the chapter identifies important control variables for the remaining analysis.

Chapter 4 examines what is often portrayed as the essential promise, trade-off, or bargain of charter schools: enhanced freedom for enhanced accountability.[55] Put simply, charter school advocates argue that in exchange for greater room to experiment and innovate, charter schools are held more accountable than public schools.

Many observers have raised questions about this trade-off and wondered whether autonomy and accountability are—to some extent at least—mutually exclusive.[56] In this light, chapter 4 explores whether charter schools foster climates in which teachers have more autonomy and are held more accountable than teachers in public schools. It also looks at two of the corollaries of autonomy: innovation and red tape. One of the main expectations about charter schools is that they reduce red tape and give teachers autonomy so they can be more innovative. Chapter 4 examines these expectations empirically. The chapter concludes by looking into the charter sector itself to ask how differences in franchising, tax status, and state charter laws might explain differences in autonomy and accountability.

Chapter 5 examines teacher leadership and collaboration. One of the initial and enduring rationales for charter schools is that they would give teachers the chance to work closer with their colleagues and to offer greater input into how their schools operated. These claims are related to, but distinct from, autonomy: whereas autonomy refers to teachers' ability to make decisions about how they teach, teacher leadership refers to the role that teachers play in running their schools. Teacher collaboration, the extent to which teachers work together, is important to study because charter schools are purposely decentralized.[57] Charter proponents expect that decentralization removes barriers to teacher collaboration, but, as others have noted, decentralization may have the opposite effect: creating disorder and reducing cooperation. This chapter uses teacher survey responses to look for evidence of differences in teacher leadership and collaboration in charter and public schools. It also asks how teacher leadership and collaboration vary within the charter sector.

Another crucial aspect of teaching climate—teacher working conditions and turnover—is the topic of chapter 6. Both supporters and critics of charter schools suggest that teachers in these schools work more hours and under more difficult conditions. For supporters, this supposition shows dedication; for critics, it suggests that teachers in charter schools are overworked (largely because they are not unionized) and that the model is not sustainable. Perhaps as a result, there has also been considerable interest in differences between charter and public schools in teacher satisfaction and turn-over. To examine the working conditions inside charter and public schools, this chapter examines various aspects of teachers' experiences, including the number of hours worked, pay, satisfaction, and turnover. The chapter concludes by asking about teacher working conditions and turnover within the charter sector.

Chapter 7 shifts the focus to the relationship between schools, communities, and parents, a central part of how schools function. Charter proponents suggest that these schools foster higher levels of parental and community engagement than do public schools. Whether this observation was true in the early days of the charter sector or more recently remains to be seen. The chapter examines these expectations empirically to determine if teachers in charter schools indicate that they work in schools with higher levels of community and parent engagement than do teachers in public schools. It also investigates the differences in community and parent engagement within the charter sector.

The final empirical chapter, chapter 8, examines teachers' experiences with administrators. It asks if teachers in charter schools are more likely to agree that their schools are guided by supportive, mission-driven school leaders than teachers in public schools. Do school leaders in charter schools use performance management techniques—the collection and use of information to enhance a school's performance—more than school leaders in public schools do? What explains the variation in teachers' experiences with leadership inside the charter sector?

Chapter 9, the conclusion, argues that the teaching climates of charter schools are different from those imagined by both proponents and critics: in some respects, charter schools appear to be meeting their promise; in other respects, they aren't. In short, the differences between the teaching climates of public and charter schools are complicated and belie simple sound bites or stereotypes. The chapter closes by considering what these findings imply for the debate over charter schools and organizational theory.

TWO

Organizational Theory
and Charter Schools

THE DEBATE over charter schools is driven by broad assumptions. Charter advocates assume that public schools are monopolies that have no incentive to improve in the absence of competition.[1] Critics of for-profit charter schools claim that introducing the profit motive creates incentives that are detrimental to student learning.[2] This chapter zeros in on expectations like these and asks why they might be true. It considers why, at the level of theory, a difference in publicness might and might not be an important factor shaping the teaching climates of charter and public schools. Additionally, the chapter analyzes the factors that might drive differences within the charter sector; specifically, it asks how franchising, tax status, and a state's charter law might affect a school's teaching climate. I begin the discussion by situating the charter school debate within the context of the larger privatization movement. In doing so, I will show how publicness came to achieve primacy in debates about education policy.

THE PRIVATIZATION MOVEMENT AND CHARTER SCHOOLS

To understand the current drive toward privatization—in education and other aspects of public policy—we need to briefly look backward and ask how we got to this point in American politics. Before the Progressive Era in the United States, public-sector jobs tended to be filled with political appointees with strong partisan allegiances.[3] As the movement for civil-service reform emerged, advocates pushed for and won a merit-based system that insulated many public workers from party control. Though largely a success for the efficacy and efficiency of public administration—the party spoils system often placed incompetent or unqualified workers throughout the government—the reforms changed bureaucratic politics. Without parties to defend them, public agencies and their workers became easy political targets. As such, public agencies needed to cobble together supporters—from inside and outside government—to fend off political challenges and to achieve some level of autonomy.[4] With the Great Depression, the New Deal, and World War II, the public sector expanded and a bipartisan consensus emerged about the need and relative competence of public agencies.

Beginning with the restiveness of the 1960s, much of this consensus unraveled. As gender and racial norms changed and as people came to see efforts like President Lyndon B. Johnson's War on Poverty as failures, there was a growing sense that public programs and agencies could not address the nation's problems.[5] The quagmire in Vietnam and the Watergate scandal accelerated uneasiness with the public sector. Around this time, conservative politicians like Barry Goldwater began to gain prominence by decrying the New Deal and vilifying government agencies. Most notably, Ronald Reagan, in his campaign for the presidency in 1980, raised the demonization of government and bureaucrats to new heights; after winning the election, Reagan, in his first inaugural address, famously proclaimed that government was the cause of, rather than the solution to, many of the nation's problems.[6]

Despite his strong language and determined efforts, Reagan's success in reducing the size and scope of government was modest.[7] In fact, even excluding the massive "shadow workforce"—the millions of employees contracted by the federal government to perform key tasks—the number of federal bureaucrats rose during the 1980s.[8] However, it would be a mistake to argue that the Reagan presidency did not have an impact on public administration and public policy making: while his administration did not massively reducing government's scope, Reagan helped change how government operated.[9] In effect, the Reagan administration helped usher in an era in which markets, competition, and nonpublic organizations played a more prominent role in US governance.[10] In this new framework, public institutions, organizations, or bureaucracies became perceived as backward, inefficient, and outdated, especially compared with the dynamism and unbridled potential of the market and nonpublic organizations.[11]

Initially, the push for charter schools did not share this hostility toward the public sector: these schools were expected to function as experimental institutions that would complement rather than compete with public schools.[12] A charter, it was expected, would be given to a school for a limited period while it tested a new idea or approach. The results from the experiment would generate new information, which could then be incorporated into existing district practice. Although not intended to supplant public schools, charter schools were soon understood as competitors, and a different sort of theory emerged: reflecting the basic logic of privatization, proponents argued that charter schools performed better than public schools because they were less public.[13]

THE PRIMACY OF PUBLICNESS

As evident in this brief history, the push for charter schools—like the broader privatization movement—elevated the importance of publicness: among all of the factors that might shape how a school functions, publicness became seen as most important. Chapter 1 briefly laid out some of the theoretical reasons this might be true; this section expands that discussion to help determine what we might expect in a comparison of the teaching climates of charter and public schools.

Even if all organizations are somewhat public—and can therefore be situated on a publicness spectrum—a variety of literatures and theories suggest that where they are located matters. To begin, consider the public administration and public management literatures.[14] The justification for these literatures is an argument about the importance of publicness in organizational life: Put simply, the reason for building separate literatures for the study of public organizations is a recognition that they are different from non-public or less public organizations. As a result, the theories used in the generic organization and management literatures are expected to be insufficient for explaining the performance of public organizations.

Perhaps most centrally, public organizations are thought to have to balance competing goals like efficiency, economy, and equity while working in a political space in which they must respond to and represent the public's wishes.[15] Although there is some debate, most works in these literatures build on this basic perspective and suggest that being public is a major challenge for administration: in effect, these political forces muddy organizational goals and amplify the number of principals to whom leaders must respond.[16] In addition, public organizations are thought to be harder to manage than private organizations. In part this difficulty stems from the afore-mentioned civil-service reforms, created to remove politics from public administration. One of the collateral effects, some argue, is that it is difficult for public managers to hire, reprimand, reward, and fire employees.[17] Without these proverbial sticks and carrots, public managers may have a harder time leading their organizations and holding employees accountable—positively or negatively—than managers in private organizations have.

Another disadvantage of the public realm—the literature contends—is more organizational red tape.[18] Because they are controlled by multiple principals and have vague and often-conflicting goals, public organizations are thought to emphasize processes over outcomes, resulting in organizations with high levels of formalization. Employees and managers tend to experience this increased formalization as a hindrance that makes it more difficult to do their work. As a result, one of the most consistent empirical finding in the public administration and management literatures accords with conventional wisdom: public organizations tend to have more red tape.[19]

Another literature that emphasizes the importance of publicness is the public choice literature in economics.[20] This literature is anchored by the expectation that people and organizations pursue their interests, whether they operate in a market or government setting.[21] However, the difference in settings is everything. In a market setting, competition drives actors toward efficiency and achievement (out of fear of loss); in a government setting, where competition is nonexistent, corruption and lethargy may come to dominate. The theory obviously has significant implications for publicness: it hypothesizes that, all else being equal, organizations that are more public are likely to perform worse than less public organizations.

In the education literature, the most famous application of public choice theory is by John Chubb and Terry Moe.[22] They argue that the political environment for public education tends to privilege the large, organized interests—like teachers unions—at the expense of unorganized groups of students and parents. Even if students and parents did have more control, the authors argue, the public education system is supposed to emphasize the needs and interests of all rather than just the needs and interests of parents and students: "The schools are agencies of society as a whole, and everyone has a right to participate in their governance. Parents and students have a right to participate too. But they have no right to win."[23] In contrast, the authors say, in the private sector parents and students are empowered to choose from among a variety of providers that must seek the families' approval if the providers hope to sustain themselves. While Chubb and Moe agree that, at the level of theory, neither public institutions nor markets are perfect, they contend that a decentralized education market would be more focused on the needs of students and parents than would be a centralized, monopolistic public school system.

QUESTIONING PUBLICNESS

Though publicness may have some important—perhaps determinative—effects on how organizations function, several prominent scholars argue that too much has been made of publicness.[24] Perhaps, as a result, when analogous public and private organizations are compared empirically, they perform roughly equally.[25] This section therefore considers a different argument: that charter and public schools' differences in publicness are unlikely to have much of an effect on a school's teaching climate.

One reason to question the relevance of publicness in a comparison of charter and public schools draws directly from the conception of it articulated in chapter 1: two organizations might be at different places on the publicness continuum, but the distance between them might not be far.[26] In other words, we should question strict delineations between public and private and expect that differences in publicness are of degree rather than kind. As discussed in chapter 1, charter and public schools have similar publicness in terms of ownership and funding but differ in how they are controlled or operated (charter schools are operated more privately, public schools are operated more publicly). With this in mind, perhaps these schools would have similar teaching climates because they are alike in two of the three components that determine publicness. To take the point further, a comparison of public and private schools (which are subject to public law but are funded, owned, and controlled privately) would seem more likely to discover a difference in teaching climate than a comparison of a public and charter schools.

A second reason to be skeptical about the primacy of publicness is, somewhat ironically, the public-sector reforms that have been undertaken as a result of the privatization movement. Since the latter part of the twentieth century, governments have undertaken a series of neoliberal reforms, like the highly controversial New Public Management, that have sought to make public organizations operate more like private companies.[27] In such an environment, public officials were positioned as quasi market actors—less concerned with big-picture public goals and more interested in performance metrics.[28] Thus, to the extent that the public and private sector have converged, we might not expect to see differences in employee behavior in public and private firms; in the aggregate, this convergence may erode any meaningful effect that publicness has on organizational performance.[29]

In education, the signal push to overhaul public education, and make it operate more like a private industry, was the No Child Left

Behind Act.[30] It did so by mandating annual testing of children in grades 3 through 8, attaching progressive sanctions for schools with repeatedly low scores, and providing alternatives to public schools (like charter schools). With these reforms, it aimed to create a competitive education marketplace where information about school performance is readily accessible and where consumers (parents and students) and elected officials would reward good schools and punish failing schools. To the extent that this law changed how public schools operate, we might not expect big differences between the teaching climates of charter schools and public schools.[31]

A third reason publicness may not matter relates to changes in the labor market in recent years. Whereas employees used to remain in one organization or sector for many years, there has been a rise in sector-switching.[32] In particular, people interested in public service are selecting into a range of organizations—from public to nonprofit or for-profit—and switching frequently over their careers. If so, we might expect some form of cross-fertilization as employees bring ideas, experiences, and patterns of practice back and forth across the sectors. Institutional isomorphism would result and, to the extent that employee self-selection drives an organization's climate, publicness would lose much of its explanatory punch.

Finally, publicness may have little effect on teaching climates because of professionalization and decision-making theory. One useful approach to understanding organizational behavior is James March and Johan Olsen's "logic of appropriateness" theory.[33] This concept suggests that as organization members decide what to do, they ask themselves three questions: Who am I as a member of this organization? What type of situation am I facing presently? What does a person like me do in a situation like this? The authors argue that in answering these questions, employees try to align their behavior with what they see as appropriate—rather than good or effort-reducing—behavior. Thus, understanding employee behavior requires reckoning with how employees see themselves and the contexts in which they work.[34]

This begs the question: where do employees learn who they are as organization members and what is appropriate behavior on the job? In many areas in which public services have been privatized, employees are not just members of organizations, they are members of professions.[35] That is, how they see themselves and their work is related not just to their organizations but also to their experiences and training before they joined the organization. In the case of schools, if teachers in charter and public schools are connected by similar professional identities or expectations—be it from training or something else—differences in publicness might have little impact on their actions inside schools. In the aggregate, this might reduce differences in the teaching climates of public and charter schools.

THE SUPERIORITY OF THE PUBLIC?

Taken in sum, the two prior sections provide conflicting guidance about how differences in publicness might influence the teaching climates of public and charter schools. To further complicate matters, several scholars stake out a third perspective: the superiority of public organizations. For example, some research suggests that although contracting, outsourcing, and privatization are meant to enhance accountability, efficiency, and performance, these practices may in fact diminish these benefits. From this perspective, when governments contract out tasks to private-sector organizations, they create another layer of bureaucracy and another set of accountability relationships.[36] The result may be less public oversight and an increase in waste and inefficiency.

To see how this might look in practice, consider the case of privatization in the military. Over the past several decades, the Pentagon has increasingly used private security companies to perform core elements of its mission. Several authors suggest that this change has been catastrophic: billions of dollars cannot be accounted for by the Pentagon, and the transparency with which the nation fights its wars—which was not high begin with—has diminished.[37]

Though military contracting is just one example, it suggests that the type of organization implementing a policy might be less important than the context in which it works. From this perspective, contracting out public tasks to the private sector would not change much about how policy is implemented: private or quasi-public organizations with muddy public goals would perform analogously to, or worse than, public organizations.[38]

Returning to the case at hand, perhaps charter schools, which are exempt from some but not all state and federal regulations, would simply add another layer of bureaucracy to a public school system that already has too many layers. Accordingly, charter schools might foster teaching climates with higher levels of red tape and less autonomy and accountability than public schools.

INSIDE THE CHARTER SECTOR

Thus far, this chapter has asked why we might expect that charter and public schools have different teaching climates. The majority of the book is devoted to examining this question empirically. However, it also devotes space in each chapter to exploring what drives differences in teaching climate within the charter sector. To guide this inquiry, this book investigates two areas that have emerged as promising (and controversial) explanations in the charter schools debate: franchising and tax status. In addition, in Chapters 4, 5, and 8, which deal with teacher autonomy, leadership, and experiences with administrators, it investigates how the flexibility or restrictiveness of state charter law could affect charter schools therein. The remainder of the chapter considers these three influences.

Franchising, Agency Theory, and Educational Management Organizations

Embracing a logic of deregulation and decentralization, charter schools were initially envisioned as independent, stand-alone institutions with which state and local stakeholders could experiment and innovate.[39] This idea was predicated on the notion that the rules and regulations, imposed by centrally controlled bureaucracies, were impeding school, teacher, and student success. Though early theorists viewed these regulations as a problem, Joe Nathan envisioned a similar danger if the charter sector moved toward a "corporate model" in which "teachers [were] hired simply to carry out a play someone else has designed"; in these cases, "teacher insight, creativity, and talent may be lost because teachers will have little motivation to use these qualities."[40] Despite these concerns, the number of students educated in schools operated by education management organizations (EMOs) has risen over time. In the 2001–2002 school year, approximately ninety thousand students attended EMO-run charter schools; ten years later, this figure had increased to an estimated nine hundred thousand students, half of the charter school population.[41]

The rise of EMOs has generated concern that charter schools will become pedagogically rigid and have less independence and school-level control.[42] Put differently, observers worry that this development may make the climate of charter schools more like that found in public schools.[43] However, others imply that the franchised approach to charter schools is promising: by experimenting with various approaches, promulgating best practices, and enabling schools to benefit from economies of scale, chains of charter schools may outperform independent schools.[44] Drawing from organizational theory, this section examines these claims and asks what the growth of charter franchises might mean for schools' teaching climates.

Franchising is a common form of organization in many business sectors. In essence, a franchise is a set of organizations that provide a relatively standardized set of goods or services through an agreement between a franchisor and a franchisee.[45] The relationship between the two parties—and the extent to which the franchisee exercises autonomy—is often understood through *agency theory,* essentially a theory that envisions a game in which a principal (the franchisor) tries to control an agent (the franchisee).[46] Perhaps the dominant way in which compliance is achieved is formalization—the creation and promulgation of rules, procedures, and enforcement mechanisms.[47] In franchises, contracts establish the rules that bind the franchisor and franchisee. As with many elements of formalization, these contracts are thought to solve some problems while creating others.[48] In particular, they may clarify a franchisee's rights and responsibilities, while constraining its ability to respond to situations as it sees fit.[49]

As this discussion hints, one of the key debates in the literature is whether franchising inhibits or encourages innovation.[50] Some scholars suggest that franchisees feel increasingly constrained by centrally determined rules and regulations that do not apply to local situations. Others imply that, in the long term, franchisees provide useful feedback to central management—feedback that enables the franchisor to adapt to changes in the market and society.

In the typical application of agency theory to franchising, there is little concern given to operative employees. However, since they play a prominent role in how organizations function, it is worth asking how this framework might shape employee experiences and, in sum, an organization's climate.[51] To do so, agency theory is extended so that the franchisee is the principal and the operative employee— in our case, the teacher—is the agent.[52] As above, the principal is expected to use formalization to standardize the behavior that he or she wants from the agent. In effect, this means that the franchisee will set up rules and routines for the operative employee to follow as well as consequent rewards and punishments. However, the franchisee does not have free rein in this respect: formalization must operate within the bounds of the contract with the franchisor. Put differently, the franchisee has a narrower range of responses than would an owner working outside a franchising agreement.

To return to charter schools, this discussion suggests that franchising could have an effect on the experiences and perceptions of teachers working in EMO-run charters. In fact, many of the theorized effects of franchising are similar to the theorized effects of publicness. Namely, teachers in EMO-run charter schools would seem likely to encounter more red tape than would teachers in non-EMO-run charters and, correspondingly, would have less autonomy and input into how the school is run. At the same time, because they work in organizations that are centrally (rather than locally) controlled, teachers in EMO-run charter schools may work for school administrators who have less control. Consequently, these teachers may be less likely than non-EMO-run charter teachers to be held accountable for their performance. These teacher experiences could have a decisive impact on teaching climates: rather than fostering experimentation and accountability, EMO-run charter schools may create schools in which principals and teachers are relatively constrained. In such an environment, teachers may have less autonomy and less room to exert leadership in their schools.

But this is an overly negative view of franchising. If franchises bring order and efficiencies to schools, perhaps teachers in EMOs would have better experiences. For example, if EMO-run charter schools have more-established protocols for the hiring and training of school leaders, perhaps teachers in these schools would be less likely to have ineffective school leaders than those in a nonfranchised setting. As this example shows, by presenting the experiences of teachers empirically, the book will demonstrate how franchising is related to a variety of aspects of a school's teaching climate.

Tax Status: Nonprofit and For-Profit Charter Schools

Another development within the charter sector has generated considerable controversy: the emergence of for-profit schools. Though many of these schools are EMOs, for the sake of analytic clarity, it is important to separate the issues of franchising and tax status—the former refers to a management approach and the latter to a particular motivation. Almost from the beginning, for-profit companies ran a portion of the schools within the charter universe. Though their national growth has not been uniform—in some states, for-profit schools make up a majority of charter schools, while in others, for-profits are nearly absent—recent estimates suggests that around 13 to 15 percent of charter schools are run by for-profit companies.[53]

What, then, does theory tell us about what we might expect in a comparison of the teaching climates of for-profit and nonprofit charter schools? Returning to the notion of publicness—in which an organization's publicness is determined by its funding, ownership, and control—the main difference between for-profit and nonprofit charter schools is that for-profit schools are even more controlled by market forces. Classical and neoclassical economic theory suggest that this is no small difference: because of their need for profit, for-profit organizations are thought to find the most efficient ways possible of providing goods and services without alienating consumers.[54]

For-profit firms, then, may have clearer goals than do public organizations or nonprofit firms, both of which are often tasked with meeting abstract political goals or missions. For-profit organizations would also have the incentive to build more direct relationships between principals and agents and would pay closer attention to the needs and desires of consumers. In this way, for-profit firms would be expected to reduce agent discretion while perhaps enhancing employee accountability (more so than would nonprofit firms).[55]

Governments have increasingly used this argument to rationalize the usage of for-profit firms for the delivery of public services. In response, scholars have raised various criticisms. Perhaps the signal concern unifying these critiques is that the profit motive creates perverse incentives for organizational practices that have traditionally been focused on nonpecuniary outcomes.[56] Put differently, the profit motive may displace other organizational goals and defeat the intended purpose of a policy. In this way, policy makers are not choosing different paths to the same destination; rather, the forms of organization that a government chooses may lead to fundamentally different experiences for citizens and, in the aggregate, public policy.

Returning to the case at hand, some have suggested that these fears have been realized in for-profit charter schools.[57] For instance, one study of for-profit providers in Massachusetts showed that these schools pushed away children with difficult-to-solve cognitive or behavioral problems, because it was in their best financial interest.[58] Similarly, a study from Michigan suggested that the profit motive led to harmful outcomes on service provision (transportation) and student composition (less integration).[59] A third study noted lower enrollment patterns of special education students in for-profit charter schools than in nonprofit charters, in California.[60]

These studies raise difficult questions for an empirical analysis like this. In chapter 1, I argued that self-selection was a potential problem for studying parent and community engagement because students and parents play some role in shaping a school's teaching climate. In much the same way, the concerns raised above could make it difficult to compare for-profit and nonprofit charter schools: if for-profit charter schools push out low-performing, hard-to-teach students, they could foster different teaching climates than non-profit charter schools have.

Though a possible problem, and one that analyzed in chapter 3, there are two factors that mitigate this concern. First, recall from chapter 1 that theorists expect that school leaders play a major role in determining a school's climate.[61] Therefore, differences in student populations alone do not completely invalidate inferences about the effect of tax status. Second, the empirical analysis controls for many student characteristics that might affect a school's teaching climate. Specifically, the analysis controls for the percentage of minority students, the percentage of students eligible for free or reduced-price lunch, and the percentage of students who have an individualized education plan or who are classified as English language learners. By controlling for these student body characteristics, the book can provide a clearer—if not perfect—picture of how the tax status of charter schools is related to their teaching climates.

The Nature of a State's Charter Law

Like many aspects of education policy, charter school governance and practice is thought to be strongly influenced by state and local law. Of particular importance are the state laws that govern how charter schools are created and overseen. After the inception of the charter idea in the late 1980s, states around the nation moved quickly to pass laws enabling the creation of charter schools. By 2015, over 80 percent of states had charter laws on the books.[62] These laws are not uniform, however, and this variation in state law may affect teaching climates within the charter sector.[63]

Many elements of a state's charter law might influence teachers' experiences. However, of particular importance in this book is the amount of operational autonomy that charter laws give to schools. For opponents of charter schools, operational autonomy is analogous to deregulation: it frees schools but also removes oversight. For supporters, it is the essence of the charter school experiment: operational autonomy enables schools to break through bureaucratic encumbrances to innovate and respond more effectively to student needs.[64]

Since the late 1990s, the Center for Education Reform (CER)—a pro-charter-school organization—has surveyed the charter landscape and rated each state according to an analysis of its charter law. Specifically, the group has given each state an operations rating based on the extent to which state law codifies independence from state and district operational rules and procedures. Like other studies in the field, this book uses these ratings to measure the operational flexibility afforded to charter schools by each state's charter law.[65] These ratings reveal the changing nature of charter laws across the states over many years. However, the effect of these laws on the teaching climates of charter schools is unknown. Though many observers assume that frontline practice naturally follows formal policy making or legislation, a rich literature suggests otherwise.[66] In fact, street-level bureaucrats have considerable autonomy as they implement policy and are influenced by a host of dispositional and institutional factors.[67]

Consequently, it is important to explore whether differences in charter law are associated with the teaching climates of charter schools. Specifically, we might surmise that teachers in states that grant charter schools more autonomy might have more classroom autonomy, play a larger role in school governance, and experience more dynamic administrators. On the other hand, decentralized control may lead to more school-level disorder, negatively affecting teachers' experiences. By investigating these expectations empirically, this book demonstrates whether differences in state charter laws filter down and impact teachers' experiences.

CONCLUSION

Using organizational theory, this chapter has sought to achieve two goals. First, moving beyond political claims and sound bites, it explored why we might expect differences in the teaching climates of charter and public schools. In effect, it suggested that theory is not clear about what we should expect in such a comparison. Second, the chapter looked into the charter sector itself to consider why some charter schools may have different teaching climates than others. Again drawing from organizational theory, it considered why a school's status as a franchise or its tax status might affect how it operates. The chapter also suggested that the amount of operational flexibility written into a state's charter law might have some effect on teaching climates within a school. In a national analysis, then, differences in the teaching climates of charter schools might be driven by differences in state law.

The following chapters will test the varied and conflicting expectations considered in this chapter. As Christopher Lubienski and Sarah Theule Lubienski note, assumptions and ideology drive this debate more often than careful empirical analysis.[68] To begin the analysis, chapter 3 explores the school, teacher, and student characteristics of charter and public schools.

T H R E E

School, Student, and Teacher Characteristics

ANYONE WHO HAS SPENT time in a variety of school settings knows that a school's demographics or location is not its destiny. For example, David Kirp's engrossing book shows how the Union City, New Jersey, school district, with a large percentage of poor, Hispanic immigrants, beat the odds and is consistently producing remarkable academic outcomes.[1] At the same time, we shouldn't forget that the characteristics of the people in a school—like the percentage of poor students or teachers' average years of teaching experience—may have generalizable effects on its processes and outcomes. For example, David Berliner and Gene Glass note that around two-thirds of the variation in student test scores is determined by sociodemographic characteristics, like neighborhood characteristics or student home life.[2] For this reason, understanding a school's climate or teaching climate requires attention to an array of school, student, and teacher characteristics.

These characteristics are particularly important in a comparison of teaching in charter and public schools because prior research suggests some systematic differences between these schools.[3] For instance, charter schools appear to be more likely to be located in urban areas than public schools are. Also, the way charter schools enroll students isn't random: students (or their parents) must apply to these schools. If there are more students than seats, the process becomes random (a lottery is run to select students). But that doesn't mean that the initial pool of applicants is a perfect cross-section of students in a particular area. On the contrary, research suggests that students in charter and public schools may differ in observed and unobserved ways, perhaps because of onerous application requirements.[4]

The second reason an analysis of these characteristics is important is methodological. Many studies in the literature don't use multivariate statistical analyses when they compare the teaching climates of public and charter schools. In other words, they don't control for factors that may systematically distinguish charter and public schools. This potentially problematic oversight increases the chances of omitted-variable bias, when two variables seem to be statistically related because other variables are left out of an analysis. For example, if charter schools are more likely to employ younger teachers, and younger teachers are more likely to change jobs, an analysis of turnover differences between charter and public schools that omits teachers' ages might generate spurious or imprecise findings. By showing how these types of schools differ—in terms of school, teacher, and student characteristics—this chapter highlights some of the factors that are necessary to control for in charter-versus-public comparisons.

We begin by focusing on school characteristics, specifically, the differences between charter and public schools in *urbanicity* (how urban the location is), enrollment, and student-teacher ratio. Following that, we look at the students attending these varied schools and, in particular, characteristics like race, poverty, special education, and English language familiarity. Then, we examine various teacher characteristics like levels of union membership, years of teaching experience, and teachers' values and motivations. We conclude by studying the differences among charter schools in light of the schools' franchising and tax status.

SCHOOL LOCATION, ENROLLMENT, AND STUDENT-TEACHER RATIO

For many years, scholars have recognized that charter schools tended to be located in urban areas; recently, however, some authors have wondered if charter schools have begun to spread to rural and suburban districts.[5] Jeffrey Henig shows that such claims are probably overblown: as of the 2009–2010 school year, few charter schools were located in suburban or rural locations.[6] This finding is helpful, but it does not compare the locations of charter schools with the locations of public schools. Nor does Henig look at how these trends have changed over time or whether there are differences in urbanicity even when controlling for a variety of school-level variables, like enrollment and student characteristics.

The left side of figure 3.1 presents the findings from a descriptive analysis that looks at how many charter and public schools were located in these different areas from school years 1999–2000 through 2011–2012. The right side of the figure presents odds ratios, derived from logit coefficients, from a multivariate analysis that controlled for other school-level factors, like enrollment size and school level (elementary, etc.).[7] Odds ratios indicate the likelihood that charter schools are differently located, controlling for school-level differences. An odds ratio above 1.0 with an asterisk indicates that, all else being equal, charter schools were more likely than public schools to be located in a particular location. An odds ratio below 1.0 with an asterisk indicates that charter schools were less likely than public schools to be located in a particular area. An odds ratio without an asterisk indicates that there were no statistically significant differences between where charter and public schools were located.

This figure confirms some elements of the conventional wisdom: since the early years of the sector, charter schools have been more likely to be located in urban areas and less likely to be located in rural areas. However, the bottom right panel adds some nuance to our understanding. In school years 1999–2000 and 2003–2004, charter

FIGURE 3.1

School locations (SASS)

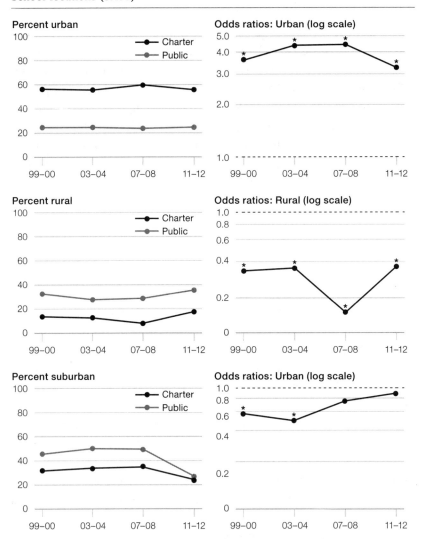

Note: SASS: Schools and Staffing Survey. Asterisks in the right panels denote a statistically significant difference between charter and public schools at the $p < 0.05$ level, controlling for other school-level influences. For information about how to interpret odds ratios, see the accompanying text. For modeling information, see the appendix.

schools were less likely to be located in suburban locations; nonetheless, in the two most recent waves, this difference evaporated. In other words, since the 2007–2008 school year, charter schools were as likely as public schools were to be located in suburban areas.

A second important school-level characteristic is enrollment. Prior research has suggested that enrollment may be related to student achievement—although there are conflicting findings in the literature, larger schools may be associated with worse student outcomes—and that charter schools tend to have smaller enrollment figures than similarly situated public schools.[8] Let's now examine whether charter schools are, on average, smaller and how any trends may have changed over time.

Figure 3.2 presents the differences in enrollment between charter and public schools over the past four waves of the SASS. The left panel shows the mean number of students per school, and the right panel indicates whether there was a statistically significant difference in enrollment between charter and public schools, controlling for a variety of school-level factors. Like the odds ratios

FIGURE 3.2

Student enrollment (SASS)

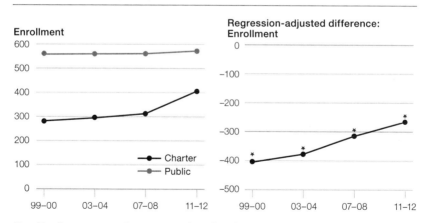

Note: Enrollment measured as mean number of students per school. Asterisks in the right panel denote a statistically significant difference between charter and public schools at the $p < 0.05$ level, controlling for other school-level influences. For information about modeling, see the appendix.

in figure 3.1, a coefficient without an asterisk indicates that there was no statistically significant difference between charter and public schools; a coefficient with an asterisk indicates a statistically significant difference.

Again, this figure confirms the conventional wisdom while adding some new information. As expected, since the early days of the charter sector, these schools have had on average many hundred fewer students per school than public schools have had. However, we see some evidence of change. The left panel shows a convergence of enrollment underway, largely due to the growing size of charter schools. The right panel shows that the regression-adjusted difference remains large in the most recent survey, but that it has been reduced by over a quarter (from approximately 400 fewer students in 1999–2000 to around 250 fewer students in 2011–2012). If this trend continues, future studies may find no statistically significant difference in enrollment between these two types of schools.

A third school-level characteristic that has the potential to shape a school's teaching climate is its student-teacher ratio. Teachers in schools with a higher student-teacher ratio may have bigger class sizes and find it harder to devote time to each student. Perhaps as a result, research shows that bigger class sizes are associated with worse student outcomes.[9] Figure 3.3 depicts the differences in the student-teacher ratios between charter and public schools. The ratios are the total number of students, divided by the total number of full-time teachers in the school. The left panel shows the mean student-teacher ratio for charter and public schools over the past four waves of the SASS. The right panel highlights the results of multivariate regressions that examined whether any differences between these schools were significant while controlling for other school-level factors.

Both parts of figure 3.3 reveal the same finding: despite having fewer enrolled students (figure 3.2), charter schools consistently had more students per teacher than did public schools. Though there was some volatility, the right panel suggests that, on average, charter schools had 1.6 more students per teacher than public schools had.[10]

FIGURE 3.3

Student-teacher ratios (SASS)

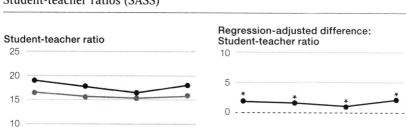

Note: Asterisks in the right panel denote a statistically significant difference between charter and public schools at the $p < 0.05$ level, controlling for other school-level influences. For information about modeling, see the appendix.

Combined, the findings from the analysis of school location, enrollment, and teacher-student ratio suggest that charter and public schools have some important structural differences. Now we turn to another way charter and public school teacher climates may differ: the characteristics of their students.

STUDENT CHARACTERISTICS

There is some evidence that charter schools attract or recruit students who are somewhat different from public school students.[11] For example, early research suggested that charter schools were more likely to enroll black and Hispanic students—and less likely to enroll non-Hispanic white students—than public schools.[12] More recent research suggests that a plurality of charter schools have a plurality of white students, although the number of schools with large Hispanic populations has increased.[13] To clarify whether any differences exist—and document any changes over time—this section presents findings from an analysis of student characteristics using SASS data.

Race and Ethnic Characteristics

This section examines the racial and ethnic composition of schools in terms of non-Hispanic white students; non-Hispanic black students; and all Hispanic students, regardless of race. The left panels of figure 3.4 present the percentage of students in these categories over the four waves of the SASS. The right panels show the results from a multivariate analysis of differences in the percentage of students in charter and public schools, controlling for other school-level factors.

The left panels of figure 3.4 show that, for all the school years studied, charter schools had a greater percentage of non-Hispanic black and Hispanic students and a lower percentage of non-Hispanic white students. Over this period, the percentage of non-Hispanic white students dropped in both settings, the percentage of Hispanic students increased in both settings, and the percentage of non-Hispanic black students stayed roughly constant. However, when other school factors are brought into the analysis (right panels), there were few statistically significant differences among the students in charter and public schools over this period. In the early years of the charter sector, there were fewer non-Hispanic white students in charter schools; nonetheless, in the most recent waves of the survey, this difference disappeared. Moreover, charter schools were no more or less likely to enroll non-Hispanic black or Hispanic students.

English-Language Learners and Students with Individualized Education Plans

Behind race, perhaps the second-biggest controversy over the composition of charter school student bodies centers along children's readiness to learn. Critics charge that for a variety of reasons—from self-selection to an interest in gaming test scores—charter schools educate fewer students with learning difficulties than do public schools.[14] Empirical analyses paint a more complex picture: some types of charter schools may enroll fewer students with disabilities or English language learners (ELL), while other charter schools are no different from public schools.[15] Also, there is great disparity in special education populations between charter and public schools

FIGURE 3.4

Student race and ethnicity (SASS)

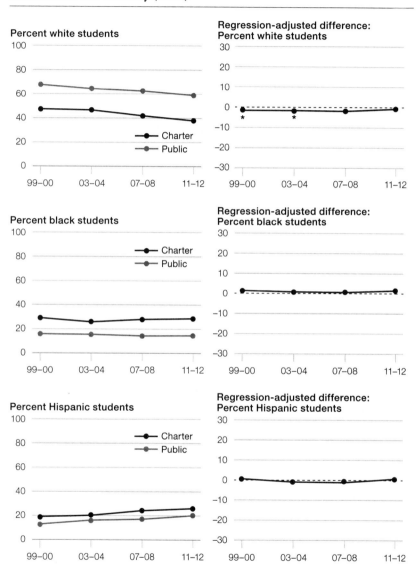

Note: Asterisks in the right panels denote a statistically significant difference between charter and public schools at the $p < 0.05$ level, controlling for other school-level influences. For information about modeling, see the appendix.

across the states.[16] For example, in Washington, DC, 15 percent of students in district schools are classified as special education students, compared with 14 percent in charter schools; however, in Arkansas, 11 percent of students in public schools are classified as special education, and 8 percent in charter schools.

To provide a national perspective, this section turns to two student characteristics measured each year by the SASS: the school's percentage of students classified as ELL or limited English proficiency (LEP) and the school's percentage of students with an individualized education plan (IEP).[17] The top of figure 3.5 displays the

FIGURE 3.5

Student ELL or LEP and IEP status (SASS)

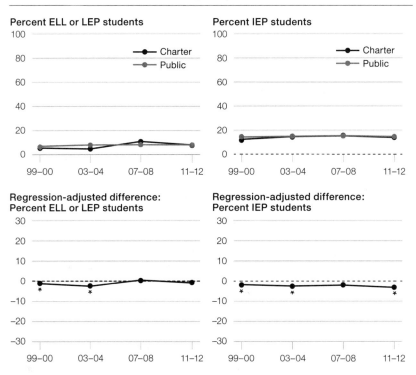

Note: ELL: English language learner. LEP: Limited English proficiency. IEP: Individualized education plan. Asterisks in the bottom panels denote a statistically significant difference between charter and public schools at the $p < 0.05$ level, controlling for other school-level influences. For information about modeling, see the appendix.

mean percentage of students in these different categories over the years of the study; the bottom panels show the differences between these types of schools, controlling for other school-level factors.

The top panels show that there were no obvious disparities between charter and public schools in terms of the percentage of students categorized as ELL or LEP or having IEPs. However, the bottom panels, which control for other school-level factors, add some nuance. In the first two waves of the survey, charter schools had around 2.5 percent fewer ELL students and 2.5 percent fewer students with IEPs. In the third wave of the survey, the differences in the percentage of ELL or LEP and IEP students in charter and public schools disappeared; in the most recent wave, charter schools enrolled 3 percent fewer students with IEPs. Taken in sum, the figure substantiates some of the critics' concerns about the student composition of charter and public schools. Therefore, the analysis will control for these student body characteristics in subsequent chapters.

Poverty

The final student characteristic examined here relates to the economic status of students' families. Specifically, it asks whether students in charter and public schools come from families with different levels of poverty. One measure of the poverty level of a school's student population is the percentage of children who qualify for free or reduced-price school lunches. The left panel of figure 3.6 describes the mean percentage of students who qualified for free or reduced-price school lunches in each wave of the SASS; the right panel shows the extent to which these types of schools differed, controlling for other school-level factors.

The left panel shows that, in the first two school years of the survey, charter schools enrolled a smaller percentage of poor students than did public schools, but, in the most recent two school years, this trend reversed. The right panel shows that the descriptive data don't tell the complete story: when other school-level factors are controlled for, there were significantly fewer poor children in charter schools for all the school years studied. Specifically, in

FIGURE 3.6

Student poverty (SASS)

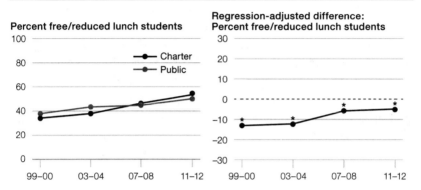

Note: Asterisks in the right panel denote a statistically significant difference between charter and public schools at the $p < 0.05$ level, controlling for other school-level influences. For information about modeling, see the appendix.

the first two years of the survey, charter schools enrolled 12.5 percent fewer students who qualified for free or reduced-price school lunches than were enrolled in public schools. In the last two waves, these differences decreased. Nonetheless, in these same last two periods, charter schools had an average of 5.5 percent fewer poor students than did public schools.

TEACHER CHARACTERISTICS

Like school and student characteristics, teacher characteristics have been the focus of some research comparing public and charter schools.[18] Among other things, this research suggests that teachers in charter schools are younger, less experienced, and less likely to be unionized than are teachers in public schools.[19] Some observers are thus concerned that teachers in charter schools are more likely to be overworked and even exploited.[20] If teachers in charter schools are overly burdened, we might expect that their morale would decrease and they would be less likely to create fertile learning environments for students.

To provide a national, temporal view, this section examines a wide range of characteristics of teachers in public and charter schools.

Race, Ethnicity, and Age

The left panels of figure 3.7 highlight the mean percentage of teachers who identified as white (any ethnicity), black (any ethnicity), and Hispanic (any race) in charter and public schools from the 1999–2000 school year through the 2011–2012 school year. The right panels present the differences between charter and public schools, controlling for other teacher and school characteristics.

The left panels align with previous research: public schools tended to have a lower percentage of black and Hispanic teachers and a higher percentage of white teachers.[21] However, the right panels show that, controlling for other teacher and school characteristics, the racial and ethnic characteristics of the teachers in charter and public schools were indistinguishable. In fact, in only one wave of the survey was there any statistically significant difference: in 2003–2004, teachers in charter schools were less likely to be white. Combined with figure 3.4, these findings suggest that, all else being equal, the racial and ethnic characteristics of students and teachers in charter and public schools were largely analogous.

Turning to age, we do see some differences between teachers in charter and public schools (figure 3.8). The left panel of the figure compares the mean age of teachers in public and charter schools in each wave of the survey; the right panel shows whether these differences were statistically significant, after controlling for other teacher and school factors.

The left panel shows that, throughout the period studied, there were steady differences in the ages of teachers in these schools: teachers in public schools were, on average, five years older than teachers in charter schools. The right panel shows that these differences were smaller but statistically significant: controlling for

FIGURE 3.7

Teacher race and ethnicity (SASS)

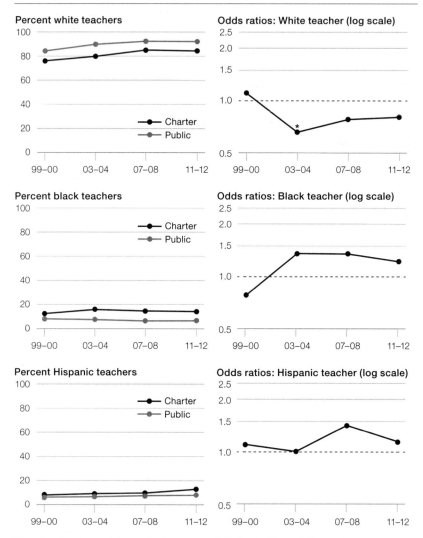

Note: Asterisks in the right panels denote a statistically significant difference between charter and public school teachers at the $p < 0.05$ level, controlling for other school- and teacher-level influences. For information about how to interpret odds ratios, see the text explanation near figure 3.1. For modeling information, see the appendix.

FIGURE 3.8

Teacher age (SASS)

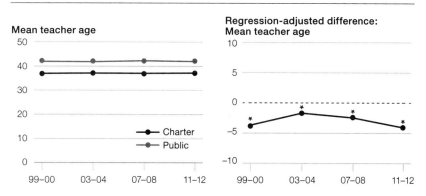

Note: Asterisks in the right panel denote a statistically significant difference between charter and public school teachers at the $p < 0.05$ level, controlling for other school- and teacher-level influences. For information about modeling, see the appendix.

other school- and teacher-level factors, charter school teachers were around three years younger than public school teachers.

Experience, Credentials, and Union Membership

Another group of characteristics important for understanding the differences between charter and public schools relates to teacher experience, credentials, and membership in teachers unions. Each of these characteristics is important to consider, but it is not obvious how we should interpret any differences therein: for each characteristic, there are arguments and evidence in support and opposition of their importance to student learning.[22] Without wading too deeply into these disagreements, this section examines the extent to which differences existed in these three areas across the years studied here.

The left of figure 3.9 details the mean reported years of experience by teachers in charter and public schools. The right panel examines whether any differences in experience were statistically significant, after controlling for other school- and teacher-level influences.

FIGURE 3.9

Teacher experience (SASS)

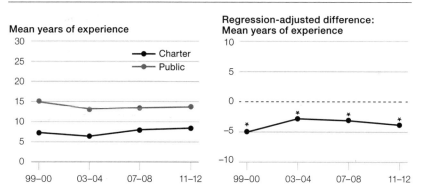

Note: Asterisks in the right panel denote a statistically significant difference between charter and public school teachers at the $p < 0.05$ level, controlling for school- and teacher-level influences. For information about modeling, see the appendix.

On the left we see a large gap in the reported years of experience between teachers in charter schools and in public schools. However, the gap seems to be narrowing somewhat in the last two waves of the survey. On the right we see that, after controlling for other factors, the difference remains statistically significant but is more modest: charter school teachers had, on average, 3.5 years less teaching experience.

Another teacher characteristic relates to credentials, the extent to which teachers have achieved particular accomplishments—like a teaching certificate or a master's degree—that might serve as an indicator of quality or ability. Figure 3.10 compares the credentials of teachers in charter and public schools, using teachers' reports of having a state-approved teaching certificate or a master's degree. The top panels describe the differences between teachers in these various settings, and the bottom panels analyze the statistical significance of any differences.

The top panels of figure 3.10 show consistent differences between teachers in these two types of schools: a higher percentage of public school teachers reported having a master's degree and a teaching

FIGURE 3.10

Teacher credentials (SASS)

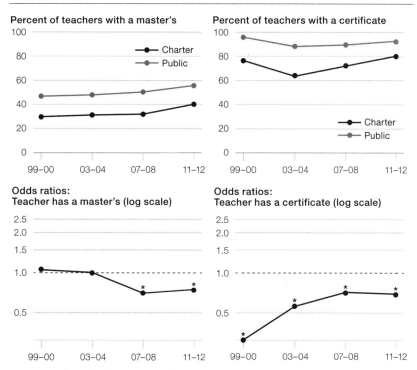

Note: Asterisks in the bottom panels denote a statistically significant difference between charter and public school teachers at the $p < 0.05$ level, after controlling for other school- and teacher-level influences. For information about how to interpret odds ratios, see the text explanation near figure 3.1. For modeling information, see the appendix.

certificate. However, the bottom panels tell a slightly different story. In the bottom left panel, we see that in the two most recent waves of the survey, there has been an increase in differences: teachers in charter schools have become less likely to have a master's degree. In the bottom right panel, we see the reverse: there seems to be a narrowing between the number of teachers in public and charter schools who hold teaching certificates. Still, throughout the periods covered by the survey, public school teachers were more likely to hold teaching certificates.

Finally, we consider teachers' unions, another controversial element of charter schools.[23] As is well known, charter schools tend to hire nonunionized teachers. However, there have been reports of recent efforts led by unions and teachers in charter schools to unionize.[24] Figure 3.11 describes the levels of unionization in charter schools (left) and analyzes the statistical significance of these differences, after controlling for other school- and teacher-related variables (right).

Both panels of the figure confirm the conventional wisdom: there was a wide gap in unionization between charter and public schools. One interesting trend, however, is that in the first year of the SASS, nearly a third of charter teachers were unionized. In the most recent survey, this figure had dropped to below 20 percent. Because of this decrease in unionization, we see a slight downward slope on the bottom: the odds that a charter teacher was unionized dropped somewhat.

Motivation and Values

Among the various teacher characteristics that might affect teaching climates in schools, two have received little attention in the

FIGURE 3.11

Teachers union membership (SASS)

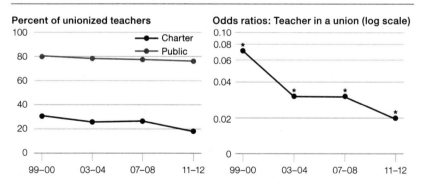

Note: Asterisks in the right panel denote a statistically significant difference between charter and public school teachers at the $p < 0.05$ level, controlling for school- and teacher-level influences. For information about how to interpret odds ratios, see the text explanation near figure 3.1. For modeling information, see the appendix.

charter school literature: teachers' motives and values. Despite the scarce attention paid these attributes, a variety of personnel theories suggests strong patterns of selection between individuals and organizations.[25] In general, people choose workplaces or organizations with which they feel, or suspect that they will feel, some interest or value congruence.[26] Though similarity of values is not the only factor considered by job seekers and recruiters—the dynamics of the labor market and the supply and demand of particular sets of skills are of obvious importance—scholars have speculated that organizations with different levels of publicness attract employees with different mind-sets.[27]

For this reason, teachers who choose a charter school might differ—for example, in their expectations, orientation, or predispositions—from those who choose a public school.[28] In fact, such arguments have been made to explain why charter schools differ from public schools: one charter school leader argued that "[being] able to attract teachers and principals that have a shared vision" nurtures a widely shared school culture.[29]

To explore teachers' motivations and values, I analyzed the data from my study of teachers in Delaware (the Delaware Teachers Survey, or DTS, described in chapter 1). My interviews with teachers in Delaware suggested that there were broad commonalities in the motivations of teachers in public and charter schools. Teachers were more drawn to the profession than to their particular school or type of school. For example, a charter teacher was looking for a job in a public school, but took a job in a charter school because he needed "a job and benefits" after the birth of a child. One of the public school teachers I spoke with was looking for a teaching job and worked a connection between a mentor and the head of a public school social studies department. For both teachers, the school's mission or type did not play a strong role in leading them to their work.

The interviews also revealed that teachers in public and charter schools were motivated by a similar set of factors: working with kids, challenging them, and getting them to think. A high school charter teacher noted that he was drawn to high schools because he "enjoyed the age group because of their ability to think, to think freely, to debate and argue and discuss." In much the same way, a public high school teacher with whom I spoke said that he has "always enjoyed sort of the intellectual debate that goes on in a classroom. I enjoy the conversation. I enjoy the humor. There's something to laugh about every day."

To provide a more systematic understanding of teachers' motivations, I asked teachers about their motives on the DTS in two ways. First, the survey adapted questions from the General Social Survey about workplace motivation.[30] Specifically, it asked teachers, "How important do you personally consider the following job characteristics?" The question was followed by five prompts: "Job security," "Employer-provided benefits," "Good opportunities for personal advancement," "An occupation in which one can help others," and "A job that is useful to society." For each prompt, respondents chose an answer on a four-point scale, from "Not important" to "Very important." Table 3.1 reports the results from a descriptive analysis of these questions.

The table shows few differences in the motivations of teachers in charter and public schools. Teachers in public schools were more motivated by job security and benefits, whereas teachers in charter schools were motivated more by personal advancement. However, none of these differences were large: in fact, if we round up to the tenth place, the mean responses across each question are identical.

TABLE 3.1

Teacher motivation: scalar (DTS)

	Public school teachers	Charter school teachers
Job security	3.64	3.58
Employer-provided benefits	3.74	3.67
Good opportunities for personal advancement	3.28	3.33
An occupation in which one can help others	3.69	3.66
A job that is useful to society	3.68	3.66

Note: DTS: Delaware Teachers Survey. Numbers are the mean responses of teachers on a four-point numerical rating scale, where 1 = "Not important" and 4 = "Very important," to the question "How important do you personally consider the following job characteristics?"

To further explore whether any differences existed, I conducted a multivariate analysis of these responses, controlling for school- and teacher-level differences. Across the five motivation areas, there were no statistically significant differences between the motivations of teachers in charter and public schools.

After the numerical-scale-based general motivation questions, respondents were asked which of the five motivations was most important to them. Table 3.2 presents the findings from a descriptive analysis of teachers' responses.

Roughly a third of teachers in charter and public schools indicated being most motivated by job security; another third were most motivated by the opportunity to help others. More teachers in public schools were motivated by benefits than were charter school teachers, more of whom were motivated by the chance for advancement. Again, however, the differences were quite small; a subsequent multivariate statistical analysis revealed no statistically significant differences across these groups for four of the five questions. Nonetheless, for one source of motivation, there was a difference: teachers in charter schools were less likely to choose job security as their top motivation than were teachers in public schools.

A second way of measuring motivation is to ask teachers about public service motivation (PSM), a concept from the public administration literature that refers to a cluster of "motives associated with

TABLE 3.2

Teacher motivation: most important (DTS)

	Public school teachers	Charter school teachers
Job security	0.33	0.34
Employer-provided benefits	0.16	0.08
Good opportunities for personal advancement	0.05	0.10
An occupation in which one can help others	0.32	0.32
A job that is useful to society	0.15	0.16

Note: Numbers are the mean proportion of teachers answering that this motivation was the most important to them, where 0 = didn't choose and 1 = did choose.

serving the public good."[31] There has been considerable effort to validate and measure PSM; borrowing from the consensus approach, the DTS employed a five-question PSM schedule: "Meaningful public service is very important to me," "I am often reminded by daily events about how dependent we are on one another," "Making a difference in society means more to me than personal achievements," "I am prepared to make sacrifices for the good of society," and "I am not afraid to go to bat for the rights of others even if it means I will be ridiculed."[32] For each question, respondents answered by choosing a response on a five-point scale, from "Strongly disagree" to "Strongly agree." Table 3.3 displays the mean responses of teachers to each of these questions.

These data show that across each question, teachers in public schools were more likely to agree with these statements than were teachers in charter schools. In most cases, the differences were small, but in the last question—about standing up for others—there was a bigger difference. To determine if these differences were significant, I conducted a multivariate analysis that controlled for teacher- and

TABLE 3.3

Teacher public service motivation (DTS)

	Public school teachers	Charter school teachers
Meaningful public service is very important to me.	4.11	4.03
I am often reminded by daily events about how dependent we are on one another.	3.75	3.69
Making a difference in society means more to me than personal achievements.	3.85	3.80
I am prepared to make sacrifices for the good of society.	3.77	3.70
I am not afraid to go to bat for the rights of others even if it means I will be ridiculed.	3.96	3.82

Note: Numbers are the mean responses of teachers on a five-point numerical rating scale, where 1 = "Strongly disagree" and 5 = "Strongly agree," to various statements about public service motivation.

individual-level covariates. I ran this analysis for each individual question and for a summary PSM index variable (which essentially adds up each teacher's answer to these five questions). The individual-question analysis revealed no statistically significant differences in the first four questions, but as table 3.3 suggested, it found that teachers in public schools were more likely to agree with standing up for others in the face of ridicule than were teachers in charter schools. The index analysis revealed no statistically significant differences between teachers in charter and public schools.

Finally, I examined the values held by teachers in these different types of schools. Adapting questions from Zeger van der Wal and Leo Huberts—who isolate key values differences between the private and public sector—the DTS asked teachers about how important the following values were to them: "Effectiveness: helping students learn," "Efficiency: helping students learn without wasting materials, time, or energy," "Compliance: closely following school policies," and "Social justice: acting out of commitment to a just society."[33] For each value, respondents chose an answer on a four-point scale, from "Not important" to "Very important." Table 3.4 displays the mean responses to these questions for teachers in charter and public schools.

TABLE 3.4

Teacher values: scalar (DTS)

	Public school teachers	Charter school teachers
Effectiveness: helping students learn	3.92	3.95
Efficiency: helping students learn without wasting materials, time, or energy	3.49	3.52
Compliance: closely following school policies	2.92	3.01
Social justice: acting out of commitment to a just society	3.11	3.16

Note: Numbers are the mean response of teachers on a four-point numerical rating scale, where 1 = "Not important" and 4 = "Very important," to questions about how important a value was to them.

The table shows that teachers in both types of schools prized effectiveness more than efficiency, compliance, or social justice. It also shows great similarity between the two groups: for all four questions, teachers in public schools appeared to care about these values the same as teachers in charter schools did. To provide a more robust comparison, I conducted a multivariate analysis that controlled for school- and teacher-level variables. The findings revealed that, in terms of compliance and social justice, there were no significantly different values expressed by teachers in charter and public schools. However, teachers in charter schools were more likely to value effectiveness and efficiency than were teachers in public schools.

As with the general motivation questions, the DTS also asked respondents about which value was most important to them. Table 3.5 summarizes the mean responses to these questions.

The table shows very few notable differences between the mean responses of teachers in charter and public schools. A multivariate analysis—which controlled for differences in teacher- and school-level factors—confirmed these descriptive findings: there were no statistically significant differences between teachers in charter schools and in public schools on which value they considered the most important.

TABLE 3.5

Teacher values: most important (DTS)

	Public school teachers	Charter school teachers
Effectiveness: helping students learn	0.83	0.84
Efficiency: helping students learn without wasting materials, time, or energy	0.07	0.03
Compliance: closely following school policies	0.01	0.00
Social justice: acting out of commitment to a just society	0.03	0.05

Note: Numbers are the mean proportion of teachers answering that this value was the most important to them, where 0 = didn't choose and 1 = did choose.

INSIDE THE CHARTER SECTOR

Thus far, this chapter has illuminated some similarities and some differences between charter schools and public schools. This section now explores variation among charter schools themselves. Specifically, it asks, to what extent were there differences among charter schools based on franchising and tax status? Because the SASS only included questions about franchising and tax status in the most recent survey, it focuses its analysis there.[34] To save space, the discussion below skips a presentation and discussion of descriptive statistics; rather, it focuses on the findings from multivariate analyses that controlled for various school, student, and teacher characteristics.

School Characteristics

The analysis found no statistically significant differences in the location (urbanicity), enrollment, or student-teacher ratios of charter schools that were run by educational management organizations (EMOs) and those that were not. In other words, there was no evidence that franchised charter schools were located in different areas from nonfranchised charters, were smaller or larger than their nonfranchised counterparts, or were employing more or fewer teachers per student.

Second, for-profit EMOs were just as likely to be located in urban or suburban areas as were nonprofit EMOs and had similar student-teacher ratios; however, for-profit EMOs were less likely to be located in rural settings. Additionally, for-profit EMOs had higher enrollments than did nonprofit EMOs: on average, for-profit schools had 154 more students, when other school-level factors were controlled for. Interestingly, a subsequent comparison of for-profit EMOs with public schools showed no differences in enrollment. Put differently, for-profit EMOs and public schools have, on average, comparable enrollments.

Student Characteristics

In terms of student composition, there were some differences between EMO-run and non-EMO-run charter schools. When other factors were controlled for, EMOs had an average of around 11 percent more Hispanic students and an average of 8 percent more poor students than did non-EMOs. However, there were no differences between the percentage of non-Hispanic black students, non-Hispanic white students, or students classified as ELL or LEP or as having IEPs in these different types of charter schools.

The second level of analysis further illuminates this story: there were some important differences between students in for-profit EMOs and nonprofit EMOs. In particular, for-profit EMOs had approximately one-fifth more non-Hispanic white students and one-fifth fewer Hispanic students than nonprofit EMOs had. In addition, for-profit EMOs had an average of 11 percent fewer students with IEPs than did nonprofit EMOs. Although we can't know for sure why these differences exist, this finding fits with concerns that for-profit charter schools will avoid enrolling students who are difficult to serve and who, therefore, might score low on standardized tests and hurt their bottom lines. Nevertheless, there were no statistically significant differences between nonprofit and for-profit EMOs in terms of the percentage of non-Hispanic black students, the percentage of poor students, and the percentage of ELL or LEP students.

Teacher Characteristics

Within the charter sector, there were differences in unionization between EMO-run and non-EMO-run schools: a multivariate analysis, controlling for other school- and teacher-level variables, revealed that teachers in non-EMOs were more likely to be members of a union than were teachers in EMOs. Interestingly, the levels of unionization were not significantly different between for-profit and nonprofit EMOs.

Moving to teacher credentials, approximately equal numbers of teachers had master's degrees in EMO-run and non-EMO-run charter schools. However, teachers in non-EMOs were more likely to have teaching certificates than were teachers in EMOs. There were no differences in teacher credentials when the tax status of the EMO running the schools was considered. Consequently, no evidence suggests that for-profit EMOs are systematically hiring teachers who are less credentialed than those hired by nonprofit EMOs.

The teaching forces of EMO-run and non-EMO-run charter schools were largely similar in race and ethnicity. Roughly similar numbers of teachers self-identified as white, black, and Hispanic. The same was true in the comparison of for-profit and nonprofit EMOs except for one area: teachers in nonprofit EMOs were more likely than those in for-profit EMOs to identify as Hispanic.

Finally, there were no statistically significant differences between teachers in EMO-run and non-EMO-run charter schools, or between teachers in for-profit and nonprofit EMOs, in terms of age or experience.

SUMMARY

If you were to look inside randomly chosen charter and public schools, would you find that they differ in any specific ways? This book answers that question by studying the teaching climates fostered by these schools. This chapter has begun to shed light on how these schools have differed over the past decade or so and how they haven't. In terms of locations, charter schools were more likely to be urban and less likely to be rural. However, in recent years there were no differences in their likelihood of being suburban. Also, though charter schools tended to have smaller enrollments, this difference appears to be waning: charter schools grew in size from below 300 in the 1999–2000 school year to around 400 in the 2011–2012 school year. Despite having smaller student populations, charter schools had higher student-teacher ratios in each of the years studied here. Thus, charter schools may provide a more intimate school experience (because of their smaller enrollments), but teachers may have less time to spend with each individual student.

Turning to the people inside these schools, charter schools had comparable percentages of non-Hispanic white, non-Hispanic black, and Hispanic students as public schools. Also, in recent years charters have had comparable numbers of students classified as ELL or LEP. However, the students in these two settings were different in two other ways: charter schools had fewer students with IEPs and fewer students classified as poor than did public schools. The number of students with IEPs was somewhat constant, with charter schools having around 2.5 percent fewer IEP students over the four waves of the survey (from 1999 to 2012). In contrast, differences in poverty narrowed: in the last two school years surveyed (2007–2008 and 2011–2012), there were 5.5 percent fewer poor students in charter schools, compared with the first years surveyed (1999–2000 and 2003–2004), when there were 12.5 percent fewer poor students in charter schools.

In terms of teachers, again these schools had some similarities and some differences. Confirming other findings, the chapter showed that teachers in charter schools were less likely to be unionized or hold a master's degree or teaching certificate. They were also more likely to be younger and have fewer years of teaching experience than teachers in public schools. However, in other respects, there were important similarities. First, there were few differences in the racial or ethnic identities of teachers in charter and public schools. Second, although the data come from only one state, the DTS responses revealed that teachers in charter and public schools largely had mostly similar motivations and values.

The chapter also showed that tax status and franchise status mattered for charter schools in some ways but not in others. EMO-run charter schools were more likely to have poor, Hispanic students than were non-EMO-run charter schools, and teachers in EMOs were less likely to be unionized or have a teaching certificate than those in non-EMOs. However, in other respects—like the percentage of non-Hispanic black, non-Hispanic white, ELL, and IEP students and the charter schools' location, enrollment size, and student-teacher ratio—EMO and non-EMO schools were indistinguishable. Nor were there any statistically significant differences in teacher race, attainment of a master's degree, years of teaching experience, or age.

Analyzing differences related to tax status within EMO-run schools, I found that the profit motive was associated with various differences. These differences corresponded to concerns critics have raised about for-profit public education: for-profit EMOs had larger enrollments, fewer Hispanic or IEP students, and more non-Hispanic white students. However, in other respects—like the student-teacher ratio, the credentials of teachers, the percentage of non-Hispanic black students, the percentage of poor students, and the percentage of ELL students—for-profit and nonprofit EMOs were comparable.

Taken in sum, this analysis has identified a few structural ways in which these schools were similar and different. Some of the findings confirm prior research, while others challenge existing beliefs about these schools. Either way, the analysis provides us with a baseline understanding of what teachers in these different settings were likely to experience, depending on whether they worked in a charter school or a public school. The chapter also demonstrated the importance of using multivariate analyses to explore differences between public and charter schools. If we are to study how school type matters—and avoid conflating it with other factors that affect what it's like to teach and learn in these different settings—we need to account for structural differences between these schools. Consequently, this book's empirical approach, as it compares the teaching climates of charter and public schools and looks within the charter sector, is to control for as many school, student, and teacher characteristics as possible.

Since the beginning of the charter movement, proponents have expected that teachers in charter schools would have more classroom autonomy while at the same time would be held more accountable. Were such differences apparent in the early days of the charter sector? Have they persisted? The next chapter turns to these questions which lie at the heart of the case for charter schools.

FOUR

Teacher Autonomy and Accountability

EARLY ADVOCATES argued that charter schools would operate differently because of a bargain struck between schools and charter-granting entities. In essence, charter schools would have more autonomy from the standard rules and regulations and, in return, would be held more accountable.[1] In this way, authorizers could encourage schools to be innovative without losing control over them. But theorists also expected that the basics of this bargain would permeate the schools themselves: they hoped that charter schools would enhance teacher autonomy and accountability. For example, Ray Budde argued that "teachers should be given more autonomy; decisions about curriculum and other school matters should be made closer to the classroom."[2] At the same time, he noted, the system of teacher evaluation had to change so that teachers would be "made more accountable for the results (or lack of results) achieved by their students. Incompetent teachers should be fired. The more able teachers should work a longer professional year and be paid substantially higher salaries."[3]

Although there have been many changes to the US public education system since these early theorists wrote, and although the charter sector has grown and evolved, these intermediate goals—enhanced autonomy and accountability—remain central to arguments in favor of charter schools.[4] Whether this promise has been achieved remains unclear. For one thing, the mechanisms that ensure school accountability may necessarily reduce autonomy.[5] For example, because charter schools face a variety of competitive pressures, innovation—at the school level or inside classrooms—may be risky and unlikely.[6] Additionally, the charter sector has become increasingly populated by centrally controlled education management organizations (EMOs).[7] Because EMO-run schools "develop curricula and instructional strategies that their teachers are expected to implement," they may reduce teacher autonomy and innovation.[8] Put differently, they may replicate the hierarchical, rules-based school districts that charter schools were founded to combat.[9]

To examine whether charter schools have fulfilled the accountability and autonomy aspects of their promise, this chapter describes and analyzes teachers' experiences. After we compare teachers in public and charter schools, we will look solely at charter school teachers to determine whether differences in autonomy and accountability are associated with differences in franchising, tax status, or the nature of a state's charter law.

AUTONOMY AND INNOVATION

A Spanish teacher in a Delaware charter school said that she had considerable flexibility inside her classroom: "I stray away when it's appropriate and stick to [the curriculum] when it is also appropriate. I look at the state standards, and I say I have to teach these topics, but the order that I teach them in, or if I add anything or take anything away, I use my judgment. Spanish is not my first language, either, so how can I show them a language that I have learned in the most effective way possible? So if something is missing from the textbook or the state standards, [and] the curriculum is telling me to teach [it], I will add things more frequently than I take things away."

Another charter school teacher made a similar observation: "We don't have to teach our standards at the same time. Another tenth-grade teacher is maybe focusing on close reading and connotations of words. I don't need to be doing that same thing in the same way she's doing it. I can do whatever I want . . . We have a lot of freedom in what we choose to read with the students, when we choose to read it, and how we choose to teach the skills that we want to use in our classes." A third charter teacher echoed this sentiment, saying that her approach to implementing her school's social studies curriculum is "entirely up to me . . . I feel very free to develop my own material."

These comments echo the claims of charter school proponents and differed from the comments about autonomy made by teachers in public schools. For example, one public school teacher I interviewed described the lack of autonomy at her job:

> We don't have much freedom in the classroom. We—and it seems really sad, I hate to talk so negatively, I really do. But you know, we were all hired, we all felt like we were hired for individual teaching styles and abilities and what we could bring to the table. And then it ended up being . . . you know, we're robots now, we're little puppets, and we're told what to do and how to teach, and that's what we're doing now. A lot of the stuff that we're teaching now ends up being scripted like our math curriculum. It's [math curriculum name], and it's scripted, and we're told what to say. We're reading a script . . . The principal, the administrators, they don't want to hear [about innovation]. They want to know that you're doing exactly . . . what's in the book—what's scripted for us. And we have binders that have scripts in it that say, 'Tell students da-da-da,' . . . as if we were all substitutes and we were following a sub place.

Two caveats are important in interpreting this comment. First, the picture painted by this teacher is something of an outlier: most public school teachers I spoke with described being constrained, but did not indicate feeling as stifled as she did. Although they did not have carte blanche to deviate and create, few reported that their jobs had descended to the level of the automaton. Second, though the teacher described herself as a puppet and a robot in this part of the interview, in another part, she said that she could go "off script" as long as an administrator wasn't in her classroom (which was fairly regularly, it seemed).

Another complication to the standard story—that charter schools foster more autonomy—is that some charter school teachers with whom I spoke reported that their autonomy was diminishing (largely because of the adoption of Common Core). For instance, a charter teacher made this comment about his school: "[We are] leashed by state mandates as far as standardized testing goes. And now that our state, the state of Delaware, has embraced Common Core, we are spending more time teaching to the test rather than teaching. So that has really taken some of the autonomy away from us as teachers and taken away some of the vision and creativity away from us that enjoyed quite freely in the past." Echoing this teacher's concern—and suggesting a larger scope—a recent report by the Fordham Institute noted that because of the encroachment of federal, state, and local rules and regulations, charter schools across the nation have considerably less autonomy than typically thought.[10] This conclusion might explain why prior studies comparing teacher autonomy in charter and public schools suggest few significant differences.[11]

To develop a more general understanding of teachers' experiences with autonomy—defined as the ability to independently make classroom decisions about teaching and learning—I conducted an analysis of SASS data.[12] On the survey, teachers were asked about how much control they had over the following areas of teaching and planning: "(1) Selecting textbooks and other instructional materials; (2) Selecting content, topics, and skills to be taught; (3) Selecting teaching techniques; (4) Evaluating and grading students; (5) Disciplining students; (6) Determining the amount of homework to be assigned."

The planning and teaching areas of the survey were the same across all four waves of the SASS (school years 1999–2000, 2003–2004, 2007–2008, 2011–2012). However, the 1999–2000 questions differed from those in subsequent surveys in two ways. First, in the 1999–2000 SASS, the questions were preceded with the following prompt: "Using a scale of 1–5, where 1 means 'No control' and 5 means 'Complete control,' how much control do you think you have

IN YOUR CLASSROOM at this school over each of the following areas of your planning and teaching?" (emphasis in original). Later surveys asked: "How much actual control do you have IN YOUR CLASSROOM at this school over the following areas of your planning and teaching?" (emphasis in original). Second, the scale for the 1999–2000 questions included five boxes with a double-sided arrow leading from "No control" to "Complete control"; the scale for subsequent surveys included four boxes from "No control" to "A great deal of control" and no arrow. To account for this difference in scale and maintain the comparability of years, respondents' answers were normalized so that 1.0 was the highest level of control for each year and 0 was the lowest level.[13] Figure 4.1 displays the teachers' mean responses to these questions over time.

The figure reveals high responses (between 0.8 and 1.0) in terms of techniques, grading, discipline, and homework and somewhat lower (below 0.8) for choosing texts and content. These findings align with other work that challenges the view that teachers have lost a massive amount of control over their classrooms in recent years.[14] The results also shows impressive consistency over a thirteen-year period in which there were remarkable changes in educational policy at the state and federal level, like the passage and implementation of the No Child Left Behind Act and the intensifying of high-stakes testing. The stability of teachers' experiences with classroom control suggests that these policy changes had little effect on this aspect of teacher practice and school life. Nevertheless, there was some downward shift in the top panels: teachers in both sectors reported less control over texts and content in 2011–2012 than they did in 1999–2000.

Figure 4.2 examines whether teachers in charter and public schools had different experiences with autonomy, controlling for school- and teacher-level covariates.[15] The vertical axis presents odds ratios, derived from ordered logit coefficients, which indicate the likelihood that teachers in charter schools answered a question differently than did teachers in public schools. An odds ratio above 1.0 with an asterisk indicates that, all else being equal, teachers in charter schools were more likely to indicate that they had

FIGURE 4.1

Teacher autonomy: mean responses (SASS)

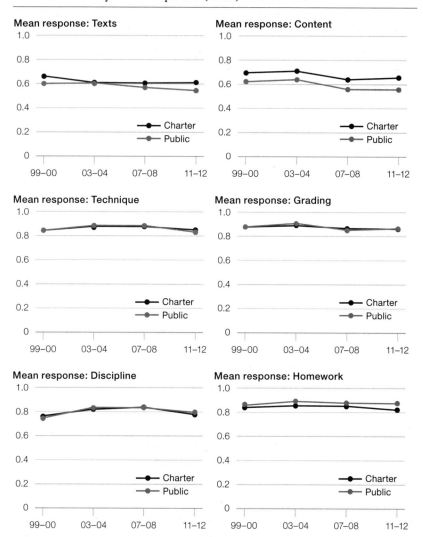

Note: SASS: Schools and Staffing Survey. Charts represent mean responses to questions about how much control teachers felt they had in the classroom with regard to six elements: textbook selection, content selection, teaching techniques, grading, discipline, and the amount of homework. The higher the number, the more control the teachers believed they had.

FIGURE 4.2

Teacher autonomy: multivariate analysis (SASS)

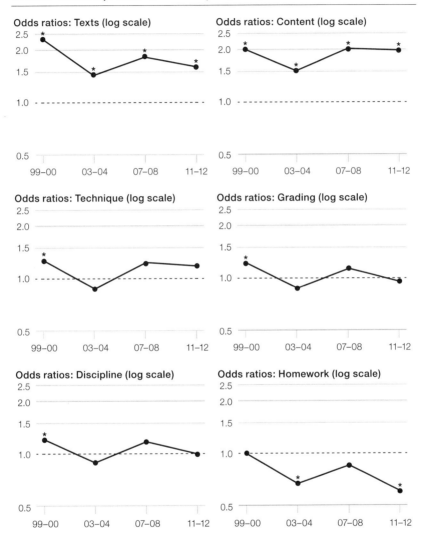

Note: Asterisks denote a statistically significant difference between charter and public school teachers at the $p < 0.05$ level, controlling for school- and teacher-level influences. For information about how to interpret odds ratios, see the accompanying text. For modeling information, see the appendix.

control over certain elements of their practice. An odds ratio below 1.0 with an asterisk indicates that teachers in charter schools were less likely to indicate that they had control than were teachers in public schools. An odds ratio without an asterisk indicates that there were no statistically significant differences between the responses of teachers in charter and public schools.

The figure shows that teachers in charter schools, from the early days of the charter sector through today, have experienced greater autonomy than teachers in public schools regarding the selection of texts and content. It also suggests that differences in text selection may have waned somewhat over the years, whereas differences in content selection remained largely the same. In terms of choosing techniques, grading, and discipline, there were few differences between teachers in these two different settings—teachers in charter schools had more autonomy in these areas in 1999–2000, but these differences evaporated in the three most recent surveys. Finally, the bottom right panel reveals interesting findings that contradict the claims of charter advocates: in two of the four surveys, teachers in charter schools reported less control over homework than did teachers in public schools.

To get a more up-to-date perspective, we now turn to TELL surveys, collected in six states during the 2012–2013 and 2013–2014 school years. Though these results cannot be used to make claims about national trends, they cover a diverse array of states and include responses from over 230,000 teachers. For these surveys, teachers were asked how much they agreed with the following statement: "Teachers have autonomy to make decisions about instructional delivery (i.e., pacing, materials and pedagogy)." Respondents chose an answer from one of four ordered responses, from "Strongly disagree" to "Strongly agree." The mean response of teachers in public schools was 2.91, and teachers in charter schools, 3.22. Because these scores are relatively high—they correspond with "Agree" on the four-point scale—they echo the SASS descriptive results and suggest that teachers generally experienced high levels of autonomy. But what about any differences in autonomy between teachers in charter and public schools? A multivariate analysis of this question, controlling for school- and teacher-level influences, revealed significant differences: teachers in charter schools were 133 percent more likely to agree that they had classroom autonomy than were teachers in public schools. This question is not as nuanced as the SASS questions, which break autonomy down into six categories; however, in directing attention to the selection of "materials and pedagogy," it's broadly consonant with the SASS finding about autonomy with respect to texts and content.

Finally we turn to the Delaware Teacher Survey (DTS)—which includes around 1,000 teachers in 180 schools—which I conducted during the 2014–2015 school year. As with the TELL, conclusions drawn from this survey are more limited than data from the SASS. Nevertheless, it is useful to gain a third vantage point on this topic. On the DTS, teachers were asked three questions pertaining to autonomy. The first two questions asked how much respondents agreed with the following statements: "Teachers are expected to closely follow their department's curriculum" and "Teachers have a lot of autonomy in planning lessons" in their schools. The third question asked teachers how much they agreed with this statement: "I diverge from the curriculum if I can help students learn more." For all questions, the respondents chose an answer from one of five ordered responses, from "Strongly disagree" to "Strongly agree." Table 4.1 displays the mean responses of teachers across these two types of schools.

Teachers' responses to the first question differ from the SASS and TELL findings: they suggest that teachers felt somewhat constrained by their department's curricula. The second question suggests a fairly sizable difference in control over lesson planning—teachers in charter schools agreed that they had control, whereas teachers in public schools were more ambivalent. Responses to the third question are consistent with the high levels of autonomy seen on the SASS and TELL surveys: teachers in Delaware indicated that they departed from the standard approach when it was helpful for students.

To determine if there were any significant differences between teachers in charter and public schools, after controlling for

TABLE 4.1

Teacher autonomy (DTS)

	Public school teachers	Charter school teachers
Teachers are expected to closely follow their department's curriculum.	4.18	3.71
Teachers have a lot of autonomy in planning lessons.	3.14	3.94
I diverge from the curriculum if I can help students learn more.	4.11	4.40

Note: DTS: Delaware Teachers Survey. Numbers are the mean responses of teachers on a five-point numerical rating scale, where 1 = "Strongly disagree" and 5 = "Strongly agree," to statements about autonomy.

school- and teacher-level influences, I conducted a multivariate analysis of these responses. Figure 4.3 presents the findings from this analysis.

Mirroring the SASS and TELL findings, the figure shows significant differences by school type: teachers in charter schools were less likely to agree that they were expected to closely follow their department's curriculum, more likely to agree that they had autonomy in lesson planning, and more likely to agree that they diverged from the curriculum if they could help students learn more.

Teacher autonomy is important in its own right; if teachers have sufficient latitude, they can use their professional training and discretion to make the best decisions for students. But autonomy is also important, charter proponents suggest, because autonomy creates the space necessary for innovation. A recent review of the innovativeness of charter school programs suggests that they are not serving as the laboratories often imagined in the charter debate; rather, they tend to employ fairly traditional approaches to education.[16]

But what about inside the classroom? Do teachers in charter schools experiment and innovate more than teachers in public schools do? Are charter schools more likely to foster environments that encourage innovation? One study of teachers in four states attempted to answer these questions. The researchers found that—all

FIGURE 4.3

Teacher autonomy (DTS)

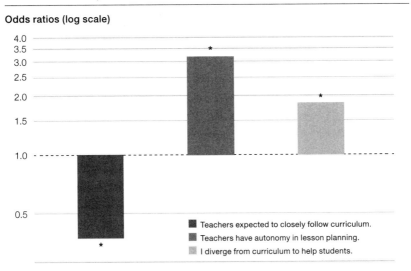

Odds ratios (log scale)

- Teachers expected to closely follow curriculum.
- Teachers have autonomy in lesson planning.
- I diverge from curriculum to help students.

Note: Asterisks denote a statistically significant difference between charter and public school teachers at the $p < 0.05$ level, controlling for school- and teacher-level influences. For information about how to interpret odds ratios, see the text explanation near figure 4.2. For modeling information, see the appendix.

other factors being held equal—teachers in charter schools were more likely than public school teachers to say that their schools fostered an environment of instructional innovativeness.[17]

In my interviews with teachers in Delaware, I sensed some differences in the level of innovativeness in charter and public schools. One charter school teacher said that administrators "always encourage us to think outside the box." When I asked for an example that came out of such encouragement, she discussed an arts integration program:

Well, this year we've been working along with [a local university], and we have arts integration. So a couple of times a month, we will have their faculty or their students come over, and they'll show us how we can integrate arts into all of our subjects. So for me, since I teach art, it's how can you integrate movement so the kids aren't just sitting there drawing. Like, what else can you do to get them out of their seats and moving that would explain the lesson better? And for the science component, I know in third grade, when they learn the life cycle of the butterfly, rather than just having them sit there and draw the pictures and talk about it, they are now acting out the life cycle so that they understand it.

Interestingly, a public school teacher whom I interviewed also said that administrators were asking teachers in his school to "think outside the box." This was important, he said, because research is showing that there are "lots of different ways to reach students just to get away from that sit-and-get, skill-and-drill-type mentality into more of a collaborative discussion with the students." Despite this approach, he, like other public school teachers, said that innovative ideas weren't always implemented, because "there's a top-down [approach] from district administration that sometimes the building administration's hands are tied. So even though they think your idea's good, it won't be implemented, because somebody else told them no. So there are just so many multiple layers that are holding things back."

While charter teachers said that they worked in somewhat more innovative teaching climates, the ability to innovate was conditional. For example, one charter teacher said that the expectation or climate of innovativeness depended on the teacher's level of experience and her students' test scores: "I think that for someone that is new—I'm thinking of someone in particular this year, whose test scores aren't very good—and so, they have been just on her, wanting her to conform and do things exactly their way so that they can get those test scores up." Interestingly, this conditional innovation theme was true for public school teachers too: the aforementioned public school teacher who wished there was more autonomy in his school noted that "as long as the kids are meeting those standards, [teachers] are sort of encouraged to do what you want to do. You're encouraged to write your own lessons as long as the kids are getting the scores."

Unfortunately, because the SASS did not ask about teacher innovation, this chapter presents no national data on this topic. Nonetheless, the TELL survey asked teachers how much they agreed with the following statement: "Teachers are encouraged to try new things to improve instruction." The teachers responded on a numerical rating scale, where 1 meant "Strongly disagree" and 4 meant "Strongly agree." The mean response for teachers in public schools was 3.19; for teachers in charter schools, 3.28. These are interesting findings, as both groups' responses are above 3 ("Agree"), suggesting that teachers in both settings felt encouraged to be innovative.

If teachers in public schools didn't experience the stultifying environment described by critics, perhaps teachers in charter schools wouldn't experience a very different environment. To determine if there were differences, I conducted a multivariate analysis of this question, controlling for school- and teacher-level influences. Despite relatively high levels of innovation in public schools, the analysis revealed that teachers in charter schools were around 50 percent more likely to agree with this statement than were teachers in public schools.

RED TAPE

Charter school advocates argue that public schools tend to be saddled with excessive rules and regulations, which, in the classroom, hinder teacher autonomy and effectiveness. Put differently, they expect that teachers in public schools experience considerable red tape: "rules, regulations, and procedures that remain in force and entail a compliance burden but do not advance the legitimate purposes the rules were intended to serve."[18] Perhaps as a result, some charter laws were specifically written to give teachers "freedom from conventional program constraints and mandates."[19] As we saw above, there was some evidence that teachers in charter schools had more autonomy than teachers in public schools. We will now investigate whether there were also differences in red tape.

When I asked teachers in Delaware charter schools about this aspect of school life, they answered somewhat uniformly that red tape wasn't a problem. One charter teacher noted that "there are plenty of rules and regulations . . . but I don't think it gets in the way of us doing our jobs . . . or . . . gets in the way of us coming up with new things and trying new things." Another charter teacher said there was virtually no red tape at her school: "I can just go down and talk to the person that needs to be spoken with about different issues. I think our issue is trying to figure out who's supposed to do what because we're a new school and where that form is and what it might look like. We just don't have the institutional history of how things get done. I would say no [red tape]: I mean, I have direct access to whoever I need, and usually, things get taken care of really quickly."

This response is interesting as it hints at what some have said is the flip side of few rules and regulations: disorder. In other words, perhaps teachers in these schools could use more guidance. We will return to this theme when considering accountability. The teacher's comment is also interesting because it points to a factor that might shape views of red tape: the age of the school. As schools age—or as the charter sector as a whole becomes established—standard operating procedures may take hold, leading to more rules and regulations, which teachers experience as red tape. For this reason, it will be interesting to see how differences between charter and public schools evolved over time; also, in the charter-sector analysis below, we will explore whether variation in the number of years a school has been in operation is associated with teachers' experiences with red tape.

Two other points from the interviews are important. First, although they were less emphatic about their responses, teachers in public schools also saw little red tape in their schools. Where it did appear, however, as one public school teacher noted, it had a lot to do with special education: IEPs created more rules and paperwork. Since chapter 3 showed that there tended to be fewer students with IEPs in charter schools, this will be an important school characteristics to control for in the statistical analysis of teachers' experiences with red tape. Second, as alluded to in the autonomy section, a number of teachers in both public and charter schools indicated that the adoption of Common Core had rigidified their teaching. As a result, it will be important to look at the TELL and DTS data—which are more recent than the SASS data—to see if any differences in red tape between charter and public schools were evident in the most recent data analyzed here.

Red tape is a multidimensional concept, containing a host of interrelated subcomponents.[20] Unfortunately, the SASS questionnaire asks teachers to respond to only one statement about a school's red tape: "Routine duties and paperwork interfere with my job of teaching." In each wave of the survey, respondents were asked how much they agreed with this statement on a four-point scale, from "Strongly disagree" to "Strongly agree." Although this approach to studying red tape is not perfect, fortunately the question asks about red tape in relation to teachers' primary classroom goal: teaching. The left panel of figure 4.4 shows teachers' mean responses to this question; the right panel presents the results of an analysis of whether there were differences in red tape in charter and public schools, controlling for school- and teacher-level covariates.

FIGURE 4.4

Teachers' experiences with red tape (SASS)

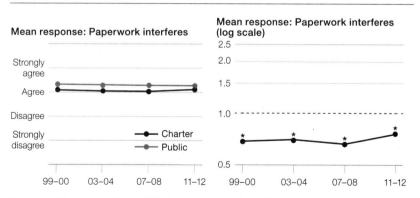

Note: Asterisks in the right panel denote a statistically significant difference between charter and public school teachers at the $p < 0.05$ level, controlling for school- and teacher-level influences. For information about how to interpret odds ratios, see the text explanation near figure 4.2. For modeling information, see the appendix.

On the left, we see that, from the first survey through the most recent, teachers in public schools reported encountering more red tape than teachers in charter schools. Although these differences were not great, the results from the multivariate analysis (right panel) reveal that they were statistically significant: in each school year, teachers in charter schools were around 30 percent less likely to agree that paperwork and routine duties hindered their ability to do their work. Since these findings come from an analysis that controls for the percentage of students with IEPs, as well as a host of other student-level variables, we can say with some confidence that these differences are related to school type.

To get a more recent view, the TELL surveys included two questions that explored teachers' experiences with red tape. Under a prompt about the use of time, teachers were asked how much they agreed with the following statement: "Efforts are made to minimize the amount of routine paperwork teachers are required to do."[21] In addition, teachers were asked how many hours they devoted to "completing required administrative paperwork" (in an average week). For the first question, respondents chose an answer from one of four ordered responses, from "Strongly disagree" to "Strongly agree"; for the latter question, respondents chose an answer from one of six ordered responses: "None," "Less than or equal to 1 hour," "More than 1 hour but less than or equal to 3 hours," "More than 3 hours but less than or equal to 5 hours," "More than 5 hours but less than or equal to 10 hours," and "More than 10 hours." The results from a multivariate analysis—which controlled for school- and individual-level influences—mirrored those from the SASS: teachers in charter schools were 129 percent more likely to indicate that efforts were made in their schools to reduce "routine paperwork" and 23 percent less likely to report spending extra time each week on administrative paperwork.

ACCOUNTABILITY AND TESTING

If you had to guess, would you think that the following quote, from an interview I conducted with a kindergarten teacher in Delaware, was from a teacher employed in a charter or a public school? "Fridays are test days, and it's very standardized. It's sad because it's not at all what we were all taught in college or preach to, or what we firmly believe. However, we are bound by the Common Core, you know. We have to do standardized testing." Then she goes on to say that because of the emphasis placed on testing, "we have to cram everything we're going to teach into four days instead of educating for five . . . It's a shame at the kindergarten level, because they should be having, they should be enjoying school and having fun and not dreading Fridays. Fridays should be a fun day."

Although critics have raised concerns that charter schools are test obsessed, this teacher was employed in a public school. She also said that teachers in her school were "held accountable for absolutely everything . . . Whether it's failing or passing, it's our fault. They're behaving badly in the classroom or great, it's our fault. If they're not bringing homework, that's our fault. Accountability is all on the teachers. It's not placed so much on the students or on the administrators. It's all on the teachers."

This teacher's comments suggest that accountability and testing are important aspects of public school life and raise questions about whether heightened performance accountability sets charter schools apart.[22] A recent review of the literature shows little evidence that charter schools are fostering high levels of performance-based accountability, at least at the systems level.[23] For example, rather than closing because of student test performance or parent discontent—as a market theory of accountability might expect—most charter schools are closed because of financial mismanagement or governance problems. But what about inside schools? If testing and accountability are firmly established in public schools—as the aforementioned kindergarten teacher observed—do teachers in charter schools feel even more pressure to devote time to testing than teachers in public schools feel?

Some comments from my interviews with charter and public school teachers in Delaware offer initial insight into these questions. Most of the teachers with whom I spoke—in charter and public schools—said that tests were crucial for accountability. For example, one charter teacher said: "Charter schools live and die by their standardized test schools. Fortunately, our school has done very well. We're usually ranked [high] in our state. But we feel the pressure to keep that up." A public school teacher whom I interviewed noted that the relationship between student testing and teacher accountability had been institutionalized in her state: "So in Delaware, we have recently adopted part of the teacher evaluations that include student test scores as a measure of performance. So if you know your students don't score high enough, your evaluation is affected and it could cost you your job if those scores are low over the course of the years."

But there were mixed views about whether this focus on test scores actually created accountability. One public school teacher voiced the concerns of school-choice proponents in noting that there was no real accountability for bad teachers in her school:

> I think that at my school, we have a lot of really great teachers. We have a lot of really great natural teachers that just love teaching and push themselves to be new and to revamp things. We also have an amount of teachers—I don't want to say it's half and half—well, it might be about half and half. This is my own view, and I'm in a lot of classrooms, and I have been in a lot of classrooms over the years. The teachers that are not that way, the teachers that are not—I hate to say this, but who I would call not good teachers—the teachers who I look at them and I question why they teach in the first place because I don't think they even like kids: um, no, I do not think they're held accountable, I think. I don't think they're held accountable. I think they have been allowed for years to continue doing bad teaching, bad relationships with kids, you know, really sometimes harmful things, I think, for students or for certain populations of students, and it just continues. Even if it was something that was brought up to an administrator's attention. It just continues. They don't want to say anything about it. They don't want to do anything. The administration doesn't want to do

anything about it. They'd rather just have someone continue to fly under the radar.

Before assuming that this is a public school problem only, consider the comments of a charter school teacher with whom I spoke. She indicated that administrators in her school focused on test scores but ignored other crucial aspects of school life: "I think that they could be much more responsive to the needs of everybody: the parents, kids, teachers. They have no real grasp of what's going on these days." In another part of our conversation, she reported liking her autonomy but being frustrated by the lack of feedback and steering from administrators as she worked to develop a new program at her school.

Echoing the theme of conditional innovation, Delaware teachers in both types of schools noted that administrative scrutiny was linked to test scores: teachers or schools with students who hadn't done well on tests received more attention from school leaders. Interestingly, however, accountability in this sense did not necessarily mean firing the teacher. One charter teacher noted that because of high teacher turnover at her school, the administrators were not forcing out teachers with low scores: "They're not trying to get people gone. Unless there's a good reason, you know?. . . They're trying to retain teachers . . . They're doing everything they can to help them improve." A public school teacher had a similar view, but at the school level: "In my school, [administrators] are more hands-off. We sort of have a culture in our school of being quite hands-off. We're always the leading school in the district, we always score really well on our tests, so, historically, it's been a very hands-off sort of approach with us, because whatever everybody was doing was working."

My conversations with teachers also suggested that the accountability systems in Delaware charter schools and public schools were different. When I asked teachers in public schools about accountability, they described a formalized, somewhat Byzantine system of oversight. In other words, public school teachers indicated high levels of process accountability, holding teachers responsible for the process of their work as opposed to the outcomes. For example, a public school teacher noted that his school had "a very complex system of teacher observation" and that "it takes a long time [for administrators] to get through observations." As a result, his principal had been in his room "three times this year. Honestly, if you add up all the time together, I'd say no more than . . . five minutes. At some point, I'll have a formal observation." But a violation of the school's rules and regulations—in this case filing lesson plans ahead of time—had real consequences for teachers: "Just to give you an example, we had a situation several years ago [when] we had teacher who by all accounts was at least a pretty good teacher, but the teacher was not writing lesson plans. He was an old guy and he just went in, did his thing. He was a chemistry teacher. There was a real conflict between the superintendent, who wanted this guy gone, and the high school administration, who were willing to keep him so long as the kids were successful. And eventually he wound up leaving us."

Another public school teacher noted that there was a good process in place to help teachers who weren't doing well. However, he said that the time and red tape associated with creating improvement plans discouraged administrators from initiating them: "I don't think—this is going to sound weird because I'm a union guy—there are enough teachers on our improvement plan . . . You can't tell me that every teacher in your building either meets or exceeds the standard . . . I think the improvement plans are way too much paperwork and way too much to do, and, oftentimes, administrators refuse to do them. Actually refuse. That's how much work it is . . . And no one holds them accountable for not doing it."

In comparison, accountability systems in charter schools sounded more informal. For instance, one charter school teacher noted that a recent administration change had ushered in a more hands-on approach from administrators. But it wasn't the type of accountability described by public school teachers. "Basically, it's very reflexive now," the teacher said, "very quick feedback, somebody coming into your classroom pretty regularly, and I think that's a lot better for teachers." Similarly, another charter teacher explained that teachers in her school are "observed at least three times per semester, so [school leaders] certainly get to view our lessons and sometimes they'll do walk-throughs. Every couple of weeks, they'll see a lesson of mine. And in general, they can tell who is doing their job and who needs a little nudge."

These potential differences between accountability in public and charter schools come from a handful of interviews in a single state at a single time. Thus, now we turn to the SASS and TELL data to determine if statistically significant differences were evident across a much larger swath of teachers, schools, and times.

To begin, I measured performance accountability by examining how teachers answered two SASS questions: "In this school, staff members are recognized for a job well done" and "I worry about the security of my job because of the performance of my students on state and/or local tests."[24] Teachers responded by choosing one of four responses on a scale, from "Strongly disagree" to "Strongly agree." These questions are useful as they capture the carrots and sticks of performance accountability; if teachers do not expect to be rewarded or punished for their work, they would be less likely to feel accountable to school leaders for their performance. The top of figure 4.5 displays the mean responses to these questions, and the bottom shows whether any differences were statistically significant, when controlling for other school- and teacher-level factors.

The upper panels show that, in general, teachers in both types of schools were more likely to agree that they would be recognized for their work than that they would be punished for low student test scores. The rise in concerns about job security—evident in the most recent survey—may be due to a change in the phrasing of the question: in 2011–2012, teachers were asked if they were concerned about their job security "because of the performance of my students or my school on state and/or local tests." Prior versions of this question didn't include the words "or my school."[25] Whether changes over time were due to how this job security question was asked or variations in the broader education landscape, the bottom panels show that teachers in charter and public schools reported largely similar experiences with performance accountability. Except for

FIGURE 4.5

Teachers' experiences with accountability (SASS)

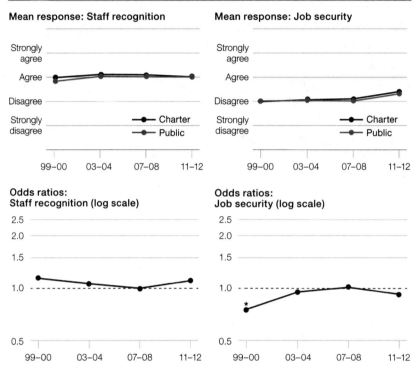

Note: Asterisk in the bottom panels denote a statistically significant difference between charter and public school teachers at the $p < 0.05$ level, controlling for school- and teacher-level influences. For information about how to interpret odds ratios, see the text explanation near figure 4.2. For modeling information, see the appendix.

1999–2000—when teachers in charter schools were less concerned than public school teachers were about their job security in relation to student test scores—there were no statistically significant differences between teachers in these two types of schools.

In the TELL survey, teachers were asked to rate how strongly they agreed with the following statements: "Teachers are held to high professional standards for delivering instruction," "The faculty are recognized for accomplishments," "The procedures for teacher evaluation are consistent," and "Teacher performance is assessed objectively."[27] As with other TELL questions, teachers were asked how much they agreed with these statements on a four-point scale, from "Strongly disagree" to "Strongly agree." Table 4.2 presents the mean responses to these questions by school type.

The table reveals that teachers generally agreed that they were held to high professional standards. However, there was less agreement that they'd be recognized for accomplishments or that they'd be assessed consistently or objectively. To explore whether there were any differences between teachers in charter and public schools, all other factors being held equal, I conducted a multivariate analysis. Figure 4.6 highlights the findings from this analysis. In three of the four questions, teachers in charter schools were more likely than teachers in public schools to agree that they were accountable for their work. Perhaps most impressively, teachers in charter schools were around 50 percent more likely to agree that they'd be held to high standards for the quality of their instruction.

Most conversations about charter schools focus on performance accountability.[27] However, this is not the only approach to understanding how schools or teachers are held responsible for their work: in addition, we need to ask to whom teachers in these different schools feel accountable. One of the major concerns about

TABLE 4.2

Teacher accountability (TELL)

	Public school teachers	Charter school teachers
Teachers are held to high professional standards for delivering instruction.	3.34	3.44
The faculty are recognized for accomplishments.	3.02	3.05
The procedures for teacher evaluation are consistent.	3.00	3.11
Teacher performance is assessed objectively.	3.06	3.20

Note: TELL: Teaching, Empowerment, Leading, and Learning surveys. With some exceptions, the surveys examined entire state populations of teachers in both charter and public schools. Numbers are the mean responses of teachers on a four-point numerical rating scale, where 1 = "Strongly disagree" and 4 = "Strongly agree," to statements about accountability.

FIGURE 4.6

Teachers' experiences with accountability (TELL)

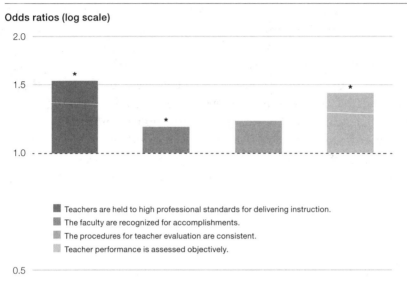

Odds ratios (log scale)

- ■ Teachers are held to high professional standards for delivering instruction.
- ■ The faculty are recognized for accomplishments.
- ■ The procedures for teacher evaluation are consistent.
- ▨ Teacher performance is assessed objectively.

Note: Asterisks denote a statistically significant difference between charter and public school teachers at the $p < 0.05$ level, controlling for school- and teacher-level influences. For information about how to interpret odds ratios, see text explanation near figure 4.2. For modeling information, see the appendix.

privatization in general, and charter schools in particular, is that employees will be more accountable to their firms or employers than to the public at large. To address this concern, we now shift to explore a DTS question that defined accountability more broadly and asked about a diverse array of school actors. The prompt read: "Accountability is the extent to which you feel responsible or answerable to others for your actions and performance as a teacher. As you think about your work in this school, please indicate the extent to which you feel accountable to the following: The Delaware Department of Education; Your school district; The people in the community that surround your school; Your principal; Your department chair; Your fellow teachers; The parents of your students; Your students." Teachers responded to these questions by choosing an answer on a four-point scale, from "Not accountable" to "Very accountable." Table 4.3

TABLE 4.3

Teachers' sense of accountability to various school stakeholders (DTS)

	Public school teachers	Charter school teachers
Delaware DOE	2.82	2.74
School district	3.27	3.02
Community	2.95	2.89
Principal	3.40	3.45
Department chair	2.56	2.81
Fellow teachers	2.87	3.03
Parents	3.39	3.52
Students	3.66	3.70

Note: Numbers are the mean responses of teachers on a four-point numerical rating scale, where 1 = "Not accountable" and 4 = "Very accountable," to questions about how accountable teachers feel to various stakeholders.

highlights the mean responses to these questions for teachers in charter and public schools.

The table reveals some general differences in the levels of accountability that teachers felt toward various school stakeholders. Teachers in both charter and public schools felt more accountable to the school district, principal, parents, and students than they did to the Delaware Department of Education (DOE) or the broader community. There were also some differences between teachers in charter and public schools: teachers in public schools reported feeling more accountable to external stakeholders like the DOE, school district, and community, while teachers in charter schools reported higher levels of accountability to internal stakeholders, like fellow teachers, department chairs, and parents. Though these initial differences are intriguing, it is important to scrutinize them using a multivariate analysis that controls for differences in schools and teachers. Figure 4.7 presents the results of this analysis.

The figure reveals three interesting findings. Although many of the accountability differences between teachers in charter and public schools (evident in the above descriptive analysis) disappeared after

FIGURE 4.7

Teachers' experiences with accountability (DTS)

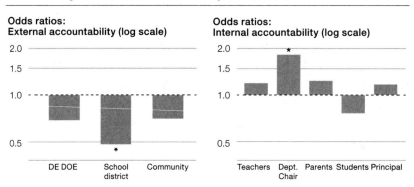

Note: Asterisks denote a statistically significant difference between charter and public school teachers at the $p < 0.05$ level, controlling for school- and teacher-level influences. For information about how to interpret odds ratios, see the text explanation near figure 4.2. For modeling information, see the appendix.

I controlled for teacher- and school-level differences, two differences persisted. The left panel of figure 4.7 shows that teachers in charter schools reported feeling less accountable to the school district in which their school was located than did teachers in public schools. This makes sense because school districts theoretically play less of a role in the day-to-day operations of charter schools. However, we might also expect that teachers in charter schools would feel more accountable to the DOE because, according to Delaware's charter law, after schools receive their charters, they are responsible for submitting an annual report to the DOE and the state board (which governs the DOE). But the figure doesn't bear out this hypothesis: Teachers in charter schools did not feel any more (or less) accountable to state officials. All of which is to say that the left panel shows modest support for the expectation that charter schools will foster climates in which teachers feel less externally accountable than public school teachers.

The right panel shows no statistically significant differences between teachers in charter and public schools in feelings of accountability toward parents, students, or other teachers. However, teachers in Delaware charter schools reported feeling more accountable to the chair of their department than did teachers in public schools. It is unclear precisely why this relationship might exist. Perhaps charter schools in Delaware are using the loosened state regulations to empower department chairs with greater control and oversight over what teachers are doing in their classrooms.

In the interviews above, we saw that test scores were important aspects of accountability in charter and public schools. To gain a more systematic perspective on teachers' experiences with testing, we now turn to the TELL survey. To begin, TELL respondents were asked how many hours they devoted to "Preparation for required federal, state, and local assessments" and "Delivery of assessments." They responded by choosing one of six ordered responses, from "None" to "More than 10 hours." On average, teachers in both types of schools reported spending from one to three hours per week preparing for tests and one to three hours per week administering tests. A multivariate analysis, which examined whether teachers in public and charter schools were likely to choose different responses, all else being held equal, found some significant differences. Specifically, teachers in charter schools were 26 percent less likely to spend more time preparing for tests and 12 percent less likely to spend more time giving tests.

Two questions on the DTS asked about the role that tests play in teachers' work. First, teachers were asked how much they agreed with the following statement: "A great emphasis is placed on test scores" in their schools; second, they were asked how much they agreed with this statement: "I cover topics that are important for students even if they won't be tested on them." For both questions, respondents chose an answer from one of five ordered responses, from "Strongly disagree" to "Strongly agree." In general, teachers strongly agreed that a great emphasis was placed on test scores (mean response for all teachers was 4.64) while also agreeing that they spent time covering nontest topics (mean response for all teachers was 4.19).

To explore whether there were differences by school type, I conducted a multivariate analysis that controlled for teacher- and school-level correlates. I found that teachers in charter and public schools had statistically indistinguishable views about the amount of emphasis that their schools placed on testing. However, the analysis also revealed that teachers in charter schools, perhaps because of their enhanced autonomy, were over 100 percent more likely to agree that they covered nontest topics than teachers in public schools.

INSIDE THE CHARTER SECTOR

Now we turn to an analysis of autonomy and accountability inside the charter sector. Because the DTS lacked sufficient variation in these characteristics to permit meaningful analysis, this section focuses only on the SASS and TELL data.

Autonomy and Innovation

To begin, let's consider the SASS data, which enable an analysis of the relationship between the grade given to a state's charter law by a pro-charter schools advocacy organization (the Center for Education Reform or CER), and teacher autonomy. A multivariate analysis of charter teacher autonomy was conducted for each wave of the SASS survey. In 1999–2000, there were no differences between teachers in higher- and lower-rated states except that teachers in higher-rated states were around 10 percent more likely to report more control over grading (i.e., student assessment). In the next wave of the survey (2003–2004), there were no differences based on state rating in five of the six areas; however, in contrast to what the CER might expect, teachers in higher-rated states were around 10 percent *less* likely to report control over choosing content. In 2007–2008, charter teachers in higher-rated states were more likely to report having autonomy over the selection of texts and teaching techniques (around 25 percent and 55 percent, respectively) than charter teachers in lower-rated states. In the most recent survey (2011–2012), there were no differences in teacher autonomy associated with the rating given to a state for the operational flexibility of its charter law.

In the most recent version of the SASS, it was also possible to examine how an institutional aspect of charter schools—whether it was run as part of a franchise—was associated with teachers' experiences with autonomy. The findings from this analysis—summarized in figure 4.8—reveal that there were some differences. This figure shows that, as theorized, teachers in EMO-run charter schools reported that they had less control than did teachers working in non-EMO-run charter schools. These findings suggest that aforementioned differences between charter and public schools (see figure 4.2) are probably driven by teachers in non-EMOs. To further explore this possibility, I ran a supplementary analysis to compare

FIGURE 4.8

Teacher autonomy in EMO-run and non-EMO-run charter schools, 2011–2012 (SASS)

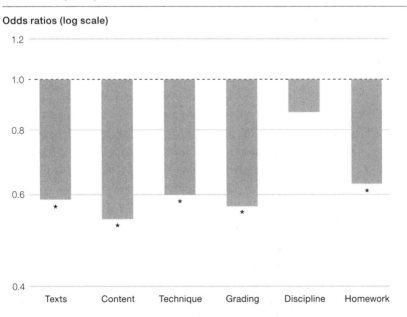

Note: Asterisks denote a statistically significant difference between teachers in EMO-run and non-EMO-run charter schools at the $p < 0.05$ level, controlling for school- and teacher-level influences. For information about how to interpret odds ratios, see the text explanation near figure 4.2. For modeling information, see the appendix.

teachers in EMO-run charter schools and teachers in public schools. This analysis showed that teachers in these different settings reported comparable levels of autonomy. In addition, I looked for differences in autonomy within EMO-run charter schools based on the tax status of the school and found no differences between teachers in for-profit and nonprofit EMOs when it came to these different types of autonomy.

Moving to the TELL survey, we can examine how teachers in different types of charter schools responded to the autonomy and innovation questions discussed above. In fact, a multivariate analysis revealed no statistically significant differences in teacher autonomy or innovation—based on franchise, tax status, or a state's charter law rating—when controlling for teacher and school-level influences.

Red Tape

Returning to the SASS paperwork question above, let's examine whether teachers in different types of charter schools had different experiences with routine duties and paperwork. At first blush, we might expect that the grade given to states by a pro-charter group —based on the amount of operational flexibility given to schools —would have an impact on teachers' experiences with paperwork: teachers in states with higher grades would seem likely to experience less paperwork than teachers in states with lower grades. In fact, in the first year of the SASS examined here (1999–2000), this expectation was borne out: a multivariate analysis revealed that teachers in higher-rated states were around 10 percent less likely to indicate that paperwork interfered with their teaching. However, in the three most recent waves of the survey, the rating had no statistically significant association with teachers' experiences with red tape. Interestingly, an analysis of the TELL survey questions revealed the same findings: teachers in states with higher charter law ratings had indistinguishable experiences with red tape.

The analysis also revealed that, although teachers working in a franchised school might be expected to encounter more red tape (as they are constrained by central operating organizations), there were no differences in red tape on the SASS or TELL surveys between teachers in EMO-run charter schools and non-EMO-run schools.

As described earlier, over the lifetime of a school, layers of standard operating procedures may ossify, which teachers could experience as red tape. Thus, as charter schools—on their own and as a sector—age, we might expect to see an increase in red tape. In the SASS analysis above, we saw little evidence that charter schools lost their red-tape advantage over time. Additionally, a multivariate analysis of the most recent SASS revealed no statistically significant relationship between the age of a charter school and teachers' experiences with red tape.

Turning to tax status, the TELL survey showed that teachers in for-profit charter schools were 50 percent less likely to agree that their schools made an effort to minimize the amount of routine paperwork they face and were 100 percent more likely to indicate that they spent more hours completing required administrative paperwork. With the SASS analysis, teachers in for-profit EMO-run charter schools were around 150 percent more likely to indicate that routine duties and paperwork interfered with their work than teachers in nonprofit EMO-run schools reported. For both datasets, a supplementary inquiry comparing teachers in public schools and teachers in for-profit EMOs revealed that the two groups were statistically indistinguishable in terms of paperwork. Put simply, levels of red tape in public schools and for-profit charter schools appear to be about the same; levels of red tape in nonprofit charter schools were relatively lower.

Accountability

Accountability among charter schools was analyzed using the SASS questions about job security and recognition. In 1999–2000, teachers in states that received higher CER ratings were less likely to indicate feeling accountable—they were around 10 percent less likely to indicate that they expected to be "recognized for a job well done" and 10 percent less likely to worry about the security of their jobs because of student test performance. In the three subsequent versions of the SASS, there were no statistically significant differences among teachers in charter schools with different state charter law ratings.

In the most recent version of the SASS, the teachers' schools' franchise status had no effect on teachers' responses to these questions. Put differently, teachers in EMO-run charter schools were indistinguishable from teachers in non-EMO-run charter schools in their responses to accountability questions. Similarly, the analysis found no differences between teachers in for-profit and nonprofit EMOs when it came to concerns about job security; however, teachers in for-profit EMOs were around 90 percent more likely to indicate that they would be recognized for doing a good job than were teachers in nonprofit EMOs.

Strangely, there were some difference in the TELL findings. To start, teachers in EMO-run charter schools were 46 percent more likely than were teachers in non-EMO-run charters to agree that there were procedures in place to ensure consistent teacher evaluation. Also, in contrast with the SASS findings, the TELL analysis revealed that teachers in for-profit charter schools reported worse accountability systems. Compared with teachers in nonprofit charter schools, they were 38 percent less likely to agree that teachers were held to professional standards, 35 percent less likely to agree that there were procedures in place to evaluate teachers consistently, and 48 percent less likely to agree that teacher performance was assessed objectively.

Testing

As noted above, the TELL survey is useful because it asked teachers how much time they spent preparing and delivering tests (see full text of questions in "Accountability and Testing" section, above). To explore charter teachers' responses to these questions, I conducted a multivariate analysis that controlled for teacher- and school-level influences on their answers. The results of this analysis revealed that the tax status of the school appeared to have a significant influence on teachers' experiences and behaviors with testing. Specifically, teachers in for-profit charter schools were 86 percent more likely to indicate that they spent more hours preparing for tests and

79 percent more likely to say they spent more hours delivering them than teachers in nonprofit charter schools. These findings confirm some of the critics' concerns about for-profit charter schools: these schools appear to be more oriented toward assessment than non-profit charter schools.

How should we interpret these findings in light of the observation that teachers in charter schools said they spend less time preparing and delivering tests than do teachers in public schools? The results here suggest that these differences are driven by nonprofit charter schools. In fact, a subsequent analysis compared teachers in public schools and teachers in for-profit charter schools; it found that teachers in for-profit charter schools were indistinguishable from teachers in public schools in the amount of time they reported spending preparing and delivering tests.

Interestingly, this difference did not appear to be driven by teachers in EMO-run charter schools. Teachers in EMOs reported experiences with testing similar to those of teachers in non-EMOs and teachers in public schools. Also, the level of operational flexibility given to a state based on an assessment of its charter school law had no statistically significant association with teachers' experiences with testing.

SUMMARY

Charter schools theoretically follow a "tight-loose" management strategy: important outcomes are specified and closely monitored, but the schools are given leeway in deciding how to accomplish them.[28] Despite this apparent strategy, some researchers have argued, charter schools are much more regulated than typically thought and lack the autonomy they need to succeed.[29] In response, this chapter has studied what teachers experience in terms of their freedom inside the classroom and the extent to which they are held to account for their work. The picture that emerges is mixed. On the one hand, teachers in charter schools reported greater autonomy (at least in some respects) and less red tape than do teachers in public schools. Also, according to the TELL survey, charter school teachers were more likely than their public school peers to work in schools that encouraged innovation.

However, there were mixed findings about accountability. The SASS data suggest that charter schools did not have significantly different climates of performance accountability: teachers in charter schools were not any more or less likely than teachers in public schools to expect that they would be rewarded or punished for their work. The TELL data tell a different story: hinting at differences in school leadership, teachers in charter schools were more likely than public school teachers to agree that they were held to high standards and assessed objectively. The DTS analysis, which looked at who teachers felt accountable to, revealed a mixed picture of accountability: teachers in charter schools were less likely than public school teachers to feel accountable to their local school district but were more likely to feel accountable to their department chairs.

Putting these findings together, we might argue that one of the major concerns about charter schools is being realized: they are creating teaching climates with greater autonomy and innovation but are doing so at the cost of oversight.[30] From this perspective, charter schools would be comparable to privatization and deregulation in other contexts: they lead to decentralized control and less accountability.[31] However, this interpretation conflicts with the findings here in an important way: teachers in charter schools were not *less* likely to be held accountable than teachers in public schools. Rather, the analysis found that teachers in charter schools reported more autonomy (in some respects) than public school teachers, but comparable levels of accountability. This could still be interpreted as problematic, of course, since charter schools are supposed to get enhanced autonomy in exchange for enhanced accountability.

The chapter closed with an analysis of three factors that might be driving some of these differences between charter and public schools. It showed that teachers in EMO-run charter schools were, in some respects, different from those in non-EMO charter schools: on the SASS, the teachers reported less autonomy. This finding is in accord with some theories about how teachers in a franchised educational setting might have different experiences (see chapter

2). Because they are implementing a playbook developed elsewhere, teachers in EMOs may have less control over some of the key aspects of their work. In terms of red tape, for-profit charter schools appear to foster environments with more administrative encumbrance than do nonprofit schools. Interestingly, the franchise status of a school appeared to have little association with red tape or accountability.

The charter sector analysis also revealed conflicting findings about tax status and accountability. The SASS analysis found that teachers in for-profit EMOs reported more accountability than teachers in nonprofit EMOs did, but the TELL analysis suggested that the reverse was true. Thus, the effect of a charter school's tax status on its accountability climate is uncertain.

These findings illuminate the importance of empirical exploration and challenging basic assumptions about organizations, publicness, and differences between charter and public schools. In the next chapter, we turn to another way in which charter and public schools have been thought to differ: teacher leadership and collaboration. Initially, charter schools were envisioned as schools in which teachers would work closely together and lead in novel ways. The next chapter asks whether such expectations have been realized over the past fifteen years.

FIVE

Teacher Leadership
and Collaboration

TEACHER LEADERSHIP and cooperation are thought to be important elements of how schools function. For example, Richard Kahlenberg and Halley Potter speak of the benefits of collaboration and leadership: "Research shows that when teachers are engaged in school decisions and collaborate with administrators and each other, school climate improves. This promotes a better learning environment for students, which raises student achievement, and a better working environment for teachers, which reduces turnover."[1]

Perhaps as a result, claims about teacher leadership and collaboration were one of the initial rationales for charter schools: these schools, it was thought, would give teachers the chance to work closer with their colleagues and offer greater input into how their schools were run. For example, in one of his early publications on the topic, Albert Shanker argued that charter schools would be formed by small groups of teachers and that the schools would emphasize "collegiality and cooperation among teachers" and "a plan for shared decision making."[2] As states passed charter laws, many included language indicating an interest in expanding teacher influence over how their schools operate.[3]

Today, teacher leadership remains a crucial selling point for charter schools. For example, the California Charter Schools Association notes that teachers, along with other school stakeholders, "shape important decisions about working conditions, including the mission, curriculum and instruction, programs and services, schedules, budgeting, and staffing—with the goal of improving educational outcomes for students."[4] Similarly, the National Alliance for Public Charter Schools argues that "charter school teachers have a say in the curriculum they teach and can change materials to meet students' needs."[5]

Some observers have questioned whether such claims are reality or rhetoric. In particular, critics have argued that charter schools systematically deny teachers power by preventing them from unionizing. As a result, Kahlenberg and Potter argue, "a lack of teacher voice" is a major problem in many charter schools.[6] In response to these conflicting expectations, this chapter turns to an empirical analysis of teacher leadership and collaboration in charter and public schools.

TEACHER LEADERSHIP

Marya Levenson notes that there are three elements of teacher leadership.[7] The most common way that teachers lead their schools is in the area of instruction: collaborating with administrators or making suggestions about their schools' approach to enhancing student learning. Second, and more rarely, teachers play a role in institutional leadership, contributing to decisions, for example, about interactions between teachers and parents, other teachers, and administrators. Finally, and most rarely, some teachers are involved in contributing to district, state, or national education policy. The questions in this section focus on the two more common types of teacher leadership.

To begin, let's consider some comments from teachers that I interviewed in Delaware. These conversations revealed that teachers in charter schools felt that they played an important role in leading their schools. For instance, one charter school teacher indicated that he and his colleagues devise and coordinate their department curriculum: "But our curriculum is pretty much designed and implemented at the department level. So we the English Department, we get together, we are beholden to the standards, because we are a public charter school so we have to do that, but standards don't dictate what we read, how we teach them. All they do is dictate a skill which we need to address. So as far as we're concerned as a department, we can address that skill through any text that we want to use. We can teach that skill the best way we want to. So we have, I think, more freedom curriculum-wise than others do. And I think that's a good thing."

Interestingly, this teacher thought his department's leadership role might be due to his discipline rather than the fact that he worked in a charter school. To examine that possibility, this chapter's SASS analysis—like all the chapters that examine SASS data—will control for the subject area in which teachers worked.

Another theme that emerged in my conversations with charter school teachers was a high level of engagement between faculty and administration. Generally speaking, charter school teachers indicated that school leaders were receptive to teacher feedback about how their schools should be run. For example, one charter teacher commented: "There is a good balance between who is an administrator and who's a staff member. It's not like there is a giant gap in power and in teachers' ability to be heard. We always have a department chair, and all the staff members will get together to speak with the department chair with no administrators in the room, and the department chairs then come together to speak with the administration so that every voice can be heard. Even if—we're not shot down by any means—but even if we didn't feel comfortable bringing it directly to administration, our department chair can bring it for us, and everyone can be heard."

Another charter teacher had a more measured view of teacher leadership in her school. When I asked her how receptive school leaders were to teacher feedback, she said, "I think we are asked for our input, but it isn't always weighted very heavily." Nonetheless, later in our conversation, she said that teachers played an important role in creating the school's curriculum.

In my conversations with public school teachers, I heard a different theme: that school leaders were receptive and sympathetic to teacher feedback, but that they were constrained from above. One public school teacher laughed when I asked whether school leaders were receptive to teacher feedback. She said that her principal listens to feedback and considers suggestions, but hasn't incorporated feedback into school policy. Rather, the principal "gives the impression that her hands are very tied from a top-down thing. They're coming from district. Messages are being sort of sent, and she is going to follow along with that. So I think, like I said, she will always sit and listen and think about it, and I always feel supported in a sense in that way. But I don't see a lot of changes happening."

These selections are just anecdotal evidence, but they suggest that there may be some differences in teacher leadership in charter and public schools. In fact, more systematic research aligns with the above teachers' comments. Comparisons of teacher leadership in charter and public schools suggest that charter teachers may play more leadership roles in their schools than public school teachers play.[8] But these comparisons use data from the 1999–2000 and 2003–2004 school years—data that is now more than ten years old—and compares teachers using mean responses. In other words, these studies don't examine teacher leadership while controlling for the systematic differences between charter and public schools, and charter and public teachers, seen in Chapter 3.

To develop a more complete view, this section examines a battery of questions asked on the 1999–2000, 2003–2004, and 2011–2012 SASS questionnaires about the level of influence teachers had over how their schools operate.[9] Teachers were asked how much influence they thought they had in each of the following areas: "Setting performance standards for students at this school," "Establishing curriculum," "Determining the content of in-service professional development programs," "Evaluating teachers," "Hiring new full-time teachers," "Setting discipline policy," and "Deciding how the school budget will be spent."[10]

Although the questions asked across the three waves of the SASS are broadly similar, the 1999–2000 questions differed from the 2003–2004 and 2011–2012 surveys. First, in 1999–2000, the questions were preceded by the following prompt: "Using a scale of 1–5, where 1 means "No influence" and 5 means "A great deal of influence," how much actual influence do you think teachers have over school policy AT THIS SCHOOL in each of the following areas?" (emphasis in original). The scale for the question included five boxes with a double-sided arrow leading from "No influence" to "A great deal of influence." In 2003–2004 and 2011–2012, the prompt was this: "How much actual influence do you think teachers have over school policy AT THIS SCHOOL in each of the following areas?" (emphasis in original), and respondents chose a point on a four-point scale, from 1 ("No influence") to 4 ("A great deal of influence"), with no arrow. To account for this difference in scale and maintain the comparability of years, respondents' answers were normalized so that 1.0 was the highest level of leadership for each year and 0.0 was the lowest.[11] Figure 5.1 compares the mean responses of teachers in charter and public schools across these three surveys.

Compared with figure 4.1—which looks at teacher autonomy—figure 5.1 suggests that teachers had less control over leading their schools than they did inside their classrooms. In particular, teachers reported little influence over the evaluation of teachers, hiring, and budgeting. They had somewhat more control over setting performance standards, determining the shape of the curriculum, and setting disciplinary policy. But in none of these areas was teacher control particularly high.

Figure 5.2 presents the findings from a multivariate analysis of differences between teachers in charter and public schools.[12] Specifically, the figure presents odds ratios, derived from ordered logit coefficients. These odds ratios indicate the likelihood that teachers in charter schools would answer a question differently, controlling for school- and teacher-level differences. An odds ratio above 1.0 with an asterisk indicates that, all else being equal, teachers in charter schools were more likely to agree with a statement. An odds ratio below 1.0 with an asterisk indicates that teachers in charter schools were less likely to agree with a statement than teachers in public schools. An odds ratio without an asterisk indicates no statistically significant differences between the responses of teachers in charter and public schools.

FIGURE 5.1

Teacher leadership: mean responses (SASS)

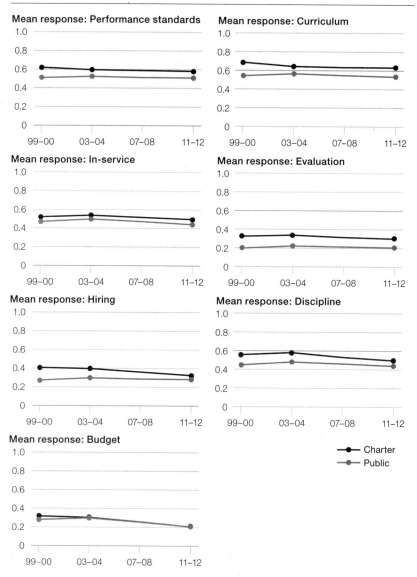

Note: SASS: Schools and Staffing Survey. Charts represent mean responses of teachers to questions about how much influence teachers felt they had over seven elements of school policy: setting performance standards, determining the shape of the curriculum, deciding on in-service training, evaluating teachers, hiring, setting disciplinary policy, and budget. The higher the number, the more control the teachers believed they had.

FIGURE 5.2

Teacher leadership: multivariate analysis (SASS)

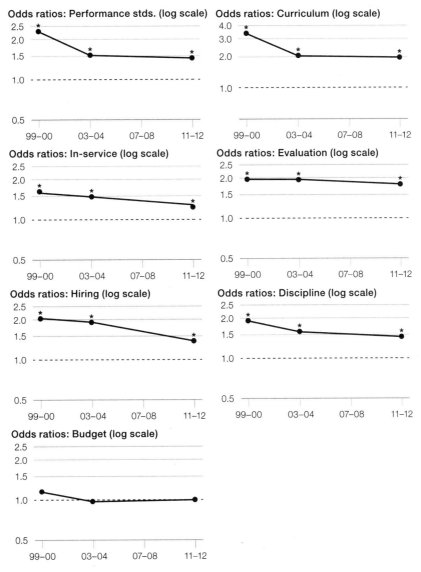

Note: Asterisks denote a statistically significant difference between charter and public school teachers at the $p < 0.05$ level, controlling for school- and teacher-level influences. For information about how to interpret odds ratios, see the accompanying text. For modeling information, see the appendix.

These findings tell an interesting story about differences between teacher leadership in charter and public schools. To begin, the findings are (somewhat) consistent from year to year. From 1999–2000 up through the last wave (2011–2012), teachers in charter schools were significantly more likely to agree that they influenced six of the seven leadership areas than teachers in public schools; in fact, in only one area were there no statistically significant differences between teachers in these different settings: teacher influence on the school budget. However, despite consistent differences in teacher leadership, the trend in each area is one of decline: the likelihood that teachers in charter schools reported greater influence than did teachers in public schools diminished somewhat from 1999–2000 to 2011–2012. Despite this decline, many of the most recent differences are large and occur in areas of school policy that are likely to be meaningful to teachers. Most important, in 2011–2012 teachers in charter schools were nearly 100 percent more likely to indicate that they had influence over establishing their school's curriculum than did teachers in public schools.

Moving to the TELL survey, we now examine two sets of questions about teacher leadership. First, teachers were asked how much they agreed with the following statements about teacher leadership in their schools: "Teachers are recognized as educational experts," "Teachers are trusted to make sound professional decisions about instruction," "Teachers are relied upon to make decisions about educational issues," "Teachers are encouraged to participate in school leadership roles," "The faculty has an effective process for making group decisions to solve problems," "In this school we take steps to solve problems," and "Teachers are effective leaders in this school."[13] For all statements, respondents indicated their agreement on a four-point scale, from "Strongly disagree" to "Strongly agree." Table 5.1 presents the mean responses for teachers in charter and public schools.

Most teachers indicated that they agreed with these statements. In particular, there were high levels of agreement about teachers being encouraged to take leadership roles and teachers being effective leaders. To determine whether there were any differences between teachers in public and charter schools, when controlling for

TABLE 5.1

Teacher leadership (TELL)

	Public school teachers	Charter school teachers
Teachers are recognized as educational experts.	2.99	3.22
Teachers are trusted to make sound professional decisions about instruction.	3.02	3.28
Teachers are relied upon to make decisions about educational issues.	2.96	3.21
Teachers are encouraged to participate in school leadership roles.	3.15	3.25
The faculty has an effective process for making group decisions to solve problems.	2.84	2.95
In this school we take steps to solve problems.	2.99	3.18
Teachers are effective leaders in this school.	3.09	3.23

Note: TELL: Teaching, Empowerment, Leading, and Learning surveys. Numbers are the mean responses of teachers on a four-point numerical rating scale, where 1 = "Strongly disagree" and 4 = "Strongly agree," to statements about teacher leadership in their schools.

teacher and school-level factors, I conducted a multivariate analysis of these questions (figure 5.3).

The findings in figure 5.3 are consonant with the SASS findings reported in figure 5.2. Across an array of leadership areas, teachers in charter schools reported exercising more leadership than teachers in public schools reported. Perhaps most impressive—and aligned with the early theories of charter proponents—teachers in charter schools felt encouraged to take up leadership roles in their schools and felt that they were relied on when educational decisions were made.

The TELL survey also examined teacher leadership by asking teachers how much of a role they had at their schools in the following areas: "Selecting instructional materials and resources," "Devising teaching techniques," "Setting grading and student assessment practices," "Determining the content of in-service professional development programs," "Establishing student discipline procedures," "Providing input on how the school budget will be spent," "The

FIGURE 5.3

Teacher leadership (TELL)

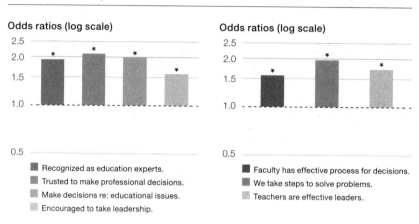

Note: Asterisks denote a statistically significant difference between charter and public school teachers at the *p* < 0.05 level, controlling for school- and teacher-level influences. For information about how to interpret odds ratios, see the text explanation near figure 5.2. For modeling information, see the appendix.

selection of teachers new to this school," and "School improvement planning." For each activity, respondents chose one of four ordered responses where 1 was "No role at all," 2 was "Small role," 3 "Moderate role," and 4 "Large role."[14] In addition, they were asked how much they agreed with the following statement: "Teachers have an appropriate level of influence on decision making in this school."[15] For this question, respondents indicated their agreement on a four-point scale, from "Strongly disagree" to "Strongly agree." Table 5.2 summarizes the mean responses of teachers in charter and public schools.

The data in this table mirror the SASS descriptive data discussed in figure 5.1: teachers reported more control over setting curriculum and teaching-related policy than other aspects of school management. In particular, teachers were generally unlikely to agree that they had control over setting the budget or determining hiring. To examine whether there were any differences between teachers in public and charter schools, I conducted a multivariate analysis that controlled for teacher and school-level influences (figure 5.4).

TABLE 5.2

Teacher roles (TELL)

	Public school teachers	Charter school teachers
Selecting instructional materials and resources.	3.00	3.25
Devising teaching techniques.	3.26	3.45
Setting grading and assessment practices.	3.00	3.27
Determining the content of in-service professional development programs.	2.43	2.60
Establishing student discipline procedures.	2.69	2.85
Providing input on how the school budget will be spent.	2.11	2.10
The selection of teachers new to the school.	2.17	2.40
School improvement planning.	2.84	2.70
Teachers have an appropriate level of influence on decision making in this school.	2.62	2.70

Note: For the first eight items, numbers are the mean responses of teachers on a four-point numerical rating scale, where 1 = "No role at all," 2 = "Small role," 3 = "Moderate role," and 4 = "Large role," to questions about how much of a leadership role they have in each area. For the last statement, numbers are the mean responses of teachers on a four-point numerical rating scale, where 1 = "Strongly disagree" and 4 = "Strongly agree," to statements about teacher leadership in their schools.

In large part, the findings here are consonant with the SASS analysis in figure 5.2: teachers in charter schools were more likely to play a substantial role in choosing instructional materials, devising teaching techniques, developing assessment schemes, and contributing to professional development. Also, like the SASS data, there was no evidence that teachers in charter schools played a bigger role providing input on their school budgets than did teachers in public schools.

However, some of the findings shown in figure 5.4 differ from those in the prior figures. For example, teachers in charter schools reported no more or less influence over the process of hiring new teachers than their public school colleagues had. As the SASS analysis in figure 5.2 showed, the difference between teachers in charter and public schools in this area was waning more precipitously than

FIGURE 5.4

Teacher roles (TELL)

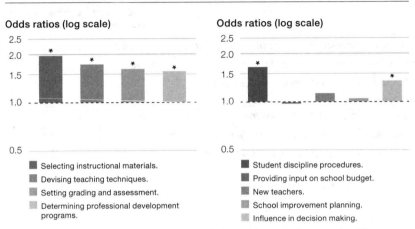

Odds ratios (log scale)

- Selecting instructional materials.
- Devising teaching techniques.
- Setting grading and assessment.
- Determining professional development programs.

Odds ratios (log scale)

- Student discipline procedures.
- Providing input on school budget.
- New teachers.
- School improvement planning.
- Influence in decision making.

Note: Asterisks denote a statistically significant difference between charter and public school teachers at the $p < 0.05$ level, controlling for school- and teacher-level influences. For information about how to interpret odds ratios, see the text explanation near figure 5.2. For modeling information, see the appendix.

the other six areas; since the TELL data are more recent (2012–2014) than the last wave of the SASS (2011–2012), perhaps they indicate that this drop accelerated.

On the DTS, teachers were asked two questions about the role that they played in two elements of school life: making recommendations to administrators about changes and shaping their department's curriculum. Specifically, teachers were asked how much they agreed with the following two statements: "I make recommendations to school administrators about changes we could make to improve student learning," and "Teachers play an important role in shaping their department's curriculum." For both, respondents answered on a five-point scale, from "Strongly disagree" to "Strongly agree." A multivariate analysis of these questions—which controlled for school- and teacher-level influences—found that teachers in charter schools were 1.3 times more likely to agree that they make recommendations to school leaders and 5.0 times more likely to agree that they play an important role in shaping their department's curriculum.

Thus far, the chapter has shown broad consonance across all three surveys: though the extent of the difference may have declined over time, teachers in charter schools appeared to exert more leadership—and take on a larger number of roles in their schools—than teachers in public schools.

TEACHER COLLABORATION

Another important aspect of how schools function is teachers' ability to collaborate. When teachers work closely, they can knit together disparate courses and disciplines and create a more cohesive learning environment for students.[16] Charter schools were originally envisioned as fostering greater collaboration because of their decentralized administrative apparatus.[17] With fewer rules and less red tape, the schools were expected to enable teachers to work together in ways that teachers in public schools could not. However, one might imagine the opposite scenario as well: in theory, organizations, and their accompanying rules, hierarchy, and structure, exist to enable cooperation among various people, departments, and tasks.[18] In this way, decentralized schools might enhance teacher autonomy (as seen in chapter 4) while also decreasing collaboration among teachers. Unfortunately, as Priscilla Wohlstetter and coauthors say, the research to date is "spotty, with little conclusive evidence of widespread practices that promote increased opportunities for teacher collaboration."[19]

To explore these divergent expectations of teacher collaboration, this section examines the SASS and teacher agreement with the following four statements: "There is a great deal of cooperative effort among the staff members," "I make a conscious effort to coordinate the content of my courses with that of other teachers," and "Rules for student behavior are consistently enforced by teachers in this school, even for students who are not in their classes." In addition, we'll explore a question about a more abstract, but no less important, aspect of how teachers work together: mission congruence. Missions are more than mere written goals: they are the belief systems or norms that guide and animate employee behavior.[20] When they are widely shared and deeply felt, missions may reduce the need for management oversight and enhance organizational effectiveness.[21] To explore whether there were differences in mission congruence among teachers in charter and public schools, I analyzed teachers' responses to the following statement: "Most of my colleagues share my beliefs and values about what the central mission of the school should be."

For all questions, teachers were asked to indicate their level of agreement on a four-point scale, from "Strongly disagree" to "Strongly agree." The coordination question was not asked in the 2007–2008 version of the survey. The left panels in figure 5.5 compare the mean responses of teachers in charter and public schools across this period; the panels on the right present findings from a multivariate analysis that controlled for teacher- and school-level factors.

The panels on the left reveal relatively high collaboration across both school types. For all four questions, the mean answers for both groups of teachers fell around or above "Agree."

The multivariate results (on the right) reveal mixed findings. In 1999–2000, teachers in charter schools were more likely to report greater cooperation and coordination than were teachers in public schools. After that, the trends diverge: in each year, teachers in charter schools were more likely than teachers in public schools were to say they were cooperating, but teachers in charter and public schools were indistinguishable in terms of content coordination. The results suggest charter schools may foster an environment of shared effort but not necessarily pedagogical synergy. The figure also shows no significant differences between charter and public schools in the consistency with which teachers enforced rules. The bottom right-most panel, which examines mission, suggests some initial differences that receded over time: in 1999–2000 and 2003–2004, teachers in charter schools were more likely than their public school colleagues to report a greater sense of shared mission; in the latter two waves, there were no statistically significant differences in mission.

The TELL survey asked three questions about the level of collaboration among faculty. One question asked teachers how much they

FIGURE 5.5

Teacher collaboration (SASS)

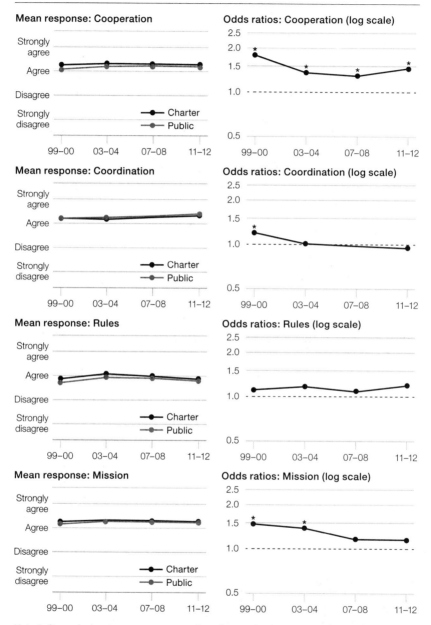

Note: Left panels denote mean responses of teachers to four statements about collaboration. Asterisks in the right panels denote a statistically significant difference between charter and public school teachers at the $p < 0.05$ level, controlling for school- and teacher-level influences. For information about how to interpret odds ratios, see the text explanation near figure 5.2. For modeling information, see the appendix.

agreed with the following statement: "Teachers have time available to collaborate with colleagues" on a four-point scale, from "Strongly disagree" to "Strongly agree." The other questions asked teachers how many hours in an average week they devoted to "Required committee and/or staff meetings" and "Collaborative planning time." For these latter questions, respondents chose an answer on a six-point scale, from "None" to "More than 10 hours." Table 5.3 presents the mean responses to these questions.

Teachers generally agreed that they had time to collaborate with their colleagues. The bottom two questions suggest that teachers generally spent around one to three hours per week in committee meetings and collaborating with colleagues.

To explore whether there were differences in collaboration between teachers in charter and public schools, I conducted a multivariate analysis that controlled for teacher and school-level influences (figure 5.6). The findings revealed that teachers in charter schools were more likely than teachers in public schools to agree that they had sufficient time to collaborate with colleagues. However, teachers from both charter and public schools reported spending approximately the same number hours in committee and staff

TABLE 5.3

Teacher collaboration (TELL)

	Public school teachers	Charter school teachers
Teachers have time available to collaborate with colleagues.[a]	2.73	2.91
Required committee and/or staff meetings.[b]	2.48	2.50
Collaborative planning time.[b]	2.58	2.69

[a]Mean responses of teachers on a four-point numerical rating scale, where 1 = "Strongly disagree" and 4 = "Strongly agree," to statements about collaboration in their schools.

[b]Mean responses of teachers on a six-point numerical rating scale, where 1 = "None"; 2 = "Less than or equal to 1 hour"; 3 = "More than 1 hour but less than or equal to 3 hours"; 4 = "More than 3 hours but less than or equal to 5 hours"; 5 = "More than 5 hours but less than or equal to 10 hours"; and 6 = "More than 10 hours," to question about how many hours per week they spend on various collaborative tasks.

FIGURE 5.6

Teacher collaboration (TELL)

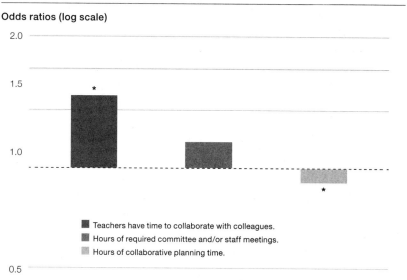

Odds ratios (log scale)

- Teachers have time to collaborate with colleagues.
- Hours of required committee and/or staff meetings.
- Hours of collaborative planning time.

Note: Asterisks denote a statistically significant difference between charter and public school teachers at the $p < 0.05$ level, controlling for school- and teacher-level influences. For information about how to interpret odds ratios, see the text explanation near figure 5.2. For modeling information, see the appendix.

meetings. Also, despite having more time to collaborate, teachers in charter schools reported spending fewer hours actually collaborating with colleagues outside of formal meetings.

INSIDE THE CHARTER SECTOR

Thus far, the chapter has revealed how charter and public schools compare in terms of teacher leadership and collaboration. We will now analyze how school franchise status, tax status, and state charter law are associated with teacher leadership and collaboration inside the charter sector. To conserve space, the section reports only the findings from the multivariate analysis of teachers' responses.

Teacher Leadership

To begin, I examined the SASS data to determine whether variation in the rating awarded to a state—for the operational flexibility of its charter law—was associated with differences in teacher leadership. Across four waves of surveys, a state's rating was not a strong predictor of teacher leadership. However, when there were statistically significant relationships, they tended to be negative: teachers in states with more flexible charter laws reported exercising less leadership. For example, in 1999–2000, teachers in states with higher charter law ratings were around 10 percent less likely to report having influence over determining in-service programming and about 20 percent less likely to report having influence over their school's budgets; in 2011–2012, teachers in states with higher charter law ratings were around 20 percent less likely to report control over the determination of performance standards.

For the 2011–2012 data, I also examined how teachers in schools run by EMOs differed from those in independently run charters. For most of the questions, there were no differences in teacher leadership. However, teachers in EMO-run charter schools were around 40 percent less likely to report having influence over setting curricula and 35 percent less likely to report having control over student disciplinary policies than teachers in non-EMO-run charter schools. The analysis revealed no differences in teacher leadership between teachers in for-profit and nonprofit EMOs.

The TELL survey data also permitted an analysis of variation within the charter sector. As with the SASS findings, the tax status of a school was unassociated with teachers' experiences with leadership. However, differing from the SASS, the TELL findings showed that teachers in EMO-run and non-EMO-run charter schools had largely similar experiences with leadership. The rating assigned to a state according to the operational flexibility of its charter law did appear to be related to teachers' experiences with leadership. Teachers in states with a higher rating were 20 percent more likely to report having influence over their school's improvement plan, the budget, student discipline procedures, and professional development programming. These teachers were also 40 percent more likely to report having control over the hiring of new teachers. However, teachers in higher-rated states were less likely to have control over devising teaching techniques.

Teacher Collaboration

Of the four school years analyzed by the SASS, teachers in higher-rated states expressed different experiences with collaboration than teachers in lower-rated states only in 2007–2008. In that year, teachers in higher-rated states were 25 percent more likely to report coordination in rule-following than were teachers in lower-rated states. Although we might expect that teachers in EMO-run charter schools would collaborate more (increased structure creates greater opportunities for collaboration) or less (increased structure creates red tape, which prevents collaboration), the 2011–2012 SASS data showed no differences in collaboration between teachers in EMO-run and non-EMO-run charter schools.

The analysis also used SASS data to look at whether differences in tax status (within EMOs) were associated with differences in collaboration and cooperation in the most recent wave of the survey. Results showed that teachers in for-profit EMOs were around 90 percent more likely to report coordinating content, 200 percent more likely to report enforcing rules collectively, and 160 percent more likely to report sharing a mission with fellow teachers.

An analysis of the TELL data revealed that, for one of the three collaboration questions, a state's charter rating was associated with teachers' responses: teachers in higher-rated states were 20 percent more likely to report having time to collaborate with colleagues for planning purposes than were teachers in lower-rated states. However, these same teachers did not report more hours of collaborative planning. In terms of franchising, the TELL survey found no differences between teachers' collaboration in EMO-run and non-EMO-run schools. There was one difference by tax status: teachers in for-profit charter schools were 38 percent less likely to indicate that they had time to collaborate than did teachers in non-profit schools.

SUMMARY

School-choice advocates expect that charter schools perform better partly because they allow teachers to play a larger role in school leadership than that played by teachers in public schools. This chapter has investigated this expectation empirically and demonstrated support for it: teachers in charter schools reported exercising greater leadership in their schools—on issues as diverse as establishing curriculum to developing professional development programming—than did teachers in public schools. Though the SASS data suggest that differences between teachers in these settings may be waning, even the most recent SASS analysis (from the 2011–2012 school year) found statistically significant differences between charter and public school teachers in six of the seven examined areas of teacher leadership. The TELL analysis echoes and expands on the SASS analysis, showing that teachers in charter schools felt they played a more important leadership role in various areas in their schools than did teachers in public schools.

In terms of teacher collaboration, the results were mixed. The SASS analysis shows that teachers in charter schools reported cooperating more than teachers in public schools; however, there were few differences in coordinating content and enforcing rules. Also, initially teachers in charter schools were more likely to report higher levels of shared mission; nonetheless, in the two most recent surveys these differences evaporated. The TELL analysis shows that teachers in charter schools reported feeling as if they had more time to collaborate but that they did not in fact spend more time collaborating than teachers in public schools did.

The charter sector analysis provided little clarity about what explains differences in teacher leadership or collaboration within these schools. In general, the three variables—state charter law rating, school governance, and tax status—did not consistently predict the outcomes examined here. However, teachers in EMO-run charter schools appeared to exercise less leadership than did teachers in non-EMOs. And according to the SASS at least, teachers in for-profit

EMOs were more likely to coordinate classroom content than were teachers in nonprofit EMOs.

Combined, the findings in this chapter and in chapter 4 suggest that teachers in charter schools had more autonomy in selecting the texts and content that they taught and played a larger role in leading their schools. These would seem to be positive developments for teachers. But there is still much to learn about what it's like to teach inside these different settings—before we start thinking of charter schools as some sort of teaching nirvana, it's important to note that prior studies have found that charter teachers are paid less and change jobs more often (relative to public school teachers). With these findings in mind, we'll now explore the working conditions of charter and public schools. How much are charter school teachers paid relative to public school teachers? Do they really work more? Are they more or less satisfied with their work? Do they turnover more?

S I X

Working Conditions
and Turnover

IN THE PRIOR TWO CHAPTERS, we saw that charter teachers had more classroom autonomy (at least in some respects), encountered less red tape, and played a bigger role in leading their schools than public school teachers did. If so, are teachers in charter schools more satisfied with their work than teachers in public schools are? Although we might expect that they are, one charter teacher whom I interviewed raised concerns about her school's teaching climate: "I like having autonomy if I know what the expectations are. But where I am right now, the job that I'm in right now, where I'm kinda creating the program? I need more feedback."

As this comment implies, autonomy may not necessarily enhance teacher satisfaction. In a similar way, teacher leadership might be exhausting rather than exhilarating. Chester Finn Jr. and his co-authors describe a progressive charter school in Minnesota in which teachers "must contend with the demands of school management, participatory governance, financial planning, and the design and application of new education methods and systems of accountability—all this while teaching!"[1] Similarly, Marya Levenson notes that teachers in some small charter schools "are expected to teach and advise students for up to fifty to sixty hours per week, longer work hours than colleagues in more traditional schools."[2] In her book *The Teacher Wars*, Dana Goldstein also notes the demanding pace of life in a charter school. She recounts a discussion with a union executive who was responsible for negotiating charter contracts across the country. The executive noted that "[charter school] teachers are expected to eat lunch with their students, and have no prep period to plan lessons. At others, when a teacher calls in sick, the school will not hire a substitute, but will instead require other teachers to fill in during their prep periods. At one Chicago charter school, teachers complained that they had so little free time during the day that they could not visit the bathroom."[3]

These comments show the importance of taking a step back and asking about a broader range of working conditions experienced by teachers in public and charter schools. This chapter begins that process by examining teacher workload, pay, burnout, and satisfaction. It then examines teachers' experiences with their schools' facilities and resources; it concludes with an analysis of teacher turnover, a metric used by scholars to understand the health of schools and other types of organizations.

WORKLOAD

Do teachers in charter schools work more than teachers in public schools? The conventional wisdom—noted in the accounts just cited—is that they do. However, one analysis, which did not control for differences in school or teacher characteristics but which used national data from the 2003–2004 school year, showed few differences in work hours.[4] To provide a more complete workload analysis, I compared teachers' reports about the number of hours that they spent working, drawing from the three most recent waves of the SASS. I measured hours in two ways. First, I looked at the number of contracted hours; teachers were asked, "How many hours are you required to work to receive BASE PAY during a typical FULL WEEK at this school?" (emphasis in original).[5] Second, teachers were asked, "Including hours spent during the school day, before and after school, and on the weekends, how many hours do you spend on ALL teaching and other school-related activities during a typical FULL WEEK at THIS school?" (emphasis in original).[6]

The top of figure 6.1 presents charter and public school teachers' mean answers over the three years of the survey; the bottom of the figure presents the findings from a multivariate regression analysis that examined whether any differences were statistically significant, after controlling for school- and teacher-level variables.[7] The regression coefficients in the bottom panels without an asterisk indicate that there was no statistically significant difference between charter and public schools; the coefficients with an asterisk next to them indicate that there was a statistically significant difference.

FIGURE 6.1

Teachers' hours contracted and worked (SASS)

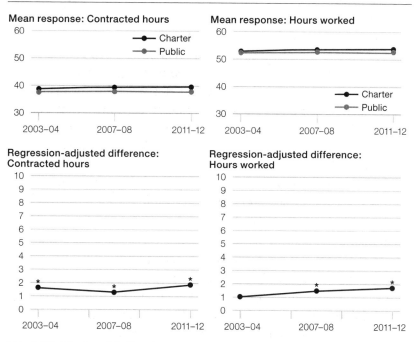

Note: SASS: Schools and Staffing Survey. Asterisks in the bottom panels denote a statistically significant difference between charter and public school teachers at the $p < 0.05$ level, controlling for school- and teacher-level influences. For modeling information, see the appendix.

The figure shows that teachers in both types of schools reported working around 10 more hours per week than their contracts stipulated (figure 6.1, top panels). Additionally, there were statistically significant differences between teachers in charter schools and public schools (bottom panels). The bottom left panel shows that in the 2003–2004 school year, teachers in charter schools reported signing contracts for around 1.5 more hours per week than did teachers in public schools. By 2011–2012, this difference increased to 1.8 more hours per week. These contractual differences resulted in real differences: in the two most recent surveys, teachers in charter schools reported working around 1.5 more hours per week than did teachers in public schools (bottom right panel). Although these differences are relatively small on a week-to-week basis, if we assume a school year of thirty-six weeks, these differences imply that, in 2011–2012, teachers in charter schools spent approximately fifty-four more hours working than teachers in public schools.

Another way of studying workload is by asking teachers how harried they felt on the job. In recent years, there has been growing concern that teachers are being saddled with bigger class sizes and are being forced to spend an ever-greater amount of their efforts preparing for standardized tests.[8] Chapter 3 showed that charter schools had more students per teacher than did public schools. If so, charter teachers might feel that they have less time to accomplish their work. On the other hand, chapter 4 showed that teachers in charter schools experienced less red tape and enjoyed greater autonomy in some ways than did teachers in public schools. If so, perhaps teachers in charter schools felt they had more time to accomplish their basic tasks.

To investigate these conflicting expectations, this section examines findings from the TELL survey, which asked teachers, "Please rate how strongly you agree or disagree with the following statements about the use of time in your school." After the prompt, teachers were given five statements: "Teachers have sufficient instructional time to meet the needs of all students," "The non-instructional time provided for teachers in my school is sufficient," "Class sizes are reasonable such that teachers have the time available to meet the needs of all students," "Teachers are allowed to focus on educating students with minimal interruptions," and "Teachers are protected from duties that interfere with their essential role of educating students."[9] For each of these statements, respondents chose an answer from one of four ordered responses, from "Strongly disagree" to "Strongly agree."

To determine if there were any differences between charter and public school teachers, all other factors being held equal, I conducted a multivariate analysis. Figure 6.2 presents the results of this analysis in the form of odds ratios derived from ordered logit coefficients; these figures indicate the likelihood that teachers in charter schools would answer a question differently, if school- and teacher-level differences are controlled for. An odds ratio above 1.0 with an asterisk next to it indicates that, all else being equal, teachers in charter schools were more likely to agree with a statement. An odds ratio below 1.0 with an asterisk indicates that teachers in charter schools were less likely to agree with a statement than teachers in public schools were. An odds ratio without an asterisk indicates that there were no statistically significant differences between the responses of teachers in charter and public schools.

Figure 6.2 shows that, in each aspect examined, teachers in charter schools were more likely to agree that they had sufficient time to do their work than were teachers in public schools. In the aggregate, this finding is surprising given that charter teachers play more roles in their schools and work in schools with more students per teacher (see chapters 3 and 5). Perhaps the associations found here result from charter teachers' working more hours or encountering less red tape. Whatever the reason, there were large differences between charter and public schools in the sufficiency of instructional time and ability to work without interruption. But the biggest difference was in class sizes: teachers in charter schools were much more likely to agree that class sizes were reasonable, thereby enabling them to do their work.

FIGURE 6.2

Teachers' experiences with time (TELL)

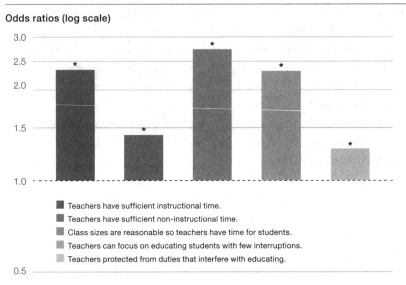

Odds ratios (log scale)

■ Teachers have sufficient instructional time.
■ Teachers have sufficient non-instructional time.
■ Class sizes are reasonable so teachers have time for students.
■ Teachers can focus on educating students with few interruptions.
■ Teachers protected from duties that interfere with educating.

Note: TELL: Teaching, Empowerment, Leading, and Learning surveys. Asterisks denote a statistically significant difference between charter and public school teachers at the $p < 0.05$ level, controlling for school- and teacher-level influences. For information about how to interpret odds ratios, see the accompanying text. For modeling information, see the appendix.

PAY

Another critical aspect of a school's teaching climate is compensation. Before the advent of teachers unions, teachers were not well paid for their work.[10] As teachers organized into unions, teacher compensation rose and unions became a lightning rod for criticism. Some have speculated that charter schools are part of a larger effort to break the power of teachers unions and reduce teacher compensation. Whether true or not, chapter 3 showed that teachers in charter schools were less likely to be unionized. Also, prior research suggests that charter school teachers receive less base pay than do teachers in public schools. For example, Finn and colleagues suggest that charter teachers earn about $9,000 less per year than teachers in district schools.[11]

Might differences in merit pay—a practice associated with charter schools in which teachers are rewarded or penalized for their performance—make up for these earning disparities? To begin to answer this question, I analyzed SASS data about where teachers said their income came from (figure 6.3). If teachers indicated that they had earned income from sources "such as a merit pay bonus, state supplement, etc.," they were coded "1"; those who didn't were coded "0." The left panel of the figure shows the mean response of teachers about their ability to earn merit pay or other supplemental pay; the right panel shows the findings from a statistical analysis of differences between public and charter school teachers, controlling for other school- and teacher-level variables.

For all the school years examined here, merit or other supplemental pay was received by a small proportion of teachers in both charter and public schools. However, there did appear to be a difference by school type. The right panel shows that in three of the four waves of the survey, teachers in charter schools were more likely

FIGURE 6.3

Teachers' experiences with merit pay or other supplemental pay (SASS)

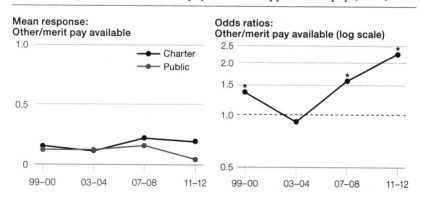

Note: The left panel shows teachers' mean scores, where 1 = "Yes" and 0 = "No," in response to question about whether they had received pay from sources "such as a merit pay bonus, state supplement, etc." Asterisks in the right panel denote a statistically significant difference between charter and public school teachers at the $p < 0.05$ level, controlling for school- and teacher-level influences. For information about how to interpret odds ratios, see the text explanation near figure 6.2. For modeling information, see the appendix.

to report earning merit pay or other supplemental pay were than teachers in public schools.

But how much did those who received merit or other supplemental pay actually earn? And how do earnings from this supplemental pay compare with base pay? The left panels in figure 6.4 present findings from an analysis of the mean base, additional, and merit and other supplemental pay reported by survey respondents in charter and public schools; the right panels present regression coefficients for the charter school variable controlling for school- and teacher-level differences. A coefficient above zero with an asterisk indicates that, all else being equal, teachers in charter schools reported more pay than did teachers in public schools. A coefficient without an asterisk indicates no statistically significant differences between the responses of teachers in charter and public schools. A coefficient below zero with an asterisk indicates that teachers in charter schools reported less pay than did teachers in public schools.

Across this entire period, teachers in charter schools earned considerably less in base pay than teachers in public schools earned (top right panel). This disparity appeared to increase over time: according to the regression-adjusted findings, in 1999–2000, the base pay difference was less than $2,000; by 2011–2012, this difference had increased to over $3,000. These differences are significant, but are around two-thirds lower than prior estimates suggest.[12] Additionally, the figure reveals no statistically significant differences in the amount of additional pay received by teachers—for things like coaching, student activity sponsorship, or teaching evening classes—and, in the last three surveys, no differences in the amount of merit pay.

BURNOUT AND SATISFACTION

If teachers in charter schools worked more hours per week and earned significantly less pay, were they also more likely to feel burned out by their work (relative to public school teachers)? To

FIGURE 6.4

Teachers' annual reported pay (SASS)

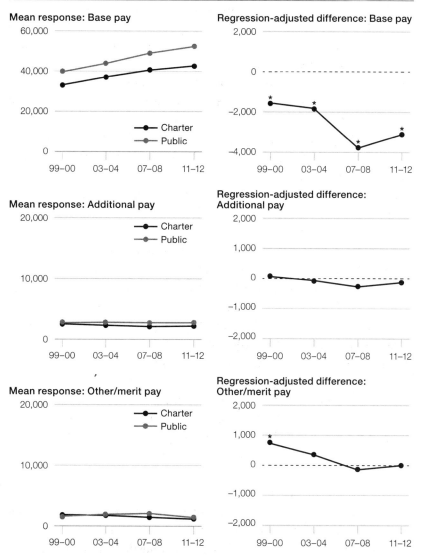

Note: Asterisks in the right panels denote a statistically significant difference between charter and public school teachers at the $p < 0.05$ level, controlling for school- and teacher-level influences. For modeling information, see the appendix.

address this question, we'll look at the SASS data and analyze questions about teacher enthusiasm and fatigue.

The SASS asked teachers to evaluate three statements and then a question: "I think about staying home from school because I'm just too tired to go," "I don't seem to have as much enthusiasm now as I did when I began teaching," "The stress and disappointments involved in teaching at this school aren't really worth it," and "If you could go back to your college days and start over again, would you become a teacher or not?" For the first three statements, teachers responded by choosing one of four options on a four-point scale, from "Strongly disagree" to "Strongly agree." For the last question, teachers chose one of five responses, from "Certainly would not become a teacher" to "Certainly would become a teacher." This last question was asked in all surveys, whereas the first three were asked only in the three most recent surveys.

Figure 6.5 presents the teachers' mean responses to these questions and the results of a multivariate analysis of the responses, controlling for school- and teacher-level factors like age and years of experience. The left panels reveal little evidence of generalized burnout in either charter or public school setting: teachers did not report feeling too tired to go to school, had not lost enthusiasm for the job, disagreed that teaching "isn't worth it," and said they would probably become a teacher if they had a chance to do it over again. The right panels show few statistically significant differences in burnout between teachers in charter and public schools. The lack of difference in fatigue is particularly interesting because, as noted earlier, in the two latest surveys, teachers in charter schools worked more hours than public school teachers did. Moreover, the one semi-consistent difference was positive for charter schools: in three of the four years, teachers in charter schools were more likely to indicate that they would become a teacher if they had to do it again.

The DTS also included a battery of questions that are helpful for discerning differences in burnout between teachers in these two settings. Specifically, teachers were asked to choose an answer on a five-point scale, from "Strongly disagree" to "Strongly agree" for the following five questions: "I feel emotionally drained from my work,"

FIGURE 6.5

Teacher burnout (SASS)

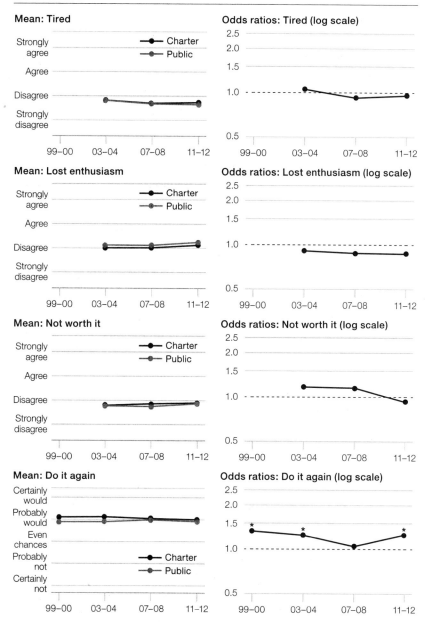

Note: Asterisks in the right panels denote a statistically significant difference between charter and public school teachers at the $p < 0.05$ level, controlling for school- and teacher-level influences. For information about how to interpret odds ratios, see the text explanation near figure 6.2. For modeling information, see the appendix.

"I've become more callous towards students since I started this job," "I feel I'm positively influencing students' lives through my work," "My job often requires me to work very hard," and "My job often leaves me with little time to get everything done." These questions were adapted from a series of questions developed by organizational scholars to explore employee burnout and workload.[13] Table 6.1 presents the mean responses of teachers to these questions.

The data in this table suggest a more mixed picture of teacher burnout: teachers in both settings felt emotionally drained by their work, thought that they worked hard, and thought that they had little time to finish their work. But they disagreed that they felt callous toward the students and agreed that they had a positive influence on students. The table also reveals no areas with major differences between teachers in charter and public schools. This lack of difference was confirmed by a multivariate analysis that controlled for teacher- and school-level influences.

Closely related to teacher burnout is teacher satisfaction. In the management literature, there is a long-running debate about whether employee satisfaction is related to employee performance.[14] Despite mixed findings in the empirical literature, scholars agree

TABLE 6.1

Teacher burnout (DTS)

	Public school teachers	Charter school teachers
I feel emotionally drained from my work.	4.14	4.01
I've become more callous towards students since I started this job.	2.40	2.33
I feel I'm positively influencing students' lives through my work.	4.35	4.36
My job often requires me to work very hard.	4.78	4.83
My job often leaves me with little time to get everything done.	4.64	4.62

Note: DTS: Delaware Teachers Survey. Numbers are the mean responses of teachers on a five-point numerical rating scale, where 1 = "Strongly disagree" and 5 = "Strongly agree," to statements about burnout.

that employee satisfaction is associated with various important organization outcomes, like motivation, absenteeism, and turnover.[15] Also, since employment contracts cannot spell out every employee activity, organizations seek to foster good "organization citizenship," an outcome strongly linked to employee satisfaction.[16] Perhaps as a result, education scholars have devoted considerable attention to teacher satisfaction.[17]

To study teacher satisfaction in public and charter schools, I turned to teachers' mean responses to four statements from the SASS: "I am satisfied with my teaching salary," "I am satisfied with my class size," "I am generally satisfied with being a teacher at this school," and "The teachers at this school like being here; I would describe us as a satisfied group." The class-size statement was only used in the first two waves of the survey; the group-satisfaction statement was not used in the first wave of the survey. For all statements, teachers responded on a four-point scale, from "Strongly disagree" to "Strongly agree." Figure 6.6 reveals the findings from a descriptive analysis of these questions (left panels) and from a statistical analysis, which controlled for teacher- and school-level covariates, of teacher satisfaction (right panels).

The left side of the figure reveals that teachers in both settings reported relatively high group, personal, and class-size satisfaction, but reported dissatisfaction with their salaries. The right side of the figure shows that there were no differences between teachers in public and charter schools in terms of personal or group satisfaction. It also shows that in the first two school years studied, teachers in charter schools were more satisfied than public school teachers were with the size of their classes. This finding is surprising, given that charter teachers faced higher student-teacher ratios than did public school teachers (figure 3.3). The right uppermost panel reveals some differences and volatility in pay satisfaction: In the 1999–2000 school year, teachers in charter schools were more satisfied with their salaries than public school teachers were; in 2007–2008, this pattern reversed.

The TELL survey had no explicit questions about teacher satisfaction. However, one prompt asked teachers about the working

FIGURE 6.6

Teacher satisfaction (SASS)

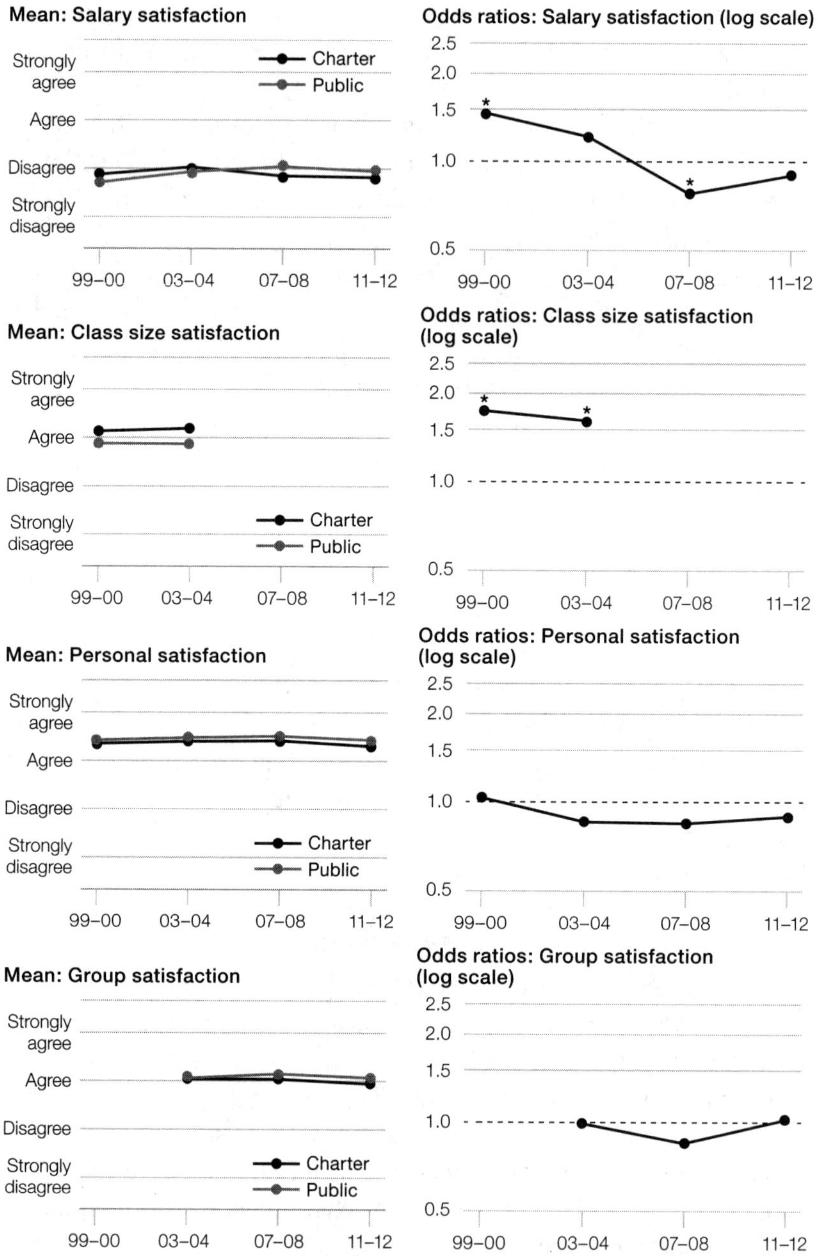

Note: Asterisks in the right panels denote a statistically significant difference between charter and public school teachers at the $p < 0.05$ level, controlling for school- and teacher-level influences. For information about how to interpret odds ratios, see the text explanation near figure 6.2. For modeling information, see the appendix.

conditions of their schools. On a four-point scale, from "Strongly disagree" to "Strongly agree," respondents were asked how much they agreed with the following statement: "Overall, my school is a good place to work and learn." Both sets of teachers are generally satisfied (public school teachers' mean response, 3.11; charter school teachers, 3.20). A multivariate analysis that controlled for school- and teacher-level factors showed that teachers in charter schools were 45 percent more likely to agree with this statement than were teachers in public schools.

Combined with the burnout findings discussed above, advocates and critics of charter schools seem somewhat off the mark. Charter schools do not appear to be the teaching paradises sometimes depicted by advocates; at the same time, these schools are hardly the stressed-out teaching sweatshops depicted by critics.

FACILITIES AND RESOURCES

Another crucial element of any school's teaching climate is its facilities and resources—what teachers have to work with inevitably shapes what they do. Perhaps because of high-profile fund-raising by charter schools in New York City, critics have argued that charters have more resources than public schools have and that, therefore, the two cannot be fairly compared.[18] Interestingly, recent research by Meagan Batdorff and colleagues suggests that charter schools receive less money per pupil—even when considering nonpublic revenue sources—than do public schools.[19] According to their most recent figures (from the 2010–2011 school year), charter schools had a funding gap of approximately 28 percent, representing around a $4,000 disparity in yearly per pupil funding.[20] The main explanation for this gap, they suggest, is that charter schools tend to receive less money from local government sources than do public schools. Moreover, because charter schools lack adequate capital funding, they are forced to lease or borrow space rather than own it outright.[21]

To summarize, there is some disagreement about whether charter and public schools operate in different resource environments. Though this chapter doesn't delve into funding differences, it contributes by exploring teachers' experiences with their schools' resources and facilities. To begin, on each wave of the SASS since 1999–2000, teachers were asked how much they agreed with the following statement: "Necessary materials such as textbooks, supplies, and copy machines are available as needed by the staff." In 1999–2000, a multivariate analysis revealed that teachers in charter schools were around 20 percent more likely to agree with this statement than were teachers in public schools. However, in each subsequent wave of the survey, there were no statistically significant differences between teachers in charter and public schools.

On the two most recent SASS questionnaires, teachers were also asked "In the LAST SCHOOL YEAR [the year range was inserted here], how much of your own money did you spend on classroom supplies, without reimbursement?" (emphasis in original). Teachers could then indicate a dollar figure up to $9,999. Prior research suggests that public school teachers spend around $500 of their own money on such expenditures each year.[22] If charter schools are more resource poor than public schools, as Batdorff and colleagues suggest, charter teachers might spend more money on classroom supplies than do public school teachers.

In the 2007–2008 school year, the SASS data show, a teacher in a public school spent on average $419 of his or her own money (0.8 percent of mean yearly base pay) on classroom supplies, whereas a teacher in a charter school spent on average $412 (1.0 percent of mean yearly base pay). In the 2011–2012 school year, the public school average dropped to $408 (0.8 percent of mean yearly base pay), and the charter school average dropped to $395 (0.9 percent of mean yearly base pay). A multivariate analysis comparing the dollar amounts spent by teachers in charter and public schools revealed no statistically significant difference in either year.

Finally, in each wave of the SASS, teachers were asked how much they agreed with this statement: "I am given the support I need to teach students with special needs." As discussed earlier in the book, teachers in charter schools were likely to work in schools with a lower percentage of students with IEPs than in public schools. When accounting for this general difference, did teachers in public and charter schools report different experiences with support for students with special needs? A multivariate analysis of this question—which controlled for school- and teacher-level covariates, including the percentage of IEP students in the school—indicated that teachers in charter schools were around 20 percent more likely than public school teachers were to agree with this statement in 1999–2000 and 30 percent more likely to agree in 2011–2012. In the other two school years, there were no significant differences between these two sets of teachers.

The TELL survey goes into considerably more depth about the resource environments in which teachers operated. Specifically, teachers were given the following prompts: "Rate how strongly you agree or disagree with the following statements about your school facilities and resources: (1) Teachers have sufficient access to appropriate instructional materials; (2) Teachers have sufficient access to instructional technology, including computers, printers, software, and Internet access; (3) Teachers have access to reliable communication technology, including phones, faxes and email; (4) Teachers have sufficient access to office equipment and supplies such as copy machines, paper, pens, etc.; (5) Teachers have sufficient access to a broad range of professional support personnel; (6) The school environment is clean and well maintained; (7) Teachers have adequate space to work productively; (8) The physical environment of classrooms in this school supports teaching and learning; and (9) The reliability and speed of Internet connections in this school are sufficient to support instructional practices."[23] They answered these questions by choosing from one of four ordered responses, from "Strongly disagree" to "Strongly agree." Table 6.2 presents the mean responses of teachers in these different settings.

The means presented in this table suggest that teachers generally agreed that their schools had sufficient resources. Although there were no massive differences, teachers in charter schools tended to report better experiences with facilities than did teachers in public schools.

To further examine these responses, I conducted a multivariate analysis that controlled for school- and individual-level differences

TABLE 6.2

Teachers' experiences with facilities and resources (TELL)

	Public school teachers	Charter school teachers
Appropriate instructional materials	2.91	3.01
Instructional technology	2.92	3.05
Communications technology	3.18	3.33
Office supplies	3.00	3.20
Professional support	2.99	2.90
Clean environment	3.15	3.31
Adequate space	3.14	3.11
Physical environment that supports teaching and learning	3.11	3.16
Reliable Internet	2.90	3.01

Note: Numbers are the mean responses of teachers on a four-point numerical rating scale, where 1 = "Strongly disagree" and 4 = "Strongly agree," to statements about their school's facilities and resources.

(figure 6.7). In most respects, teachers in charter schools had more favorable views about their schools' facilities and resources than teachers in public schools had. In particular, it is notable that charter teachers were more likely than public school teachers to agree that the physical environments of their classrooms were conducive to teaching and learning and more likely to agree that they had sufficient access to instructional materials.

TURNOVER

One of the most useful ways of understanding the working conditions inside a school is by looking at turnover: the rates at which teachers leave their schools and the teaching profession. Consequently, there has been considerable scholarly interest in—and empirical analysis of—the rates of turnover at charter schools and at public schools.[24] These studies suggest that teachers in charter schools tend to leave

FIGURE 6.7

Teachers' experiences with facilities and resources (TELL)

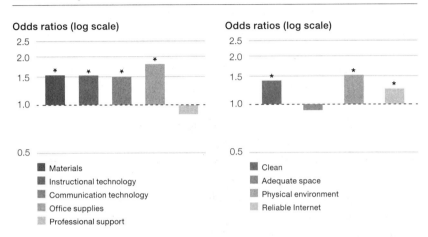

Note: Asterisks denote a statistically significant difference between charter and public school teachers at the $p < 0.05$ level, controlling for school- and teacher-level influences. For information about how to interpret odds ratios, see the text explanation near figure 6.2. For modeling information, see the appendix.

their schools or their profession more than do teachers in public schools.[25] But it is unclear how much of this difference is driven by factors associated with charter schools—like the age of teachers or the student-teacher ratio inside schools—and how much is driven by differences in school type (being a charter school or not).

David Stuit and Thomas Smith looked at data from sixteen states from the 2003–2004 school year and found higher rates of turnover for teachers in charter schools.[26] However, they found that nearly two-thirds of the difference between the two rates is explained by teacher characteristics (like age and certification status) and personnel policies (like union status). In a study of Wisconsin teachers, and an analysis of national-level data from the 1999–2000 school year, researchers found that controlling for teacher and school variables removed any statistically significant differences in turnover between the sectors.[27] In fact, the Wisconsin study suggests that charter schools did a better job of retaining teachers in urban settings than did public schools.

To contribute to our understanding of turnover, I used TELL and SASS data to examine turnover intent and actual turnover across a number of years. To begin, the TELL surveys asked teachers to respond to the following question about their future professional plans: "Which of the following best describes your immediate professional plans? (Select one.)" They were provided with six choices: "Continue teaching at my current school," "Continue teaching in this district but leave this school," "Continue teaching in this state but leave this district," "Continue working in education but pursue an administrative position," "Continue working in education but pursue a non-administrative position," and "Leave education entirely." These responses were coded so that those who intended to continue teaching in their current schools received a "1" and all other respondents received a "0." A descriptive analysis revealed that the mean response for teachers in public schools was 0.80, and the mean response for teachers in charter schools was 0.79. A multivariate analysis of this question—controlling for school and individual-level factors—revealed that teachers in charter schools were 14 percent more likely to indicate that they would continue working in their current schools than were teachers in public schools.

On the SASS, teachers were asked to respond to two questions about their intention to stay in their current schools: "If I could get a higher paying job I'd leave teaching as soon as possible" and "I think about transferring to another school." For both questions, teachers chose a response on a four-point scale, from "Strongly disagree" to "Strongly agree." The top of figure 6.8 reveals the results of a descriptive analysis of these questions for each year they were asked (neither group of teachers was asked these questions in the 1999–2000 survey). The bottom presents the results from a multivariate analysis, which asked if any differences were statistically significant, when controlling for other school- and teacher-level covariates.

Teachers in both charter schools and public schools generally disagreed that they would leave teaching for better pay or that they thought about transferring to another school (top panels). Nonetheless, there were some statistically significant differences between teachers in public and charter schools (bottom panels). In

FIGURE 6.8

Teacher turnover intent (SASS)

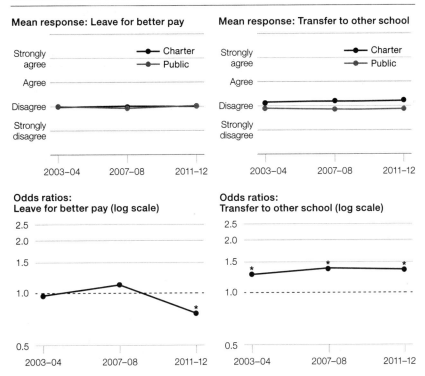

Note: Asterisks in the bottom panels denote a statistically significant difference between charter and public school teachers at the *p* < 0.05 level, controlling for school- and teacher-level influences. For information about how to interpret odds ratios, see the text explanation near figure 6.2. For modeling information, see the appendix.

2011–2012, teachers in charter schools were less likely to indicate that they would leave teaching for a higher paying job. The bottom right panel points in the opposite direction: teachers in charter schools were consistently more likely to indicate that they thought about transferring to another school. It is not clear what to make of this finding. Since teachers in charter schools weren't radically different in terms of satisfaction and burnout, perhaps thoughts about transferring stem from their consistently lower pay.

Whatever the case may be, we should explore actual differences in turnover across these two types of schools. To do so, we now examine questions asked by the US Department of Education's National Center for Education Statistics on the Teacher Follow-Up Survey (TFS)—a survey sent to a sample of SASS respondents in the year following each wave of the SASS to measure attrition rates and personnel change across a range of schools. We will examine professional turnover and school turnover on the TFS. The top of figure 6.9

FIGURE 6.9

Teacher turnover (SASS)

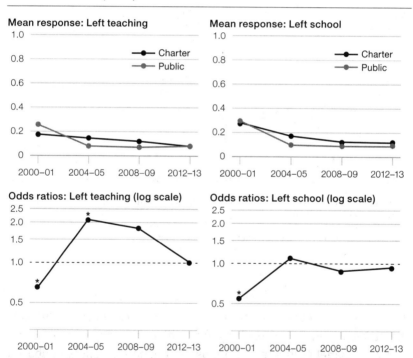

Note: Top panels show mean responses of teachers asked whether they left teaching (top left panel) or left their school (top right panel), where 1 = "Yes" and 0 = "No." The higher the number, the more likely that the teachers left. Asterisks in bottom panels denote a statistically significant difference between charter and public school teachers at the $p < 0.05$ level, controlling for school- and teacher-level influences. For information about how to interpret odds ratios, see the text explanation near figure 6.2. For modeling information, see the appendix.

presents the findings of a descriptive analysis of whether teachers left the teaching profession altogether (top left panel) and left their schools (top right panel). If teachers left the profession or their schools, they were coded as a "1"; if they did not, they were coded as a "0." The bottom panels examine whether there were any statistically significant differences between teachers in charter and public schools, after controlling for school and teacher covariates.

For both sets of teachers, the 2000–2001 school year was the high-water mark of turnover; after that, fewer teachers left the profession and their particular schools. The bottom panels show that there were few statistically significant differences in turnover between teachers in charter and public schools. In the first wave of the survey, teachers in charter schools were less likely to leave their schools and the profession than were teachers in public schools. In the second wave, charter teachers were more likely to leave teaching than were public school teachers. In the two most recent waves of the survey, there were no statistically significant differences in turnover between teachers in charter and public schools.

INSIDE THE CHARTER SECTOR

Now we shift to explore the working conditions and turnover rates among charter schools. Returning to the explanations developed in chapter 2, this section asks how different types of charter schools might shape teachers' experiences.[28] This section therefore focuses on schools' franchise status (EMO versus non-EMO) and profit-nonprofit status. As with other chapters, for the sake of brevity, this section only reports the findings from its multivariate analyses.

Workload and Pay

Analyzing SASS data for the 2011–2012 school year, I found that teachers in EMO-run schools reported signing contracts that required them to work an additional 1.3 more hours per week, relative to teachers in non-EMO-run schools. Interestingly, however, they did not report working more hours than teachers in non-EMO-run charter schools reported. Also, there were no differences between teachers in nonprofit and for-profit EMOs in the hours contracted or worked. There were nevertheless some interesting differences in pay: teachers in for-profit EMOs received over $4,000 less in base pay than did teachers in nonprofit EMOs. Although this difference might have been mitigated with additional pay, merit pay, or other supplemental pay, teachers in both for-profit and nonprofit EMOs saw no statistical differences in the amount of this pay they received.

Despite no differences in the number of hours that teachers worked in for-profit and nonprofit EMOs, the TELL analysis revealed some interesting differences in the experiences of teachers in these two types of schools. Returning to the time questions asked earlier (see figure 6.2), teachers in for-profit EMOs were less likely to agree that they had sufficient instructional time, that class sizes were reasonable, and that they could focus on educating students with minimal interruptions. The TELL analysis revealed no differences between teachers' experiences with time in EMO-run and non-EMO-run charter schools.

In sum, the TELL analysis suggests that teachers in charter schools indicated generally having more time to meet their goals than teachers in public schools did and that teachers in for-profit charters had less time than teachers in nonprofit charters had. Apparently, then, teachers in nonprofit charters were driving the differences observed between public and charter schools. But how do teachers in for-profit charter schools and public schools compare? An analysis showed that teachers in for-profit charter schools were around 1.0 time more likely than public school teachers to agree both that they had sufficient instructional time to meet the needs of students and that they could focus on educating students with minimal interruptions. In the other three ways that the TELL survey investigated time, there were no differences between teachers in public schools and for-profit charter schools. In other words, in most ways, teachers in for-profit charter schools and in public schools had comparable experiences with time.

Burnout and Satisfaction

Turning to burnout and satisfaction, few statistically significant differences were evident for teachers in different types of charter schools. For example, on the 2011–2012 SASS, teachers in EMO-run charter schools and non-EMO-run schools reported comparable levels of fatigue and enthusiasm. However, teachers in EMO-run charter schools were 50 percent less likely to be satisfied with their salaries than were teachers in non-EMO-run schools. Within the EMO-run category, the school's tax status (profit versus nonprofit) was not associated with teachers' sense of burnout. This finding is surprising, given the pay disparities noted above. Also surprisingly, teachers in for-profit EMOs were over 100 percent more likely to indicate that "teachers like it here."

On the TELL survey, teachers responded to a question about their satisfaction with their schools as overall places to learn and work. Teachers in EMO-run and non-EMO-run schools showed no statistically significant differences in their satisfaction, but teachers in for-profit charter schools were around 40 percent less likely than teachers in nonprofit charter schools were to agree that their schools were good places to work and learn.

Facilities and Resources

In the above charter-public analysis, we saw mixed evidence about facilities and resources: the SASS data showed few differences while the TELL data showed that teachers in charter schools reported better experiences with facilities and resources (relative to teachers in public schools). Inside the charter sector, the SASS data revealed no statistically significant differences between teachers in EMO-run and non-EMO-run charter schools in terms of their experiences with resources or the amount of their own money that they spent on school supplies. Also, within EMO schools there were no differences in experiences with resources between teachers in for-profit and nonprofit schools.

The TELL analysis revealed a few differences: teachers in EMO-run schools were 40 percent more likely to report having access to appropriate instructional materials and were around 50 percent more likely to agree that they had access to office supplies. Meanwhile, teachers in for-profit charter schools were around 40 percent less likely to agree that their schools' physical environment contributed to teaching and learning, 30 percent less likely to agree that they had sufficient space, and 60 percent less likely to agree that they had access to office supplies.

Turnover

The 2011–2012 SASS data revealed that teachers in EMO-run charter schools were around 40 percent more likely than were teachers in non-EMO-run schools to indicate that they would leave teaching for a job with better pay. Perhaps the higher likelihood of turnover intent in EMO-run schools reflects these teachers' above-noted dissatisfaction with their salaries. However, teachers in for-profit EMOs were no different in turnover intent than were teachers in nonprofit EMOs. The TELL data showed no associations between teacher turnover intent and their school's tax status or its franchise status.

The actual turnover data had too few respondents for a statistically valid multivariate analysis. For this reason, I compared the means while varying the values of the relevant independent variables. In 2011–2012, about 17 percent of teachers left EMO-run charter schools, compared with 7 percent of teachers who left non-EMO-run schools. However, there were no differences in the percentage of either group of teachers who left the profession (around 7 percent). Within EMOs, around 23 percent of teachers in for-profit schools left their schools, whereas 14 percent of teachers in nonprofits left their schools; their rates of leaving the profession were quite similar (between 7 and 8 percent).

SUMMARY

This chapter has covered a lot of ground. It showed that teachers in charter schools worked more hours for less pay than teachers in public schools did. Despite this difference, there was little evidence of consistent differences in burnout, satisfaction, and turnover. On their face, these observations present something of a puzzle: all else being equal, we would expect that teachers who work more and are paid less would be less satisfied and more likely to leave their work. There are a few ways that this puzzle might be explained. Perhaps teachers in charter schools are unaware that they make less money and work more than teachers in public schools do. Under this theory, charter teachers would not feel as if they were being taken advantage of. Alternatively, perhaps charter teachers are aware of this disparity, but the advantages of teaching in a charter school—like having more autonomy over the content that they teach or playing a bigger role in leading their schools—have outweighed the dissatisfaction that could come with relatively low pay.

Within the charter sector, teachers in EMO-run schools reported feeling less satisfied with their salaries and said that they would leave teaching for jobs that paid more money. Accordingly, perhaps, the charter sector turnover analysis hinted that teachers in EMOs may have been more likely to leave their schools than were teachers in non-EMOs. Further parsing the data, we see that teachers in for-profit EMOs rated their schools as worse places to work and learn and appeared to have left their schools at higher rates than did those teaching in nonprofit EMOs.

At the close of this chapter, we have now completed four empirical chapters that have examined differences in the teaching climates of charter and public schools. If there is a single theme that has emerged so far it's this: despite some important differences, the teaching climates of charter and public schools do not match the enthusiastic expectations of proponents or the worst fears of critics.

Now we turn to another crucial part of a school's teaching climate: the extent to which teachers believed that their schools were engaged with parents and the broader community. Charter schools, at their founding, were expected to arise organically from their surrounding communities. The trajectory of the sector, as noted in chapter 2, hasn't developed that way: Currently, a majority of students in charter schools are in schools run by centrally operated EMOs.

Despite this organizational reality, claims about charter schools and community and parental involvement persist. In the next chapter, we examine these claims empirically and ask whether teachers in charter and public schools reported different levels of community and parent engagement.

SEVEN

Parent and Community Engagement

PARENT AND COMMUNITY involvement in schools are thought to have a direct, substantial impact on student and school success.[1] One meta-analysis found a "positive and convincing relationship between family involvement and benefits for students, including improved academic achievement. This relationship holds across families of all economic, racial/ethnic, and educational backgrounds and for students at all ages. Although there is less research on the effects of community involvement, it also suggests benefits for schools, families, and students, including improved achievement and behavior."[2] There are varied explanations for why parental support is important, but two essential components are coordination and reinforcement: when parents and teachers work together, parents can reinforce in-school messages and play a more active role overseeing student progress.

In recent years, departments of education around the nation have seized on the importance of family and neighborhood connections and have formed offices devoted to enhancing linkages between schools, parents, and communities.[3] These offices develop models detailing how schools can conduct outreach to engage with the parents of students, especially in struggling schools. Some departments have gone even further than directing schools on how to conduct outreach. In New York City, for example, Schools Chancellor Carmen

Fariña has led an effort to make parental engagement a component of a school's annual rating.[4]

Recognizing the importance of family-school connections, many states have used charter legislation to "[increase] opportunities for parental involvement" in charter schools.[5] Some advocates suggest that this goal has been achieved. For example, the National Alliance for Public Charter Schools notes: "Charter schools foster a partnership between parents, teachers, and students. They create an environment in which parents can be more involved."[6]

Despite claims like this, there is relatively little empirical proof that charter schools foster higher levels of parent and community engagement. For example, a study of parents in charter and public schools in Washington, DC, showed that charter school parents were more likely than public school parents were to report being in touch with teachers and administrators but were no different in terms of their likelihood to volunteer for a school event or be a member of a PTA.[7] Studies like this suggest that we need a national perspective on whether charter and public schools foster different levels of parent and community engagement. However, as noted earlier in the book, studying differences in engagement is difficult: perhaps charter school parents, who made an affirmative choice about where their children attended school, would be more engaged than parents who did not make an affirmative choice.[8] In other words, perhaps any observed differences in engagement aren't driven by the type of school a student enrolls in but by the characteristics of the student's parents.

This possibility poses a problem for this chapter. To deal with it, like other chapters, the statistical analysis presented here controls for as many of a school's student characteristics as possible—like poverty, race, and special education. However, it obviously cannot control for unobserved differences, which may affect the findings here. This is a problem, but it isn't fatal: few would suggest that self-selection, or the characteristics of a school's students or parents, is all that affects a school's climate. Rather, most theorists think, a school's leadership, policies, and procedures explain important aspects of why schools function as they do.[9] In other words, a school's level of parental engagement is likely linked to institutional choices within the school. For example, research suggests that charter schools are embracing some innovate techniques—including the use of technology, contracts, and incentives—to ensure that parents are involved in their children's school lives.[10]

Whether these approaches have demonstrable effects is beyond the scope of this chapter. Rather, we'll set a more modest goal: to use teachers' experiences to ask whether there are differences in the level of parental and community engagement in charter and public schools.

PARENTAL SUPPORT AND INVOLVEMENT

In some of my interviews with Delaware teachers during the 2014–2015 school year, there appeared to be a higher level of parental engagement in charter schools. For example, one charter school teacher noted that back-to-school night in his room was often "standing room only" and that parents across the school were "super involved." Another charter teacher with whom I spoke had previously worked in charter and public schools in a nearby state. During our conversation, she noted that, in her current school, "parents actually show up for conferences and IEPs. When I was [teaching in schools in the other state], I think there were parents that I had never met before. I couldn't tell you who they were if I was walking down the street. So I feel that the parents here are really involved." Since she didn't specify whether she was comparing her current school to her previous experiences in charter or public schools, I asked her whether the high level of engagement in her current school was similar to that at the charter school she taught at in the other state. She replied: "They were not very involved at all. I would sit at conferences, and maybe two people would show up in a twelve-hour day." This comment suggests that school type may not be the driving difference in parental engagement across schools.

Whether school type was affecting teachers' experiences or not, public school teachers in Delaware said that parental involvement was more mixed. For them, it was hit or miss and depended on the students or families. One public school teacher noted that the "parents that show for open house and parent conferences are not the parents that we need to see. It's not that we're not grateful that they're there, but they're typically not the parents that we need to see. Their students are high performing, their students are engaged in the process ... If we can get more parent engagement at the low end of the spectrum as far as the struggling learners, it would be much more beneficial." Similarly, a public school teacher who rotated among a few different schools noted: "I have two schools that are primarily Spanish-speaking, and we have more trouble getting parents involved. I don't know, they don't feel as comfortable coming to teacher events because they can't speak the language, or teachers don't feel as comfortable. You're not going to call them on the phone, because you can't talk to them."

These comments hint that higher levels of parental engagement in charter schools—if they indeed exist—might be more driven by student- or family-level differences than by what a school is doing. If so, self-selection could be an important driver of differences in parental engagement between charter and public schools. In fact, a charter teacher with whom I spoke indicated that self-selection fostered high levels of engagement in her school: "The vast majority of our students come from families that really place an emphasis on education, and they really work hard, and they really—just choosing to enter the lottery, to come to the school, would be an indication of that." However, she later noted that the school itself played a role in fostering high engagement. She said that parent engagement was one of the school's "driving principles," so "pleasing the parents is very high on the agenda" for administrators and teachers.

These comments highlight the difficulty—perhaps the impossibility—of teasing out whether any differences between charter and public school engagement are driven by self-selection or institutional characteristics like school policy. Although this chapter will not investigate why there were or weren't differences, it will ask the more fundamental question: do charter and public schools have different levels of parental involvement and support?

To begin to systematically answer that question, we turn first to the SASS data. Specifically, teachers were asked whether they agreed with the following statement: "I receive a great deal of support from parents for the work I do." Respondents chose an answer from one of four ordered responses, from "Strongly disagree" to "Strongly agree." Teachers were also asked, "To what extent is each of the following a problem in this school?"[11] One of the items listed was "Lack of parental involvement."[12] Following this prompt, teachers chose from one of four ordered boxes, from "Serious problem" to "Not a problem." The top of figure 7.1 compares the mean responses of teachers to these prompts across the four waves of the SASS. The bottom panels present odds ratios indicating the likelihood that teachers in charter and public schools had different experiences with parental support, controlling for school- and teacher-level differences.[13] An odds ratio above 1.0 with an asterisk next to it indicates that, all else being equal, teachers in charter schools were more likely to agree with a statement than public school teachers were. An odds ratio below 1.0 with an asterisk indicates that charter school teachers were less likely to agree with a statement than were public school teachers. An odds ratio without an asterisk indicates no statistically significant differences between the responses of teachers in charter and public schools.

On average, teachers in both types of schools weren't wildly enthusiastic or concerned with parental support and involvement. The upper left panel of figure 7.1 suggests similarities between charter and public school teachers, while the upper right suggests some differences: teachers in charter schools were closer to agreeing that parental involvement was a "minor problem," whereas teachers in public schools were closer to agreeing it was a "moderate problem." The bottom panels, which control for school- and teacher-level covariates, show that in each wave of the survey, teachers in charter schools were more likely than teachers in public schools were to agree that they received support from parents and that involvement wasn't a problem. It is notable that the size of the odds ratios in these bottom panels are among the largest and most consistent of all the areas of teaching climate examined in this book.

Another indicator of parental involvement is the amount of time teachers actually spent communicating with parents. Do higher

FIGURE 7.1

Teachers' views of parental support and involvement (SASS)

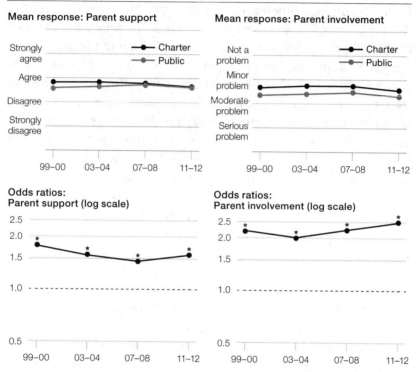

Note: SASS: Schools and Staffing Survey. Asterisks in bottom panels denote a statistically significant difference between charter and public school teachers at the $p < 0.05$ level, controlling for school- and teacher-level influences. For information about how to interpret odds ratios, see the accompanying text. For modeling information, see the appendix.

levels of parental support and involvement translate into more time that teachers spend interacting with parents? In the TELL, teachers were asked how many hours, in an average week, they devoted to "Communicating with parents/guardians and/or the community."[14] Respondents chose an answer to this question on a six-point scale, from "None" to "More than 10 hours." A descriptive analysis of teachers' responses to this question revealed that the mean response for teachers in both settings was around 3, which indicates that most teachers spent from one to three hours per week communicating with parents. To further investigate these differences, I conducted a multivariate analysis using TELL data; this analysis found that teachers in charter schools were more likely to spend a greater amount of time communicating with parents and the community (relative to public school teachers).

The TELL survey also asked a variety of questions about the role that parents play in the school's life and more general questions about school-parent interactions. Specifically, teachers were asked how much they agreed with the following statements: "Parents/guardians are influential decision makers in this school," "This school does a good job of encouraging parent/guardian involvement," "Teachers provide parents/guardians with useful information about student learning," "Parents/guardians know what is going on in this school," "Parents/guardians support teachers, contributing to their success with students." In response, teachers chose an answer on a four-point scale, from "Strongly disagree" to "Strongly agree." Table 7.1 displays the mean responses to these questions for teachers in charter and public schools.

There were no large differences between charter and public school teachers in their responses. However, across each of the examined questions, teachers in charter schools saw parents as more involved with their schools than did teachers in public schools.

To determine if any of these differences were statistically significant, I conducted a multivariate analysis of the teachers' responses to these questions (figure 7.2). The findings echo and expand on the findings discussed so far. Like the SASS analysis (bottom panels of figure 7.1), the TELL analysis showed that teachers in charter schools were more likely than their colleagues in public schools to agree that parents support them. However, the SASS question only indicated whether parents supported teacher work; the TELL data go a bit further, showing that teachers in charter schools were more likely to perceive that this support contributed to student success. In addition, figure 7.2 deepens our understanding of what higher levels of parent involvement in charter schools (than in public schools)

TABLE 7.1

Teachers' views of interactions between parents and schools (TELL)

	Public school teachers	Charter school teachers
Parents/guardians are influential decision makers in this school.	2.82	3.05
This school does a good job of encouraging parent/guardian involvement.	3.19	3.36
Teachers provide parents/guardians with useful information about student learning.	3.30	3.42
Parents/guardians know what is going on in this school.	3.07	3.25
Parents/guardians support teachers, contributing to their success with students.	2.79	3.04

Note: TELL: Teaching, Empowerment, Leading, and Learning surveys. Numbers are the mean responses of teachers on a four-point numerical rating scale, where 1 = "Strongly disagree" and 4 = "Strongly agree," to statements about interactions between parents and the teachers' schools.

might mean in practice. In short, the TELL findings suggest that these interactions are meaningful: teachers in charter schools were more likely to agree that parents know what is happening in their children's schools and that parents are given useful information about their learning. Figure 7.2 also shows that teachers in charter schools were much more likely than teachers in public schools to agree that parents are important decision makers in their schools.

But perhaps the most important finding from this figure relates to the question of school encouragement of parent involvement. Recall from above that the higher levels of engagement evident here may arise from student self-selection, school policies and practices, or both. The TELL data show that teachers in charter schools were more likely to agree that their schools did a good job of encouraging parental involvement (relative to public school teachers). Consequently, though this question doesn't prove that higher engagement is due solely to administrative practices, it suggests that they may have contributed to the high levels of engagement seen here.

FIGURE 7.2

Teachers' views of interactions between parents and schools (TELL)

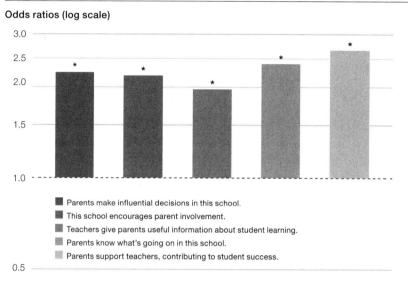

Odds ratios (log scale)

■ Parents make influential decisions in this school.
■ This school encourages parent involvement.
■ Teachers give parents useful information about student learning.
■ Parents know what's going on in this school.
▨ Parents support teachers, contributing to student success.

Note: Asterisks denote a statistically significant difference between charter and public school teachers at the $p < 0.05$ level, controlling for school- and teacher-level influences. For information about how to interpret odds ratios, see the text explanation near figure 7.1. For modeling information, see the appendix.

COMMUNITY SUPPORT AND ENGAGEMENT

Thus far, the chapter has focused on teachers' perceptions of parental involvement in schools. Now we zoom out slightly to consider how they saw interactions between their schools and the broader community. A school's community is harder to define than its parents: it may refer to people in the geographic proximity of the school and/or those directly associated with it. Despite the term's slipperiness, it is an important study for two reasons. First, as noted above, student success is thought to be influenced not just by parents but also by the communities in which they learn.[15] This is because students and parents are connected to their broader social environments which, research suggests, affect everything from family norms and expectations to brain development.[16] Second, at the outset of the movement, charter theorists envisioned schools that would emerge from and be tightly bound to the communities they serve.[17] Whether these expectations were met remains unclear.

Unfortunately, the SASS included no questions that directly assessed teachers' interactions with—and perceptions of support from—the broader community. As a result, it is not possible to provide a snapshot of national differences between charter and public schools or determine how they have evolved since the early days of the charter sector. Luckily, the TELL survey asked three questions of teachers about how they and their schools were tied to their communities. Specifically, the teachers were asked how much they agreed with three statements: "This school maintains clear, two-way communication with the community," "Community members support teachers, contributing to their success with students," and "The community we serve is supportive of this school."[18] In response, teachers chose an answer on a four-point scale, from "Strongly disagree" to "Strongly agree." Table 7.2 summarizes the mean responses of teachers in charter and public schools to these questions.

TABLE 7.2

Teachers' views about ties to the community (TELL)

	Public school teachers	Charter school teachers
This school maintains clear, two-way communication with the community.	3.11	3.26
Community members support teachers, contributing to their success with students.	2.91	3.01
The community we serve is supportive of this school.	3.02	3.18

Note: Numbers are the mean responses of teachers on a four-point numerical rating scale, where 1 = "Strongly disagree" and 4 = "Strongly agree," to statements about the interaction between the community and the teachers' schools.

The data in the table suggest that teachers in charter schools perceived somewhat stronger ties and communication with their communities than did teachers in public schools. However, these differences weren't massive. To determine whether there were statistically significant differences between the experiences of teachers in public and charter schools, figure 7.3 displays the results of a multivariate analysis of teachers' responses to these questions.

Even when school and teacher factors were controlled for, teachers in charter schools saw a considerably closer relationship between their schools and the community than did teachers in public schools (figure 7.3). Notably, charter school teachers described their schools as having more two-way communication with their communities

FIGURE 7.3

Teachers' views about ties to the community (TELL)

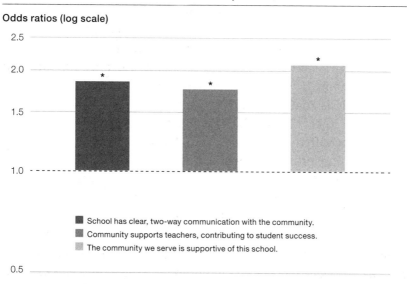

Note: Asterisks denote a statistically significant difference between charter and public school teachers at the $p < 0.05$ level, controlling for school- and teacher-level influences. For information about how to interpret odds ratios, see the text explanation near figure 7.1. For modeling information, see the appendix.

and being more supported by the communities. And most important from the standpoint of academic achievement, charter school teachers were more likely than public school teachers to agree that they were supported by their communities and that this was beneficial for student learning.

INSIDE THE CHARTER SECTOR

This chapter shows that teachers in charter schools indicated stronger engagement with parents and communities than did teachers in public schools. We now shift our attention to what drives variation in community and parent engagement within the charter sector. Specifically, we examine how the two factors introduced in chapter 2—school franchise status (EMO-run versus non-EMO-run) and tax status—are associated with teacher leadership and coordination. Because of the need to conserve space, the section reports only the findings from the multivariate analysis of teachers' responses.

Turning to the SASS questions analyzed above—from the 2011–2012 school year, the only year in which we can examine differences in franchising and tax status—an analysis revealed no differences in parent involvement or support between EMO-run and non-EMO-run charter schools. This is surprising, given that one criticism of EMO-run schools is that they are centrally managed and, according to some, disconnected from their neighborhoods. Similarly, the analysis found no differences in parent support and involvement between teachers in nonprofit and for-profit EMOs.

Using the TELL questions analyzed above, we can also investigate teachers' perceptions of parental and community support. Again, this analysis revealed that teachers in EMO-run and non-EMO-run charter schools—as well as teachers in for-profit and nonprofit charter schools—reported comparable experiences with parents and their schools' communities. The one difference was that teachers in EMO-run charter schools were around 30 percent more likely than those in non-EMO-run schools to report that parents' support of teachers contributed to student success.

SUMMARY

The findings presented in this chapter are relatively unambiguous: they suggest higher levels of engagement with parents and communities in charter schools than in public schools. These differences do not appear to be new. Since the early days of the charter sector, teachers have described their schools as being more supported by parents and having more parental involvement than public schools enjoyed. Teachers in charter schools were also more likely than their public school peers to indicate that the high levels of parental and community involvement have led to positive outcomes for students.

Although the findings here are generally positive for charter schools, it is important to recall the caution discussed in the introduction: student and parent self-selection is likely to play some role here. In other words, teachers in charter schools may have reported greater support from parents and communities because the parents who enrolled their children in these schools were more involved in their children's education than parents who did not. There was some evidence of this connection in the interviews that I conducted with Delaware charter school teachers. As a result, it is still unclear whether charter schools—as educational institutions—are cultivating different climates of engagement. This question cannot be resolved here, but the TELL analysis suggested that charter schools may be doing more than what public schools are doing to encourage parent engagement.

Interestingly, the charter sector analysis indicated that nonprofit and for-profit schools had similar levels of parental and community support and involvement. Moreover, even though EMOs are centrally controlled chains of schools—and they are often portrayed as interlopers in the communities in which they run schools—there were few differences between the levels of community and parent engagement in EMO-run and non-EMO-run charter schools. As a result, these factors provide little information about what might be driving differences in parent and community engagement between charter and public schools.

Now we turn to the final empirical chapter, which examines teachers' experiences with school leadership. This topic is central to the theory of charter schools: advocates suggest that charter schools differ from public schools in part because they have more dynamic, responsive administrators. But is there evidence to support these expectations? Do teachers in charter schools have significantly better experiences with school leaders than do teachers in public schools?

EIGHT

Administrative Leadership

MANY WORKS in the education literature suggest that the approaches taken by principals can influence schools, teachers, and, in the aggregate, student learning.[1] For instance, Robert Kelley, Bill Thornton, and Richard Daugherty argue that principal leadership is "possibly the most important single determinant of an effective learning environment."[2] Perhaps for this reason, proponents of charter schools have highlighted the important role played by school leaders in how charter schools operate. With less state and district control, charter administrators are thought to play a heightened role in guiding school operations and all other activities.[3] In fact, there is some scholarship to support this claim: charter principals report greater autonomy, or freedom from state and district control, than public school principals do.[4] Marytza Gawlik underscores this observation: "Perhaps the most distinctive feature of charter schools compared with traditional public schools is the significant autonomy granted to principals."[5]

Despite the potential importance of principals in teaching climates, we have little information about how teachers in charter schools view principals compared with teachers in public schools. This is an important gap in our understanding, as there may be some slippage between the rhetoric of charter advocates—and the experiences of principals—and the reality experienced by teachers inside these schools. In other words, although principals may feel that they have greater freedom from state or district rules, they may not use this autonomy to inspire or support teachers, who are the key to student learning.

To further our understanding of this issue, we will begin by examining teachers' views about how well principals articulated a mission for their schools and supported teacher work. We will then look at performance management, an increasingly popular approach across public organizations. In performance management, managers collect performance information about employees and use it to maintain accountability and improve performance.[6] The chapter also considers Bernard Bass's theory of leadership, a prominent theory in management science, and the differences between laissez-faire, transactional, and transformational leadership in different schools. Finally, as we have done in previous chapters, we will look at differences within charter schools.

MISSION AND SUPPORT

In my interviews with charter teachers in Delaware, I heard few rave reviews about administrators or how their schools were run. Rather, the themes voiced by teachers sounded similar to what one might hear in a teachers' lounge in any school: administrators were fine but far from inspiring or visionary. For example, one charter school teacher indicated that he wished administrators would show more of a "willingness to be a little risky at times rather than settle for the same old, same old, and be safe." Later, he added, "Right now, I would say that as far as our administration is concerned, they're more concerned with structure and policy and compliance." Other charter teachers raised concerns about leadership turnover, relatively small administrative apparatuses (preventing leaders from fully engaging with teachers), and general organizational discord. Comments like these contrast in obvious ways with the rhetoric of charter advocates about the dynamism or deftness with which these schools are led.

Nonetheless, some of the teachers' concerns with charter leadership were connected to Delaware's recent embrace of the Common Core, which led to a new set of state mandates. What's more, not all charter teachers were critical of administrators. One charter teacher said that administrators in her school both were supportive of teachers and held teachers accountable for their work. Another felt that administrators strongly encouraged her to be creative and to add her "personal flare" to her lessons.

I got a similar set of responses in my conversations with public school teachers: despite mostly positive experiences with administrators, few teachers were glowing or enthusiastic about their school leaders. Like charter teachers, public school teachers recognized that their administrators' hands were tied. For example, one public school teacher said that he generally trusted school leaders to do what was best for students but recognized that "they're under a lot of the same pressures we're under. The test scores shape what their jobs are a lot. Sometimes, they have to do uncomfortable things to make sure that they stay high. I get that." Another teacher said that she believed administrators were reasonable but were stuck having to always respond to state and federal mandates. She argued that, in response, her schools' administrators "want to insulate the teachers from [new initiatives] because two years from now, it might be something different. They don't want everyone to panic or have this big upheaval if in three years it might be the next thing. That's the philosophy."

These conversations indicated few generalizable differences between teachers in public school and those in charter schools. To better understand teachers' experiences with school leaders, we now examine data from the SASS. Specifically, we will look at how much teachers agreed with these four statements: "The school administration's behavior toward the staff is supportive and encouraging," "My principal enforces school rules for student conduct and backs me up when I need it," "The principal knows what kind of school he or she wants and has communicated it to the staff," and "I like the way things are run at this school" (the last question was not asked in the 1999–2000 survey). As with the other questions, respondents were asked whether they agreed with these statements on a four-point scale, from "Strongly disagree" to "Strongly agree."

The left side of figure 8.1 displays teachers' mean responses to these questions; the right side displays odds ratios from multivariate analyses that controlled for teacher- and school-level influences.[7] Odds ratios, derived from ordered logit coefficients, indicate the likelihood that teachers in charter and public schools answered questions differently. An odds ratio above 1.0 with an asterisk next to it indicates that, all else being equal, teachers in charter schools were more likely to agree with a statement. An odds ratio below 1.0 with an asterisk indicates that teachers in charter schools were less likely to agree with a statement. An odds ratio without an asterisk indicates that there were no statistically significant differences between the responses of teachers in charter and public schools.

The findings in this figure align with the interviews that I conducted with teachers in Delaware: teachers were generally happy with school leaders but, on average, were not ecstatic. Across public and charter settings, teachers were likely to agree that they received administrative support, that their principals enforced rules and backed them up, that principals articulated a mission, and that their schools were well run (left panels of figure 8.1). In comparison, the right panels reveal that teachers in charter and public schools had largely similar experiences with administrative leadership. In the first wave of the survey, charter teachers were more likely than their public school peers to agree that they received support from administrators. In the second wave, the difference in support disappeared, but charter teachers were more likely to believe that their principals articulated a mission. In the two most recent surveys, there were no statistically significant differences in mission or support. It's also interesting to see that in one year of the survey (2007-2008), there is bad news for charter school administration: that year, charter teachers were less likely than public school teachers were to agree that their schools were well run.

Administrative leadership is also an important emphasis of the TELL surveys. One section of questions asked teachers to rate

FIGURE 8.1

Teachers' experiences with administrators (SASS)

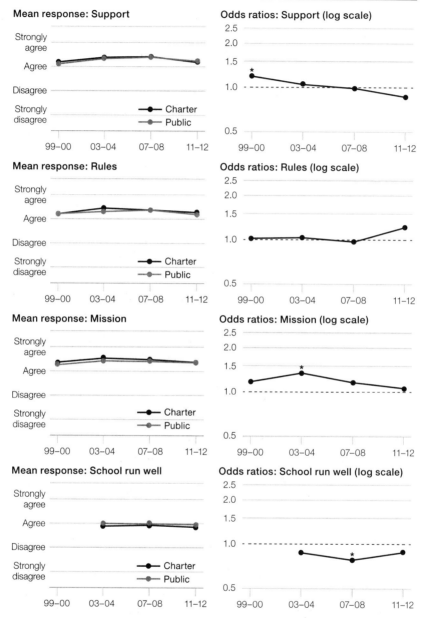

Note: SASS: Schools and Staffing Survey. Asterisks in the right panels denote a statistically significant difference between charter and public school teachers at the $p < 0.05$ level, controlling for school- and teacher-level influences. For information about how to interpret odds ratios, see the description in the accompanying text. For modeling information, see the appendix.

how much they agreed with five statements about school leadership: "The faculty and leadership have a shared vision," "There is an atmosphere of trust and mutual respect in this school," "Teachers feel comfortable raising issues and concerns that are important to them," "The school leadership consistently supports teachers," and "Teachers receive feedback that can help them improve teaching."[8] Respondents chose one of four ordered responses, from "Strongly disagree" to "Strongly agree" (table 8.1).

The findings from the TELL data are quite similar to those from the SASS analysis: on average, teachers agreed that administrators did a decent job. But there was no indication that teachers in either setting strongly agreed with these statements. To examine whether teachers in charter and public schools had different experiences with leaders, I conducted a multivariate analysis of teachers' responses to the TELL questions (figure 8.2).

The TELL analysis paints a much more optimistic picture of the charter sector than the SASS does. Across all five statements, teachers in charter schools were more likely to articulate favorable views about school leaders than were teachers in public schools (figure 8.2). Most impressive is the reciprocity reported by teachers

TABLE 8.1

Teachers' experiences with administrators (TELL)

	Public school teachers	Charter school teachers
The faculty and leadership have a shared vision.	2.96	3.09
There is an atmosphere of trust and mutual respect in this school.	2.85	3.03
Teachers feel comfortable raising issues and concerns that are important to them.	2.80	2.91
The school leadership consistently supports teachers.	2.95	3.08
Teachers receive feedback that can help them improve teaching.	3.08	3.14

Note: TELL: Teaching, Empowerment, Leading, and Learning surveys. Numbers are the mean responses of teachers on a four-point numerical rating scale, where 1 = "Strongly disagree" and 4 = "Strongly agree," to statements about teachers' experiences with administrators.

FIGURE 8.2

Teachers' experiences with administrators (TELL)

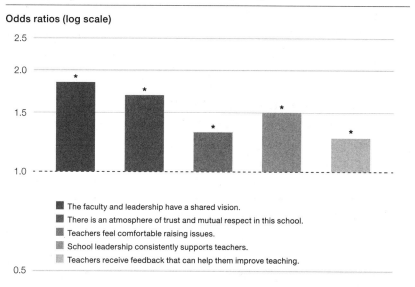

Note: Asterisks denote a statistically significant difference between charter and public school teachers at the $p < 0.05$ level, controlling for school- and teacher-level influences. For information about how to interpret odds ratios, see the text explanation near figure 8.1. For modeling information, see the appendix.

in charter schools: they were much more likely than public school teachers were to agree that they shared with administrators a vision of how the school should operate and to indicate that there was respect between teachers and administrators. Although the findings here are clear, it is important to recall that they come from a survey of teachers in six states, whereas the SASS findings are nationally representative.

PERFORMANCE MANAGEMENT

A major reason charter schools are thought to be different is accountability: with the opening and closing of schools—and family choice—charter schools will be held more accountable than public schools. Accountability is also thought to manifest inside charter schools:

because of differences in school administration and red tape, teachers are thought to be held more accountable for their performances. Earlier in the book, we found no national evidence that teachers in charter schools believed that they were held more accountable for their students' performance than did teachers in public schools (chapter 4).

This section continues the inquiry by asking about performance management, perhaps the most popular leadership tactic used to ensure personnel accountability.[9] This approach consists of three main activities: setting goals, identifying and monitoring performance indicators, and taking managerial action to achieve goals in light of information gleaned from performance indicators.[10] In effect, managers (in this case, principals) use performance indicators to understand how their employees (teachers) are performing and what major or minor changes managers need to make to enhance performance. Put differently, managers are theorized to achieve improved performance in part by making sure that employees are accountable.

In American schools, student standardized test scores are the sine qua non of performance management: most conversations and policies that seek to evaluate the performance of teachers, administrators, and schools rely on test scores.[11] Given the importance of accountability for charter schools, we might expect that charter administrators use student assessment data more than public school administrators do.[12] However, teachers and administrators in public schools also face significant testing pressures.[13] For example, chapter 4 showed that test scores did not play a more prominent role in charter school teaching climates than such scores did in public schools. In fact, the TELL analysis suggested that teachers in charter schools reported spending less time preparing for and administering tests than teachers in public schools reported.

This section uses SASS data from 2011–2012 (the only year possible) to compare public and charter school teachers' experiences with test- and non-test-based aspects of performance management. Specifically, we ask if teachers in charter schools reported being evaluated more or less frequently than teachers in public schools and whether student test scores or growth were included as criteria in these evaluations. On the SASS, teachers were asked three questions about performance management: "How often are you rated in a formal evaluation?," "How often are you informally evaluated?," and "Are student test score outcomes or test score growth included as an evaluation criterion in your FORMAL evaluation this school year?" (emphasis in original). For the first two questions, respondents' answers were collapsed into two categories: not evaluated yearly (coded as "0") and evaluated yearly (coded as "1"); for the third question, respondents' answers were also collapsed into two categories: test scores not included ("0") and test scores included ("1"). Table 8.2 presents findings from a descriptive analysis of these questions.

The table shows that most teachers in both settings said that they were formally and informally evaluated on a yearly basis. However, less than half of teachers said that student test scores were included in their formal evaluations.

Figure 8.3 shows the differences between teachers' experiences in charter and public schools as determined by a multivariate analysis that controlled for school- and teacher-level factors. The two statistically significant differences shown suggest that performance management was different in charter and public schools. Charter teachers were more likely than public school teachers to say that they would be formally evaluated on a yearly basis and that test scores would be included as a criterion in their formal evaluations. The test-score finding is interesting to consider in conjunction with

TABLE 8.2

Teachers' experiences with performance management (SASS)

	Public school teachers	Charter school teachers
Yearly formal evaluation?	0.74	0.93
Yearly informal evaluation?	0.83	0.91
Students' test scores included in evaluation?	0.29	0.43

Note: Numbers are teachers' mean scores, where 1 = "Yes" and 0 = "No," in response to questions about performance management.

FIGURE 8.3

Teachers' experiences with performance management, 2011–12 (SASS)

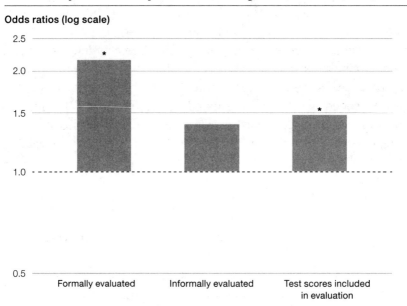

Note: Asterisks denote a statistically significant difference between charter and public school teachers at the $p < 0.05$ level, controlling for school- and teacher-level influences. For information about how to interpret odds ratios, see the text explanation near figure 8.1. For modeling information, see the appendix.

the earlier finding that teachers in charter schools reported spending less time preparing and administering tests (chapter 4). Perhaps, taken together, they the two results suggest that charter schools have achieved a nice middle ground: they use the data from student test scores to evaluate teachers without forcing teachers to spend all of their time on test-related activities.

In the TELL survey, teachers were asked to evaluate four statements relating to performance management in their schools. On the leadership battery, they were asked how much they agreed with the following statement: "The school leadership facilitates using data to improve student learning." In a section about instructional practices and support in their schools, teachers were asked how much they agreed with these statements: "State assessment data are available in time to impact instructional practices," "Local assessment data are available in time to impact instructional practices," and "Teachers use assessment data to inform their instruction."[14] For each question, teachers responded on a four-point scale, from "Strongly disagree" to "Strongly agree" (table 8.3).

The data in table 8.3 suggest that teachers were likely to agree that administrators facilitated the use of data and that the teachers used the data to inform their instruction. However, there was less agreement that the data were available in time to affect how teachers operated their classrooms. To compare the experiences that teachers in charter and public schools had with performance management, I conducted a multivariate analysis (figure 8.4).

The figure suggests important differences between charter and public schools in the full cycle of performance management. In charter schools, school leaders were more likely to encourage teachers to use assessment data, state assessment data were more likely to be available in a timely manner, and teachers were more likely to use these data in their instruction.

TABLE 8.3

Teachers' experiences with performance management (TELL)

	Public school teachers	Charter school teachers
The school leadership facilitates using data to improve student learning.	3.32	3.38
State assessment data are available in time to impact instructional practices.	2.52	2.68
Local assessment data are available in time to impact instructional practices.	2.93	3.08
Teachers use assessment data to inform their instruction.	3.17	3.24

Note: Numbers are the mean responses of teachers on a four-point numerical rating scale, where 1 = "Strongly disagree," 2 = "Disagree," 3 = "Agree," and 4 = "Strongly agree," to statements about their experiences with performance management.

FIGURE 8.4

Teachers' experiences with performance management (TELL)

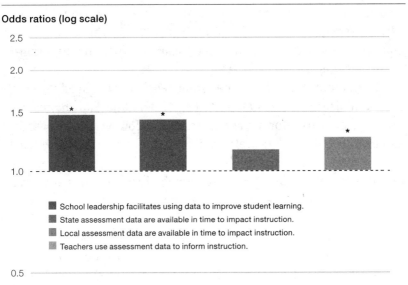

Odds ratios (log scale)

■ School leadership facilitates using data to improve student learning.
■ State assessment data are available in time to impact instruction.
■ Local assessment data are available in time to impact instruction.
■ Teachers use assessment data to inform instruction.

Note: Asterisks denote a statistically significant difference between charter and public school teachers at the $p < 0.05$ level, controlling for school- and teacher-level influences. For information about how to interpret odds ratios, see the text explanation near figure 8.1. For modeling information, see the appendix.

LAISSEZ-FAIRE, TRANSACTIONAL, AND TRANSFORMATIONAL LEADERSHIP

Bernard Bass's concept of a full range of leadership has received attention inside and outside education circles.[15] According to the theory, teachers will perform better when principals establish patterns of transactional leadership, that is, rational, organized approaches for rewarding and punishing teacher behavior. Transactional leadership establishes a basic administrative competency: principals pay attention to what teachers do and respond in kind. This approach stands in contrast with laissez-faire leadership, in which principals pay little or no attention to positive or negative teacher behavior.

Though transactional leadership is important, Bass thinks it has limited potential. For greater success, principals must adopt transformational leadership—a more proactive approach that inspires teachers and generates high levels of commitment to the school's goals. However, Bass argues that transformational leadership need not supplant transactional leadership. Rather, the two are complementary: transactional leadership establishes the foundation that enables a school to function, and transformational leadership leads to the achievement of greater outcomes, because teachers feel fully realized as school members.[16]

Because leadership is central to the theory of charter school success, transformational leadership has, not surprisingly, begun to receive attention in studies of charter schools.[17] To date, however, few studies have used Bass's full model to explore teachers' experiences with leadership in charter and public schools. Accordingly, on the DTS, I asked teachers five questions drawn from Bass's model. To study whether school leaders were adopting laissez faire styles of management, I asked teachers how much they agreed with the following statement: "School administrators are content to let teachers continue doing things the same ways as always." To examine teachers' views of transactional leadership by school administrators, I asked them how much they agreed with this statement: "School administrators are clear about what I need to do to be rewarded for my work." Finally, teachers' responses to three statements plumbed teachers experiences with transformational leadership: "I have confidence in this school's administrators (principal, assistant principal, etc.)," "School administrators help me find meaning in my work," and "School administrators help me think about old problems in new ways." For all questions, respondents chose an answer on a five-point scale, from "Strongly disagree" to "Strongly agree." Table 8.4 presents teachers' mean responses to these questions.

In both charter and public schools, teachers disagreed that school leaders let teachers continue doing the same thing without any change (statement 1 in the table) and were unclear about what teachers needed to do be rewarded (statement 2). Turning to transformational leadership, they indicated having confidence in school leaders (statement 3) but neither agreed nor disagreed that leaders helped teachers find meaning in their work (statement 4) or helped teachers think about old problems in new ways (statement 5).

TABLE 8.4

Teachers' experiences with administrators (DTS)

	Public school teachers	Charter school teachers
1. School administrators are content to let teachers continue doing things the same ways as always.	2.12	2.29
2. School administrators are clear about what I need to do to be rewarded for my work.	2.95	3.12
3. I have confidence in this school's administrators (principal, assistant principal, etc.).	3.58	3.65
4. School administrators help me find meaning in my work.	3.03	3.32
5. School administrators help me think about old problems in new ways.	3.14	3.32

Note: DTS: Delaware Teachers Survey. Numbers are the mean responses of teachers on a five-point numerical rating scale, where 1 = "Strongly disagree" and 5 = "Strongly agree," to statements about their experience with administrators.

To explore whether there were any differences between teachers in public and charter schools, I conducted a multivariate analysis that controlled for individual- and school-level influences. This analysis uncovered no statistically significant differences in any of these three types of leadership between charter and public schools. Put differently, if we were to walk into any charter or public school in Delaware, we'd be equally likely to find transformational, transactional, and laissez-faire school leaders.

INSIDE THE CHARTER SECTOR

To analyze whether there were differences in teachers' experiences with administrative leadership in different types of charter schools, we turn to the SASS from 2011–2012 and the questions surrounding support, mission, and performance management. An analysis revealed no differences between teachers in EMO-run charter schools and non-EMO-run schools for these questions. In other words, teachers in franchised and nonfranchised charter schools reported largely similar experiences with school leaders.

However, within the EMO sector, there were some important differences based on tax status. Contrary to what critics might expect, teachers in for-profit EMOs reported better administrative leadership than did teachers in nonprofit EMOs. In particular, teachers in for-profit EMOs were over 1.5 times more likely to agree that principals in their schools had a mission for the school and had communicated it to teachers; they were also over 2 times more likely to agree that their schools were run well. There were also differences in performance management: teachers in for-profit EMOs were 10 times more likely to indicate that they had been informally evaluated by school leaders and over 2 times more likely to indicate that student test scores were factored into their teaching evaluations.

Moving to the TELL findings, I conducted a multivariate analysis of the leadership questions shown in table 8.1. As with the SASS data, the results showed that teachers in both EMO-run and non-EMO-run charter schools reported mostly comparable experiences with school leaders. There was one difference, though: teachers in EMO-run schools were 0.6 times more likely to indicate that they received feedback from school leaders to improve their teaching. But in contrast to the SASS data, the TELL analysis showed that teachers in for-profit charter schools reported experiences that were more negative with leaders than teachers in nonprofit charters did: they were 0.5 times less likely to agree that their schools had an atmosphere of trust and mutual respect with school leaders and 0.4 times less likely to indicate that they felt supported by administrators.

An analysis of the TELL performance management questions (see table 8.3) revealed that teachers in EMO-run schools were 0.3 times more likely than teachers in non-EMO schools to indicate that leaders facilitate the use of data to improve student learning. Also, teachers in for-profit charter schools were 0.4 times less likely than their nonprofit peers were to agree that teachers use local data and to agree that teachers use assessment data to inform their instruction. In all other respects, there were no significant differences between charter teachers on the basis of franchise status or tax status of their schools.

In addition to franchise and tax status, we might expect that teachers' experiences with school administrators are tied to the flexibility that administrators are given via their state's charter law. Specifically, do states whose charter laws are looser than other states' charter laws enable more dynamic school leadership? To answer this question, we explore if a state's rating by a pro-charter-school group—a rating based on the operational flexibility written into each state's law—was associated with teachers' experiences with administrators. An analysis of SASS data from four school years—1999–2000, 2003–2004, 2007–2008, and 2011–2012—showed no relationships between a state's rating and charter teachers' experiences with administrators. In other words, teachers' experiences with administrators in high-rated states did not significantly differ from teachers' experiences in low-rated states. An analysis of TELL data mirrored these findings: the rating for operational flexibility was unassociated with teachers' experiences with administrators.

SUMMARY

This chapter has investigated teachers' experiences with the administrators in their schools. Across the datasets, some of the findings are clear, while others are more muddled. One of the unambiguous findings is that performance management techniques appear to have been used more in charter schools than in public schools. In the SASS analysis, we saw that teachers in charter schools were more likely than teachers in public schools to be formally observed and to have student test scores incorporated into their yearly evaluations. The TELL analysis showed that administrators in charter schools were more likely to facilitate the usage of assessment data to improve student learning. For this reason, perhaps, charter teachers were more likely to use assessment data to inform their instruction. The teachers might have used these data because of efficiencies within the school: teachers in charter schools were more likely to indicate that state and local assessment data were available in time to affect how they taught.

It is interesting to compare these findings with the accountability findings from chapter 4. That chapter showed mixed evidence about whether teachers in charter schools felt more accountable for their work: on the SASS, there were no differences, and on the TELL, charter teachers felt more accountable. This leaves us with a puzzle: if teachers in charter schools were more likely to encounter administrators using performance management techniques, why didn't they feel more accountable for their work (as the SASS analysis showed)?

In contrast with performance management, there was inconsistent evidence about the type of leadership exerted in these different schools. The SASS analysis showed no differences in how much the teachers felt supported or in whether teachers believed that their administrators articulated a mission. Similarly, the DTS revealed few differences in the types of administrative leadership experienced by teachers in charter and public schools. However, the TELL analysis found that charter teachers were more likely than public school teachers to feel supported and that teachers and administrators had a shared vision.

Looking inside the charter sector, there was agreement among the datasets that the rating given to a state based on its charter law was not associated with teachers' experiences with administrators. This is interesting because, as in chapter 4, we again see little evidence that state-level legislative choices about charter school operational flexibility filter down to affect teaching climates. This is not to say that state laws don't matter: in fact, the interviews in this chapter and in chapter 4 suggest that teaching is shaped by state mandates. However, perhaps because charter and public schools have high levels of publicness, the evidence here suggests that the composition of charter laws did not have a major impact on charter schools' teaching climates.

The evidence about franchising in the charter sector analysis was mixed. The SASS analysis found no differences in mission and support or performance management between teachers in EMO and non-EMO schools. However, in the TELL analysis, teachers in EMO schools reported getting better feedback from administrators than non-EMO teachers did. The findings of the SASS and TELL analyses of the tax status of charter schools also conflicted. The SASS analysis revealed that teachers in for-profit EMOs were more likely than teachers in nonprofit EMOs to agree that their principal had a mission for the school and had communicated it to teachers and that their schools were run better. The teachers in for-profit EMOs were also more likely to indicate that they had been informally evaluated by school leaders and that student test scores factored into their teaching evaluations. On the TELL, teachers in for-profit schools tended to report worse experiences with administrators and less performance management than did teachers in nonprofit schools.

This chapter has clarified our understanding of some but not all aspects of teachers' experiences with administrators. Clearly, some of the well-worn arguments and expectations about charter schools need revisiting. Other familiar characterizations seem to accurately represent life inside these schools. With the empirical inquiry, we now turn to the final chapter, which synthesizes the book's findings, draws implication for scholarship and practice, and lays out directions for future research.

NINE

The Teaching Climates of
Charter and Public Schools

DO CHARTER SCHOOLS foster different teaching climates than public schools do? Have they met advocates' enthusiastic expectations, or do they overburden teachers and deny them voice in their schools, as feared by critics? The evidence in this book more closely aligns with the views of charter advocates: teachers in charter schools had more autonomy over choosing content and texts, described their environments as more innovative, faced less red tape, played a bigger role in leading their schools, and reported better connections with parents and communities.[1] This expanded role, perhaps unsurprisingly, took more of their time. Charter teachers reported working more hours than public school teachers did and doing it for less pay. They also worked in schools with fewer teachers per student and reported having fewer professional credentials, like teaching certificates and master's degrees. One might hear these findings and imagine a sweatshop-like school filled with overwhelmed, perhaps even exploited, teachers. But there was little evidence that teachers experienced it that way: charter teachers were no less satisfied and no more burned out than their public school peers were. Also, they did not leave their schools or the teaching profession at a higher rate than did teachers in public schools.

While these results more closely align with the picture painted by charter advocates, this book also challenges rhapsodic claims about the teaching and learning environments inside charter schools. For instance, although charter teachers weren't less satisfied than public school teacher and didn't change schools or profession more, neither were they *more* satisfied, and they didn't turn over *less*. Also, contrary to the claims of charter advocates, teachers in charter schools weren't more accountable than public school teachers, didn't collaborate more, and their experiences with administrators were generally comparable to those reported by public school teachers.

Taking all this evidence into account, it appears that charter schools have made strides toward meeting the goals set by early advocates. But they haven't completely fulfilled their promise. In fact, the evidence here suggests, the benefits that come with charter schools are associated with real costs, like higher student-teacher ratios and teachers who are paid less and have less experience and training. As a result, the teaching climates inside charter and public schools aren't "better" or "worse"; they're different. And choosing between these models requires us to weigh distinct trade-offs. A recognition of these trade-offs is important because the charter debate is usually cast as a horse race between sectors, in which test scores take center stage.[2] This book presents a different view, positioning charter and public schools as different models of public education, each with its attendant strengths and weaknesses.

If this view is right, three questions follow. First, if we *exclude* any positive or negative systemic effects that charter schools are having on public school systems, which model do we prefer? It's not a simple choice. For example, do we want teachers who are more empowered even if they have less experience, training, and education? Though this book doesn't argue which model is more desirable, the charter debate should, at least in part, consider why the particular advantages and costs of one model are preferable to the particular advantages and costs of the other.

To move this debate forward, we will need to dive more deeply into an early assumption articulated in the book: that the teaching climates within a school affect student learning and development.

There is, of course, empirical research supporting this notion.[3] But the research points to how particular parts of a school's teaching climate are associated with student test scores, rather than reckoning with its entirety. For example, research suggests a strong, statistically significant relationship between student achievement and community support and involvement.[4] This finding is helpful, but what if high levels of connectedness are paired with low teacher pay and lesser credentials? In the end, if public and charter schools cultivate different teaching climates, we need to see the schools as they are (rather than as we want them to be) and understand how their climates shape students' experiences and learning.

Second, if we *include* any systemic effects that charter schools are having on public school students, do the differences in teaching climate identified here justify further expansion? To answer this question, we must reckon with claims about the effects that charter schools may be having on students in other parts of the public school system. Unfortunately, there's little scholarly or popular consensus about the systemic effects wrought by the charter experiment.[5] For example, in October 2016, the National Association for the Advancement of Colored People (NAACP) ratified a resolution calling for a moratorium on new charter schools; it argued that, among other things, charter schools were diverting public funds from public schools and increasing de facto segregation of the highest-performing students.[6] In response, the editorial boards of several major newspapers—including the *New York Times, Wall Street Journal,* and *Washington Post*—strongly criticized the NAACP's decision. They contended that it wasn't fair or accurate to blame charter schools for systemic problems like increased segregation or public school funding deficits.[7]

These arguments and counterarguments illustrate the lack of agreement about what effects, if any, charter schools are having on students in public schools. But let's assume, for the sake of argument, that research in the near future definitively supports the NAACP's case, and we can agree that charter schools exacerbate performance segregation (where high- and low-performing students attend different schools). In deciding the fate of the charter experiment, we would need to weigh the findings about how these schools function internally—the focus of this book and the implicit focus of most test-focused research—against our understanding of these systemic effects.

Finally, will the differences in teaching climate identified here remain in the future? Although the SASS covered over a decade, the findings are now somewhat dated (the most recent SASS examined the 2011–2012 school year). In some respects, the SASS results showed, the teaching climates of charter and public schools were consistently alike or different; in other areas, there seemed to be some change over time and, perhaps, a minimizing of the initial differences between these schools. For this reason, researchers must continue to compare the teaching climates of these types of schools to inform any discussion about which model is preferred.

Later in this chapter, I will expand upon this last point and make recommendations for scholars, school leaders, and policy makers. But now we turn to the theories that have run throughout the book. What do the findings here imply about the role that publicness, profit, franchising, and state law play in shaping the life of schools?

THEORIZING PUBLICNESS

At least since the Reagan era, the publicness of an organization has achieved tremendous prominence in political debates. The basic argument—which was initially put forward by conservatives but is now made by politicians of various political stripes—is that publicness has a crucial, if not decisive, influence on how organizations operate. In many respects, the movement for privatization and school choice flows directly from this expectation. By portraying public schools as beset by inefficiency and mismanagement, advocates for school choice argue for using private or quasi-public school forms. In essence, these arguments are about institutions and markets: institutions develop sets of protocols and norms that shape the behavior of the people therein; institutions that are responsive to market forces must adapt to consumer needs—and focus more on output than process—if they are to maintain market share.

The findings presented in the book suggest that publicness can be associated with how organizations function. These findings are impressive because charter schools and public schools did not sit far apart on the publicness spectrum: as noted in chapter 1, in two of the three ways that publicness is delineated—ownership and funding—charter and public schools are largely the same. Thus, changing one of the characteristics of publicness (control) may filter down to the level of operative employees, leading to different experiences and perceptions. In other respects, teachers in public and quasi-public institutions described indistinguishable teaching climates. Perhaps if public and charter schools were further apart on the publicness continuum, we would see greater differences between their teaching climates.

Another way of understanding what these findings mean, at the level of theory, is to revisit the drivers of publicness, as discussed in chapter 1: red tape, administrative leadership, and self-selection. The most unambiguous association between these factors and publicness was red tape. As popular myth suggests, higher levels of publicness did appear to be associated with higher levels of interfering duties and paperwork. Why might this be the case? In the public administration literature, there are varied hypotheses as to how public organizations differ from private organizations and, as a result, why red tape is associated with higher levels of publicness.[8] One argument is that public organizations have more red tape because they have vague and often-conflicting goals. Another is that differences arise from accountability: because public organizations are under more scrutiny, they tend to formalize processes, a practice that leads to more supervision and red tape.

The findings here contribute by process of elimination. Although they do not point directly to an explanation about why experiences with red tape differed, they raise questions about claims about goal differences: because teachers across these settings have largely the same goals, it would not seem to be goals *per se* leading to differences by sector. They also question claims that red tape is driven by accountability and supervision: the findings here showed that teachers in less public settings reported experiencing less red tape but feeling equally accountable.

If it's not goals and accountability to leaders, perhaps differences in red tape are being driven by political constraints.[9] In other words, red tape may appear in more public forms of organization because they are more closely monitored and controlled by political stakeholders. One might argue that this is a reasonable if annoying side effect of accountability: more accountability requires more formalization, which employees experience as red tape. The flaw with this account, as noted above, is that increased red tape was not associated with increased accountability. As a result, public organizations might get all the pain that accompanies higher levels of scrutiny, without concomitant gains in performance accountability.

The second reason publicness might matter is administrative leadership. Because they are relatively free from political interference, leaders in more private organizations would be able to manage with fewer encumbrances: they would have more flexibility in choosing directions for their units and more power to hire, fire, reward, and punish. As noted above, the book revealed conflicting evidence about these aspects of administrative leadership. For this reason, it is not clear whether leaders in less public, policy-oriented organizations are more able to articulate a mission, reward employees, or help employees find meaning in their work (relative to leaders in more public, policy-oriented organizations). This ambiguity is crucial to recognize because claims about differences in leadership are central to the case for privatization and charter schools. Also, public management scholarship has explored in depth whether differences in publicness affect manager behavior and experience.[10] Implicit in much of this literature is an expectation that management practices will affect the experiences of operative employees. This book's findings suggest that greater attention is needed here: if we are to more fully grapple with how differences in publicness matter, we need more studies about how differences in publicness and management matter for frontline employees.

In another sense, the publicness of an organization was associated with a key administrator practice: performance management.

As discussed, administrators in charter schools were more likely than those in public schools to formally evaluate teachers, include student test scores in teachers' evaluations, and make assessment information available to teachers quickly. This observation is in line with expectations about how less public organizations will operate. What does the difference in performance management mean for our understanding of charter schools? It could be seen as tempering concerns about the accountability non-finding and the criticism about giving uncertified teachers considerable autonomy. If charter teachers are observed more and have performance data included in their assessments, they are, arguably, held to account even if they do not feel that they are.

The performance management findings are also helpful in light of the concern that when public and quasi-public organizations embrace performance management, they will foster cultures that lead to perverse incentives and behavior on the part of operative employees, in this case, teachers.[11] This is only one case, but the evidence here runs contrary to this account: although student testing was more likely to be incorporated into charter teachers' assessments, and the assessment data were made available to them, teachers did not report that testing dominated their work. In fact, they had more autonomy than public school teachers did in selecting texts and content, and charter teachers spoke of their ability to diverge from the curricula when needed.

The third explanation for how differences in publicness might lead to different teaching climates is teacher self-selection. Within the public administration literature, there is considerable evidence that the leaders of public organizations see personnel attraction and recruitment as a key culture-shaping factor.[12] Some empirical evidence also suggests that entrants remain mostly tied to the views they express before entering their organizations.[13]

Regrettably, few scholars have examined the socialization of similar workers into organizations with varying levels of publicness, and the data analyzed here were not set up to investigate socialization. However, employees' motivations and values are thought to be relatively stable over time. For this reason, it is useful to note that the findings in chapter 3 showed broad similarities between the values and motivations of teachers in Delaware's charter and public schools. Therefore, the book reveals little evidence that self-selection was driving the differences in teaching climate identified here.

PROFIT MOTIVE AND CLIMATE

It is also useful to think about what the book's findings about tax status—from the charter sector analysis—imply for our understanding of publicness. Chapter 2 argued that for-profit charter schools would be further away from public schools on the publicness continuum, with nonprofit schools somewhere in between. The argument was that nonprofits and for-profits had different exposure to market forces: classical and neoclassical economic theory suggests that for-profit firms aim to maximize profits in a way that nonprofit organizations do not.[14] Because of this need for profit, these firms theoretically find the most efficient ways possible of providing goods and services without alienating consumers.[15]

As part of this process, they are thought to build more direct principal-agent relationships and pay closer attention to the needs and desires of consumers. To ensure that consumers' needs are met, they may reduce employee discretion and build tighter webs of accountability than do nonprofit firms. However, when applied to public policy via the contracting system, the profit motive may displace other organizational goals and defeat the intended purpose of a policy. In particular, because of long or tenuous feedback loops between citizens and policy makers, for-profit firms that deliver public services might sacrifice quality for the bottom line. Whether these hopes or concerns have merit is unclear; exploring whether they do is important for the charter school debate and for an understanding of public policy generally.[16]

So how much does a charter school's profit motive affect how it functions? If you have two comparable charter schools—one for-profit and one nonprofit—is it likely that they foster different teaching climates? The results here show one definitive way in which profit motive does matter, some ways profit motive might matter, and others in which profit motive doesn't appear to matter. Contrary to the expectations of neoclassical economic theories, for-profit schools were less efficient in an important way: they had more red tape. Consequently, perhaps organizations at the polar ends of the publicness continuum adopt red tape, albeit for different reasons. In public organizations, red tape may result from the oversight of external political actors and a need to ensure equitable process; in more private organizations, red tape may come from the need of centralized owners to ensure standardized output. Whatever the reason, this finding—that teachers in for-profit charters felt more embroiled in red tape than teachers in nonprofit charters did—questions the typical association between public organizations and red tape.

In other areas we examined in this book, the teaching climates of for-profit and nonprofit schools were indistinguishable. For example, despite the expectation that for-profit groups would make teaching more rigid, there was no evidence that schools with a profit motive fostered lower levels of teacher autonomy. Also, the concerns of critics of for-profit schools were not met in an important way: working conditions. Although they were paid less, teachers in for-profit charter schools were neither less satisfied nor more burned out than were teachers non-profit charters.

Finally, the analyses in this book had mixed findings in many areas. Most striking, the nationally representative SASS analysis suggested a generally positive view of for-profit charter schools— or found no differences between for-profit and nonprofit schools— while the TELL analysis pointed to potential problems with for-profit schools. As I will discuss later in the chapter, this notable dissonance highlights a key area that future scholars should further investigate.

FRANCHISING

The charter sector analysis also looked at franchising, when a set of organizations such as an EMO provides a relatively standardized set of goods or services. As discussed in chapter 2, scholars have sought to understand franchises using agency theory: they envision a game in which the franchisor tries to control the franchisee by promulgating rules, procedures, and enforcement mechanisms. The contracts that link franchisor and franchisee solve some problems—for instance, the agreements can set forth predetermined responses to thorny problems—while creating others. One particular problem is that the contracts may constrain the ability of franchisee to respond to situations and contexts as they see fit.[17]

Inside organizations, where superiors and employees interact, the relationships may become more complicated. Employees in franchised organizations are likely to be managed by superiors who, because of the franchise contract, are more constrained than superiors in nonfranchised organizations. For this reason, employees in franchised organizations would have less autonomy and would experience more red tape than would employees in stand-alone institutions.

The empirical analysis showed that teachers in EMO-run charter schools played less of a leadership role than did those in non-EMO-run charters; they may also have turned over at higher rates. In two other areas, the evidence was conflicted: it was unclear whether teachers in EMOs had less autonomy and accountability than did teachers in non-EMOs. But the dominant finding in my analyses was that franchising had little bearing on the teaching climates of charter schools. Put simply, in areas like collaboration, use of time, and experiences with facilities, red tape, and performance management, there were no differences between the teaching climates of franchised and non-franchised charter schools. Though more work is needed, the implication for theory is that of all the things that might shape how an organization functions—including its tasks, goals, technology, resources, history, and leadership—franchises may not exert much influence.

This has clear implications for the debate over charter schools—in which EMOs play an important part—but also for the utility of agency theory for explaining organizational performance. In other words, the cat-and-mouse game between franchisors and franchisees, and between superiors and employees, may explain little about how operative employees act. This is a finding that resounds with findings from the implementation and street-level bureaucracy literatures. Scholars in these fields have long expected that the patterns of behavior at the front lines are dictated as much by interactions between people, and the exigencies of particular situations, as they are by abstract, distant forces like organizational structure.

THE IMPACT OF LAW ON ORGANIZATIONAL CLIMATES

To continue this last point, the book also showed that a remote force that is often seen as affecting operative employee behavior—legislation—had no consistent influence on how teachers functioned. This finding is surprising, because the character of charter laws has figured prominently in the literature on charter schools.[18] The general view is that charter laws are important because they can affect schools and, by extension, teachers and students. The findings here showed that the operational flexibility of a charter law didn't matter for charter school teachers in a few important ways, like teacher autonomy, leadership, and accountability.

A note of caution in interpreting these findings: perhaps they are related to the metric used in this book—an analysis of the operational flexibility of state charter school laws by a pro-charter-school group (the Center for Education Reform, or CER). In other words, charter laws may matter for teachers in ways not measured by this group. Nonetheless, the findings here suggest the importance—for lawmakers, advocacy organizations, and scholars—of determining whether charter laws affect the experiences and actions of teachers and students.

Again, this finding has deep resonance with the research in public administration and political science that emerged after the start of the War on Poverty.[19] At the time, scholars were shocked to discover that loudly trumpeted dicta, set forth in legislation made by state and national policy makers, made barely a peep in the ears of the bureaucrats in the cities and towns that the pronouncements were meant to affect. This observation doesn't mean that legislation is always ignored or is irrelevant to policy making. Rather, scholars and advocates who think that laws circumscribe or empower frontline bureaucrats have a responsibility to determine if that is in fact the case.

RECOMMENDATIONS

When charter schools originated, they were seen as an experimental form of school that would encourage new approaches and inform public school practice. Somewhere along the way, the context changed significantly, and as many others have noted, there is now considerable competition between charter and public schools.[20] For instance, public school teachers in some cities are going door-to-door to recruit children for their schools.[21] Though charter and public schools probably cannot go back to a time of comity and information sharing, public school policy makers and administrators can learn from the results discussed in this book. In this section, I make recommendations—for leaders in public and charter schools and for scholars interested in furthering our understanding of these schools—based on my analyses throughout this book.

Implications for Public School Leaders

Several findings in this book are useful for public school leaders. First, leaders should pay attention to the results regarding red tape. The charter school movement was significantly galvanized by a desire to remove the institutional confines of public schools, both to enhance innovation and to free teachers to do their work. It remains unclear whether true innovation has resulted from this approach. As this book makes clear, however, teachers in charter schools reported having more time to complete their work, fewer encumbrances from paperwork, and more control over choosing the texts and content that they teach. Thus, administrators in public schools would be wise to think about how teachers could be freed up from some of the onerous rules and regulations that they face. The evidence here suggests that doing so would likely have a minimal impact on accountability—which is probably why the regulations were created in the first place—but might empower teachers to use more of their professional discretion in the classroom.

Related to this, public schools could empower teachers to play more significant roles in how their schools are run. One of the striking findings of this book is that charter schools foster climates in which teachers have more say over key aspects of how their schools are governed. In other words, it is not just that charter schools give teachers more classroom autonomy, they foster teacher leadership, giving them more of a say in how their schools are run. For public school policymakers, it seems clear that teachers could be included more in conversations about school governance. There would be obvious difficulties in doing so—like running afoul of teachers' contracts—but it might help improve teacher morale and help align teacher and school priorities.

Finally, the results of my analyses suggest that public schools might do well to forge deeper connections between schools, communities, and parents. It may be difficult for public schools to achieve the high levels of interconnectedness enjoyed by charter schools, partly because of the self-selection of parents and students into particular schools. Nonetheless, observers have noted that charter schools have greater parent engagement than do noncharter magnet schools that also require parent involvement in selection.[22] What's more, teachers in charter schools were more likely to indicate that their schools made an effort to connect with parents. Therefore, at least some of the difference found here probably stems from different approaches taken by charter schools. If so, public schools should pay close attention to the tactics used by charter school administrators and teachers in fostering parent and community engagement.[23] If public schools could move toward greater parent and community engagement, research suggests, students would experience a significant benefit.

Although public school leaders would benefit from thinking about moving their schools in these directions, their hands may be tied, because their schools are publicly controlled. In my interviews with Delaware public school teachers, some commented that school leaders were confined by the rules and regulations coming from above. Whether the leaders are bound or not, the results here at least highlight a problem and give public school leaders a reason to try to improve in these three respects, if at all possible.

Suggestions for Charter School Leaders, Policy Makers, and Advocates

What might charter school policy makers and administrators learn from this book? Perhaps most obviously, charter schools do not appear to be meeting a core component of their promised bargain: greater teacher accountability. If this bargain is to remain a key aspect of charter school theory—and remain the sales pitch used to defend existing charters—policy makers and school officials must find ways to improve teacher accountability. In particular, charter schools should use their greater flexibility to develop human resources strategies that recognize teachers who are achieving the desired results. At the same time, they should focus on identifying teachers who are not meeting expectations and determine how these teachers can improve or be dismissed. Although charter schools may have difficulty moving toward greater teacher accountability, administrators may have an easier time achieving it; they appear to gather and use performance management information more than do administrators in public schools.

Another area that could be improved is teacher collaboration. A major advantage of school decentralization is that leaders and administrators can implement schoolwide programs place together teachers from different departments and backgrounds.[24] This practice could foster curricular richness and interdisciplinary study. Although teachers in charter schools appear to cooperate more with one another than do public school teachers, little evidence showed that they coordinate content. This area seems ripe for improvement if charter schools are to achieve their full potential.

Moving to working conditions, there is a fascinating puzzle in the empirical findings from this book. In many ways, the teaching climates of charter schools are more teacher friendly. Teachers have greater autonomy in choosing texts and content, a deeper involvement in how their schools operate, and better connections with parents and communities. Despite these advantages, teachers in charter schools did not report greater satisfaction than did teachers in public schools; nor did charter teachers have lower turnover rates. Although we cannot be sure of why this tension exists, one possible explanation has to do with pay and hours. Perhaps because of lower rates of unionization or funding disparities, teachers in charter schools work longer hours for lower pay than do teachers in public schools. If there is one way that charter schools might enhance teacher satisfaction, it would be to compensate them more fairly for their work.

As with my recommendations to public school policy makers, charter school leaders might be frustrated by this recommendation. They might reply, "If we had more money, we'd be happy to pass it along to teachers. But charter schools are systematically underfunded." Underfunding may be real and is an issue that merits further attention. Still, the pay gap between charter and public school teachers may be an important factor preventing charter schools from meeting their full promise. To the extent that charter leaders and administrators can find ways of improving the pay and benefits of teachers, they should do so.

Another surprising empirical finding in this book had to do with administrative leadership: the SASS analysis revealed few differences between charter and public schools in their administrators' articulation of a mission or support for teachers (see chapter 8). As this is a much-discussed pathway by which charter schools presumably forge different types of schools, charter school administrators and policy makers must reflect on this finding. The charter school literature, fortunately, has many terrific case studies illustrating in-depth accounts of successful leadership. It will be helpful moving forward for policy makers to distill the lessons from these disparate studies to show how charter school leaders can play a larger role in their schools.

Finally, the movement for charter schools is at least partly motivated by frustration with the status quo and an interest in disruption. But too often, experiments are driven more by a priori assumptions and ideology than by careful analysis and evaluation. My findings indicate a general need to understand how organizational forms affect schools, teachers, and students. Before leaders advocate for, or implement, new types of charter schools, they need to carefully study them. Pilot studies could be used to experiment on a smaller scale before leaders enshrine a new type of charter school in state law.

Research

This book's approach to studying the differences between charter and public schools—examining teaching climates—will hopefully inspire similar future research. Though the findings here help clarify our understanding of how these schools function, more research is needed to flesh out how these schools compare, and why. Perhaps the most obvious need is for more nationally representative research. Unfortunately, such research is expensive and difficult to conduct. Therefore, it would be helpful if the US Department of Education's National Center for Education Statistics (NCES) would revise the SASS (which, after the 2011–2012 survey, will be known as the National Teacher and Principal Survey, or NTPS) to provide greater insight into teachers' experiences with, among other things, testing, innovation, and resources. Also, it would be useful if the NTPS indicated how teachers spent their time weekly and to which stakeholders in their schools and communities they felt accountable.

But most importantly, NCES should incorporate in the NTPS the insights from the school climate literature.[25] With help from the National School Climate Center (NSCC), our understanding of school climate has improved considerably over the years. And the evidence suggests that there are particular things that schools and teachers can do to increase the likelihood of student success. Unfortunately, several key elements of NSCC's school climate concept are not measured on the SASS, so we cannot use teachers' experiences to determine how or whether charter and public schools have different school climates. If the NCES incorporated some of the NSCC's school climate questions on its surveys, the information obtained would be more helpful to researchers and policy makers.[26]

In addition to nationally representative research, researchers should collect and make greater use of longitudinal data. A cursory glance at education policy shows that the world in which teachers and students interact is, in a variety of ways, dynamic. Perhaps the one constant across the public education landscape—especially among troubled, urban schools—is change.[27] As a result, it is often difficult to know whether educational policy innovations that demonstrate short-term gains or failures are representative of long-term trends.[28] Despite this challenge, education researchers often generalize from cross-sectional research. To provide a better understanding of how charter and public schools differ, we will need to make greater use of longitudinal data and analysis. This book, which aggregates and compares cross-sectional data over time, provides one approach. Another would be to use panel data that track particular schools and teachers over time.

Another key question for future research is about scale. The growth of the charter sector has been explosive over the last decade. In some cities, like New Orleans, charter schools educate the majority of public school students. Cities like this offer a crucial test for this book: when charter schools must absorb all students in an area, and all teachers wanting to teach in public schools must select a charter, what types of teaching and school climates develop? Do the differences observed here between charter schools and public schools persist in the context of a majority-charter area? Future research can focus more directly on the organizational questions raised in this book by carefully studying schools in such areas.

Finally, this book highlights a need for greater research into the charter sector. The 2011–2012 version of the SASS included questions about the governance of schools (EMO versus non-EMO schools), charter-granting authorities, and tax status. Researchers should rerun these questions in the future and explore other potential drivers of variation within the sector (e.g., whether a school is a cyber charter or not). In this way, we can better understand what is happening with the charter experiment and the extent to which the teaching climates of these schools resemble and diverge from those fostered in public schools.

CHARTER SCHOOLS AND DEMOCRATIC CONTROL

Baked into the charter school theory is an understanding that when schools are public, they are at a disadvantage: they are guided by shortsighted politicians and constrained by red tape. Charter schools are supposed to work better—in large part—because public authorities exert less control over their day-to-day operations. This is, of course, another way of saying that charter schools reduce the level of democratic control over education. For critics, this decreased public control is one of the signal concerns with charter schools. By granting control over education to out-of-state franchises or unaccountable operators, critics argue, communities are losing control over how their children are educated.[29]

Concerns about the level of democratic control over governance are as old as the nation. The desire for more input from "the people" fits neatly with core American values like popular sovereignty and self-determination and is a recurring political impulse. However, another long-running strain of American thought is a concern with too much democracy. For James Madison, this was one of the central rationales for creating a republican government that separated powers and balanced responsiveness and stability.[30] In more recent times, many key aspects of public policy—from the development of monetary policy by the Federal Reserve to the implementation of environmental regulations—have been delegated to bureaucratic or quasi-bureaucratic entities. These organizations are, to some extent at least, purposively insulated from popular control.

Supporters of such arrangements, and those who generally advocate for charter schools, might note that making a bureaucracy, an institution, or a school less public does not make it nonpublic. For example, in every state, they would argue, charter schools are ultimately accountable to a public entity. And even if charter schools are under less day-to-day public control, this lessened control may be preferable if the schools produce better outcomes for students.

In this response, we get to the heart of the matter: Do the results flowing from comparisons of charter and public schools support a continuation of the experiment? Are any benefits created by, or observed in, charter schools worth the loss of day-to-day democratic control over how public schools are run? Ultimately, it is citizens— the people with the most to lose or gain—who must answer this question. As researchers and scholars seek to inform this deliberation, we must look beyond tests scores to a broader set of educational processes and outcomes. By closely studying the ways that schools operate—and the experiences of teachers, parents, principals, and students—we can create a stronger base of evidence for assessing whether any benefits of charter schools are worth the loss in democratic control that comes with them.

APPENDIX

SURVEYS

The instruments used to create the Schools and Staffing Survey (SASS) can be found online on the NCES website https://nces.ed.gov/surveys/sass. The website also includes detailed information about sampling frames for each year as well as response rates, validity, and reliability. The survey instruments used to create the Teaching, Empowerment, Leading, and Learning (TELL) surveys are available on request from the New Teacher Center, as is information about sampling, response rates, validity, and reliability.

The full survey instrument used to create the Delaware Teacher Survey (DTS) is available upon request from the author. The DTS was created and distributed using Qualtrics survey software. As indicated throughout the book, where possible I adapted questions that were already determined to be valid and reliable. For example, the values questions are adapted from Zeger van der Wal and Leo Huberts, the motivation questions are drawn from Tom Smith and other scholars in public service motivation, and questions about burnout are adapted from Christina Maslach and Susan Jackson.[1] Before administering the survey, I piloted it with a group of public and private school educators who, in addition to completing it, gave me feedback about the phrasing and flow of questions.

To administer this survey, I created a dataset including the names and e-mail addresses of all public school teachers in the state of Delaware, excluding teachers in early childhood centers, preschools, vocational schools, and intensive learning centers. I then sent an introductory e-mail followed up by an e-mail from Qualtrics with a link to the survey. Taking into account spam filters, incorrect e-mails, and other unknown problems, I estimate that I contacted 6,500 teachers in 181 schools across the state. Of that estimated total, 1,241 teachers from 180 schools completed the survey, for a response rate of 19 percent. To encourage participation, in my introductory and survey e-mails, I informed teachers that completing the survey would enable them to enter a lottery to win one of five $100 gift cards.

ESTIMATION

The estimation approach used for the SASS analysis varied, depending on the nature of the dependent variable: when the dependent variable was continuous, I used regression; when the dependent variable was ordered, I used ordered logit; and when the dependent variable was binary, I used dichotomous logit. In all cases, I used Stata's survey command, set the school as the primary sampling unit, and used the final teacher survey weights calculated by NCES (except for the outcomes that used schools as opposed to teachers as the unit of analysis in chapter 3; for these analyses, I used the final school survey weights). The estimation approach used for the TELL and DTS analyses—which did not use sampling weights, because they were population surveys—was multivariate ordered or dichotomous logit with standard errors clustered by school.

MODELS

This section highlights the models used to analyze the survey data from the SASS, TELL, and DTS datasets. My modeling decision rule was to ensure that the analyses—across questions and datasets—were as uniform as possible. However, for certain questions and with certain datasets, there were some discrepancies because of data limitations. The only general modeling difference across the empirical chapters was in the school and student characteristics analysis in chapter 3, which did not include teacher-level data (because the unit of analysis was the school rather than the teacher). The following sections list the models for each of the datasets and their levels of analysis.

SASS: Charter Versus Public School

The basic model used for the SASS charter-versus-public-school comparison included the following sets of school- and teacher-specific variables.

School-specific variables:

- Charter (binary)
- Urban (binary)
- Rural (binary)
- Enrollment size (continuous)
- Student-teacher ratio (continuous)
- Percentage of students who are non-Hispanic white (continuous)
- Percentage of students who are non-Hispanic black (continuous)
- Percentage of students who are Asian (continuous)
- Percentage of students who are Hispanic (continuous)
- Percentage of students having an individualized education plan (IEP) (continuous)
- Percentage of students categorized as having limited English proficiency (LEP) or English language learners (ELL) (continuous)
- Percentage of students who qualified for free or reduced-price lunches (continuous)
- Elementary school (binary, based on if it had at least one of the following grades: K–5)
- Middle school (binary, based on if it had at least one of the following grades: 6–8)
- High school (binary, based on if it had at least one of the following grades: 9–12)
- State, district, or territory (binary)
  - *Note:* In certain years, the inclusion of some state, district, or territory variables prevented the analysis from completely

determining all observations. To maintain consistency across years, the following state, district, or territory variables were excluded: AK, AL, AR, AS, CT, GU, IA, IL, KS, KY, MD, ME, MO, MS, MT, ND, NE, NH, NV, OK, OR, PR, RI, SD, TN, VA, VI, VT, WA, WV, and WY. However, teacher and schools from these states remained in the analysis. Supplementary analysis revealed that the exclusion or inclusion of state dummy variables had little impact on the findings reported here.

Teacher-specific variables:
- Years of teaching experience (continuous)
- Birth year (continuous)
- Hispanic teacher (binary)
- White teacher (binary)
- Black teacher (binary)
- Asian teacher (binary)
- Teacher gender (binary)
- Union member (binary)
- Certification status (binary)
- Master's degree (binary)
- Main teaching area: general education (binary)
- Main teaching area: art (binary)
- Main teaching area: English (binary)
- Main teaching area: English as a second language (ESL) (binary)
- Main teaching area: foreign language (binary)
- Main teaching area: health (binary)
- Main teaching area: physical education (binary)
- Main teaching area: math (binary)
- Main teaching area: natural science (binary)
- Main teaching area: social science (binary)

SASS: Charter School Only

For the 2011–2012 school year, the basic model used for the SASS charter-schools-only analysis included the following sets of school- and teacher-specific variables.

School-specific variables:
- Center for Education Reform rating (continuous)
- Education-management-organization-run (EMO-run) school (binary)*
- For-profit EMO (binary)*
- Years of operation (continuous)*
- Originally a charter school, versus converted (binary)*
- Charter granted by school district (binary)*
- Charter granted by state (binary)*
- Charter granted by a university (binary)*
- Charter granted by a charter-granting agency (binary)*
- Urban (binary)
- Rural (binary)
- Enrollment size (continuous)
- Student-teacher ratio (continuous)
- Percentage of students who are non-Hispanic white (continuous)
- Percentage of students who are non-Hispanic black (continuous)
- Percentage of students who are Asian (continuous)
- Percentage of students who are Hispanic (continuous)
- Percentage of students categorized as IEP (continuous)
- Percentage of students categorized as LEP or ELL (continuous)
- Percentage of students who qualified for free or reduced-price lunches (continuous)
- Elementary school (binary, based on if it had at least one of the following grades: K–5)
- Middle school (binary, based on if it had at least one of the following grades: 6–8)
- High school (binary, based on if it had at least one of the following grades: 9–12)

Teacher-specific variables:
- Years of teaching experience (continuous)
- Birth year (continuous)
- Hispanic teacher (binary)

- White teacher (binary)
- Black teacher (binary)
- Asian teacher (binary)
- Teacher gender (binary)
- Union member (binary)
- Certification status (binary)
- Master's degree (binary)
- Main teaching area: general education (binary)
- Main teaching area: art (binary)
- Main teaching area: English (binary)
- Main teaching area: ESL (binary)
- Main teaching area: foreign language (binary)
- Main teaching area: health (binary)
- Main teaching area: physical education (binary)
- Main teaching area: math (binary)
- Main teaching area: natural science (binary)
- Main teaching area: social science (binary)

For the first three years of the survey (1999–2000, 2003–2004, and 2007–2008), the model is the same but did not include the school-specific variables with asterisks (questions about these variables were not asked on the SASS in those years). Also, since the number of charter school teachers in each wave of the analysis was smaller than the general charter-versus-public comparison, I could not include state control variables (which were included in the charter-versus-public analysis). Finally, because there were fewer charter school teachers in the 2003–2004 and 2007–2008 surveys, some models from these years excluded the main teaching area variable.

TELL: Charter Versus Public School

The basic model used for the TELL charter-versus-public school comparison included the following sets of school- and teacher-specific variables. The percentage of LEP/ELL and IEP students per school—for teachers in Maryland and North Carolina—was drawn from the Department of Education's Civil Rights Data Collection (http://ocrdata.ed.gov). Unfortunately, these data are collected every two years and were not collected in 2012–2013, the year of the Maryland TELL survey. Consequently, the percentage of LEP/ELL and IEP students per school in the Maryland dataset refers to the 2013–2014 school year. A supplementary analysis, which excluded the Maryland data, revealed few substantive differences from the one presented in the book.

School-specific variables:
- Charter (binary)
- Enrollment size (continuous)
- Percentage of students who are non-Hispanic white (continuous)
- Percentage of students who are non-Hispanic black (continuous)
- Percentage of students who are Hispanic (continuous)
- Percentage of students who are female (continuous)
- Percentage of students categorized as IEP (continuous)
- Percentage of students categorized as LEP or ELL (continuous)
- Percentage of students who qualified for free or reduced-price lunches (continuous)
- Elementary school (binary, based on if it had at least one of the following grades: K–5)
- Middle school (binary, based on if it had at least one of the following grades: 6–8)
- High school (binary, based on if it had at least one of the following grades: 9–12)
- State (binary)

Teacher-specific variables:
- Years of teaching experience (continuous)
- Years of experience in current school (continuous)

TELL: Charter School Only

The basic model used for the TELL charter-school-only analysis included the following sets of school- and teacher-specific variables.

The percentage of LEP/ELL and IEP students per school—for teachers in Maryland and North Carolina—was drawn from the Department of Education's Civil Rights Data Collection (http://ocrdata.ed.gov). Unfortunately, these data are collected every two years and were not collected in 2012–2013, the year of the Maryland TELL survey. Consequently, the percentage of LEP/ELL and IEP students per school in the Maryland dataset refers to the 2013–2014 school year.

School-specific variables:
- Center for Education Reform rating (continuous)
- Education-management-organization-run (EMO-run) school (binary)
- For-profit school (binary)
- Year opened (continuous)
- Enrollment size (continuous)
- Percentage of students who are non-Hispanic white (continuous)
- Percentage of students who are non-Hispanic black (continuous)
- Percentage of students who are Hispanic (continuous)
- Percentage of students who are female (continuous)
- Percentage of students categorized as IEP (continuous)
- Percentage of students categorized as LEP or ELL (continuous)
- Percentage of students who qualified for free or reduced-price lunches (continuous)
- Elementary school (binary, based on if it had at least one of the following grades: K–5)
- Middle school (binary, based on if it had at least one of the following grades: 6–8)
- High school (binary, based on if it had at least one of the following grades: 9–12)
- State (binary)

Teacher-specific variables:
- Years of teaching experience (continuous)
- Years of experience in current school (continuous)

DTS: Charter Versus Public School

The basic model used for the DTS charter-versus-public school comparison included the following sets of school- and teacher-specific variables.

School-specific variables:
- Charter (binary)
- Enrollment size (continuous)
- Percentage of students who are non-Hispanic white (continuous)
- Percentage of students who are non-Hispanic black (continuous)
- Percentage of students who are Hispanic (continuous)
- Percentage of students who are female (continuous)
- Percentage of students categorized as IEP (continuous)
- Percentage of students categorized as LEP or ELL (continuous)
- Percentage of students who qualified for free or reduced-price lunches (continuous)
- Elementary school (binary, based on if it had at least one of the following grades: K–5)
- Middle school (binary, based on if it had at least one of the following grades: 6–8)
- High school (binary, based on if it had at least one of the following grades: 9–12)
- Arts school (binary)
- Magnet school (binary)

Teacher-specific variables:
- Years of teaching experience (continuous)
- Gender (binary)

INTERVIEWS

To further my understanding of the teaching climates of public and charter schools in Delaware, I conducted interviews with a subset of survey respondents. At the completion of the survey, respondents were directed to an online form and asked to indicate their e-mail address—if they wanted to be entered in the lottery for one of the gift cards—and asked if they would be interested in speaking at further length with me about their experiences. They were also told that all interviewees would be given a $10 gift card. Around four hundred teachers indicated an interest in conducting an interview. Of that initial group, I randomly selected thirty teachers to contact. Ultimately, I interviewed around one-third of this group.

I used the following interview protocol with each interviewee. The advantage of using this approach is that I asked a standard set of questions in each interview but also had the flexibility to use follow-up questions and detour as I saw fit. All interviews were recorded and transcribed.

Interview Protocol

Ask details about what they teach and for how long they have been teaching (in general and in their current school).

1. First, can you tell me a little bit about why you're a teacher?
2. How did you pick your school?
3. Next I'd like to ask you a little bit about your school.
   a. Do you think that school leaders—principal, etc.—have a good understanding of what's happening in classrooms on a day-to-day basis, or are they more "hands-off"?
   b. Do school leaders encourage teachers to be creative and come up with new approaches to teaching, or do they emphasize using standardized approaches?
      i. Can you think of any innovations that have come from the teachers in the school?
      ii. How much are teachers expected to teach to the test?
   c. How receptive are school leaders to feedback from teachers?
      i. Can you think of an example when a teacher's input helped change the school's policy or curriculum?

d. Do you think teachers in your school are held accountable for the quality of their teaching?
   i. If yes, how so?
e. Do you trust school leaders to generally do what's best for students when they make schoolwide decisions?
   i. Example?
f. What's the relationship between parents and the administrators and teachers in your school?
   i. How closely do administrators and teachers work with parents?
g. How much red tape do you have at your school? In other words, [are there] rules and regulations that get in the way of teachers doing their jobs?
   i. If yes, can you think of an example when it made it more difficult to do your job?

4. The next questions are about your approach to teaching.
   a. Do you follow the curriculum closely or diverge when you think it's necessary?
   b. Can you tell me a bit about the role you play in shaping your department's curriculum?
   c. Can you tell me a little bit about your approach to education?
      i. Do you push students to think critically and challenge conventional wisdom?

NOTES

PREFACE

1. J. R. Henig, *Spin Cycle: How Research Is Used in Policy Debates; The Case of Charter Schools* (New York: Russell Sage Foundation/Century Foundation, 2008).

2. Ibid.; M. Berends, "Sociology and School Choice: What We Know After Two Decades of Charter Schools," *Annual Review of Sociology* 41 (2015): 159–180; P. Wohlstetter, J. Smith, and C. Farrell, *Choices and Challenges: Charter School Performance in Perspective* (Cambridge, MA: Harvard Education Press, 2013).

CHAPTER 1

1. R. Budde, "Education by Charter: Restructuring School Districts" (Andover, MA: Regional Laboratory for Educational Improvement of the Northeast and Islands, 1988); Ted Kolderie, "Beyond Choice to New Public Schools: Withdrawing the Exclusive Franchise in Public Education," policy report 8 (Washington, DC: Progressive Policy Institute, 1990); Joe Nathan, *Charter Schools: Creating Hope and Opportunity for American Education* (San Francisco: Jossey-Bass, 1996). I say "at least in part" to acknowledge that teaching isn't the only way that charter schools are supposed to create different learning environments.

2. As quoted by R. Kahlenberg and H. Potter, *A Smarter Charter: Finding What Works for Charter Schools and Public Education* (New York: Teachers College Press, 2014), 12.

3. Nathan, *Charter Schools*, xv–xvi.

4. Ibid., 18.

5. See, for example, A. Bryk et al., *Organizing Schools for Improvement: Lessons from Chicago* (Chicago: University of Chicago Press, 2010); D. Berliner and G. Glass, *50 Myths and Lies That Threaten America's Public Schools: The Real Crisis in Education* (New York: Teachers College Press, 2014).

6. R. Ferguson and E. Hirsch, "How Working Conditions Predict Teaching Quality and Student Outcomes," in *Designing Teacher Evaluation Systems: New Guidance from the Measures of Effective Teaching Project*, ed. T. Kane, K. Kerr, and R. Pianta (New York: Wiley, 2014), 332–80; H. Ladd, "Teachers' Perceptions of Their Working Conditions: How Predictive of Policy Relevant Outcomes?" working paper 33 (Washington, DC: Urban Institute, 2009); New Teacher Center, "Research Brief: TELL Maryland Student Achievement and Teacher Retention Analyses" (Durham, NC: New Teacher Center, 2014). Drawing from the school climate literature, a school's teaching climate is theoretically one part of the overall climate

that students experience, J. Cohen et al., "School Climate: Research, Policy, Practice, and Teacher Education," *Teachers College Record* 111, no. 1 (2009): 180–213; A. Thapa et al., "A Review of School Climate Research," *Review of Educational Research* 83, no. 3 (2013): 357–85.

7. National Alliance for Public Charter Schools, "What Are Public Charter Schools?," *National Alliance for Public Charter Schools*, 2015, www.publiccharters .org/get-the-facts/public-charter-schools; New York City Charter School Center, "About Charter Schools," 2016, www.nyccharterschools.org/about.

8. "Restructuring Our Schools," *Peabody Journal of Education* 65, no. 3 (1988): 97.

9. D. Ravitch, *Reign of Error: The Hoax of the Privatization Movement and the Danger to America's Public Schools* (New York: Knopf, 2013).

10. Kahlenberg and Potter, *A Smarter Charter.*

11. K. Taylor, "At Success Academy School, a Stumble in Math and a Teacher's Anger on Video," *New York Times*, February 13, 2016, www.nytimes.com/2016/02/13/ nyregion/success-academy-teacher-rips-up-student-paper.html.

12. Nathan, *Charter Schools*, xvii.

13. A. Wells, "Why Public Policy Fails to Live Up to the Potential of Charter School Reform," in *Where Charter School Policy Fails: The Problems of Accountability and Equity*, ed. A. Wells (New York: Teachers College Press, 2002), 2.

14. Ravitch, *Reign of Error*, 159.

15. C. Lubienski and P. Weitzel, eds., *The Charter School Experiment: Expectations, Evidence, and Implications* (Cambridge, MA: Harvard Education Press, 2010), 4.

16. J. Betts and Y. Tang, "The Effect of Charter Schools on Student Achievement: A Meta-Analysis of the Literature" (Seattle, WA: Center on Reinventing Public Education, 2014); Center for Research on Education Outcomes, "National Charter School Study" (Stanford, CA: Stanford University, 2013); W. Dobbie and R. Fryer Jr., *Are High Quality Schools Enough to Close the Achievement Gap? Evidence from a Social Experiment in Harlem* (Washington, DC: NBER, 2009); B. Gill et al., *Rhetoric Versus Reality: What We Know and What We Need to Know About Vouchers and Charter Schools* (Santa Monica, CA: RAND, 2007); C. Lubienski and S. Lubienski, *The Public School Advantage: Why Public Schools Outperform Private Schools* (Chicago: University of Chicago Press, 2013).

17. M. Berends, M. Springer, and H. Walberg, introduction to *Charter School Outcomes*, ed. M. Berends and H. Walberg (New York: Lawrence Erlbaum Associates, 2008), xiii–xviii; Lubienski and Weitzel, *The Charter School Experiment*; G. Miron and C. Nelson, *What's Public About Charter Schools? Lessons Learned About Choice and Accountability* (Thousand Oaks, CA: Corwin Press, 2002).

18. C. Goodsell, *The Case for Bureaucracy: A Public Administration Polemic* (Washington, DC: CQ Press, 2004); C. Risen, "The Lightning Rod," *Atlantic*, November 2008.

19. B. Bozeman, *All Organizations Are Public: Bridging Public and Private Organizational Theories* (Washington, DC: Beard Books, 2004); M. Murray, "Comparing Public and Private Management: An Exploratory Essay," *Public Administration Review* 35, no. 4 (1975): 364–71; H. Simon, *Administrative Behavior: A Study of Decision-Making Processes in Administrative Organizations* (New York: Free Press,

1997); M. Weber, *Economy and Society* (Berkeley: University of California Press, 1968).

20. H. Rainey and B. Bozeman, "Comparing Public and Private Organizations: Empirical Research and the Power of the a Priori," *Journal of Public Administration Research and Theory* 10, no. 2 (2000): 447–69; M. Sanger, *The Welfare Marketplace: Privatization and Welfare Reform* (Washington, DC: Brookings Institution Press, 2003); J. Soss, R. Fording, and S. Schram, *Disciplining the Poor: Neoliberal Paternalism and the Persistent Power of Race* (Chicago: University of Chicago Press, 2011).

21. R. Andrews, G. Boyne, and R. Walker, "Dimensions of Publicness and Organizational Performance: A Review of the Evidence," *Journal of Public Administration Research and Theory* 21, no. supplement 3 (2011): i301–19; Y. H. Chun and H. Rainey, "Goal Ambiguity and Organizational Performance in US Federal Agencies," *Journal of Public Administration Research and Theory* 15, no. 4 (2005): 529; K. Meier and L. O'Toole, "Comparing Public and Private Management: Theoretical Expectations," *Journal of Public Administration Research and Theory* 21, no. supplement 3 (2011): i283–99; J. Perry and H. Rainey, "The Public-Private Distinction in Organization Theory: A Critique and Research Strategy," *Academy of Management Review* (1988): 182–201.

22. M. Batdorff et al., *Charter School Funding: Inequity Expands* (Fayetteville: School Choice Demonstration Project, University of Arkansas, 2014).

23. Miron and Nelson, *What's Public About Charter Schools?*; P. Wohlstetter, J. Smith, and C. Farrell, *Choices and Challenges: Charter School Performance in Perspective* (Cambridge, MA: Harvard Education Press, 2013). Though the greater leeway for charters is a key general difference, states provide varied levels of autonomy to charter schools in terms of teacher hiring and firing and other important aspects of human resources (Alison Consoletti, ed., *Charter School Laws Across the States* [Washington, DC: Center for Education Reform, 2012]).

24. M. Ford and D. Ihrke, "Comparing Nonprofit Charter and Traditional Public School Board Member Perceptions of the Public, Conflict, and Financial Responsibility: Is There a Difference and Does It Matter?," *Public Management Review* 18 (2016): 972–92 (published online March 31, 2015), www.tandfonline.com/doi/abs/10.1080/14719037.2015.1028975; Miron and Nelson, *What's Public About Charter Schools?*

25. C. Burris, "Why Charter Schools Get Public Education Advocates so Angry," *Washington Post*, July 24, 2016, www.washingtonpost.com/news/answer-sheet/wp/2016/07/24/why-charter-schools-get-public-education-advocates-so-angry.

26. W. Hoy, "Organizational Climate and Culture: A Conceptual Analysis of the School Workplace," *Journal of Educational and Psychological Consultation* 1, no. 2 (1990): 149–68.

27. Bozeman, *All Organizations Are Public*.

28. J. Chubb and T. Moe, *Politics, Markets, and America's Schools* (Washington, DC: Brookings Institution Press, 1990); Goodsell, *The Case for Bureaucracy*.

29. J. Donahue, *The Privatization Decision: Public Ends, Private Means* (New York: Basic Books, 1989); L. Salamon, *Partners in Public Service: Government-Nonprofit Relations in the Modern Welfare State* (Baltimore: Johns Hopkins University Press, 1995).

30. P. Ingraham, P. Joyce, and A. Donahue, *Government Performance: Why Management Matters* (Baltimore: Johns Hopkins University Press, 2003); K. Meier et al., "Strategic Management and the Performance of Public Organizations: Testing Venerable Ideas Against Recent Theories," *Journal of Public Administration Research and Theory* 17, no. 3 (2007): 357–77; D. Moynihan and S. Pandey, "Testing How Management Matters in an Era of Government by Performance Management," *Journal of Public Administration Research and Theory* 15, no. 3 (2005): 421–39; N. Riccucci, *How Management Matters: Street-Level Bureaucrats and Welfare Reform* (Washington, DC: Georgetown University Press, 2005); T. Trottier, M. Van Wart, and X. Wang, "Examining the Nature and Significance of Leadership in Government Organizations," *Public Administration Review* 68, no. 2 (2008): 319–33.

31. Bozeman, *All Organizations Are Public*; R. Davis and E. Stazyk, "Developing and Testing a New Goal Taxonomy: Accounting for the Complexity of Ambiguity and Political Support," *Journal of Public Administration Research and Theory* 25, no. 3 (2014): 751–75; Meier and O'Toole, "Comparing Public and Private Management"; H. Rainey and Y. Chun, "Public and Private Management Compared," in *The Oxford Handbook of Public Management*, ed. E. Ferlie, L. Lynn Jr., and C. Pollitt (New York: Oxford University Press, 2005), 72–102.

32. R. Davis, "Blue-Collar Public Servants: How Union Membership Influences Public Service Motivation," *American Review of Public Administration* 41, no. 6 (2011): 705–23.

33. J. Broadbent and R. Laughlin, "Evaluating the 'New Public Management' Reforms in the UK: A Constitutional Possibility," *Public Administration* 75, no. 3 (1997): 487–507.

34. B. Bozeman, *Bureaucracy and Red Tape* (New York: Prentice Hall, 2000), 12.

35. "Stakeholder Red Tape: Comparing Perceptions of Public Managers and Their Private Consultants," *Public Administration Review* 69, no. 4 (2009): 713.

36. J. Carpenter, D. Doverspike, and R. Miguel, "Public Service Motivation as a Predictor of Attraction to the Public Sector," *Journal of Vocational Behavior* 80, no. 2 (2012): 509–23; B. Schneider, "The People Make the Place," *Personnel Psychology* 40, no. 3 (1987): 437–53.

37. Z. Oberfield, *Becoming Bureaucrats: Socialization at the Front Lines of Government Service* (Philadelphia: University of Pennsylvania Press, 2014).

38. Donahue, *The Privatization Decision*; B. Wright and R. Christensen, "Public Service Motivation: A Test of the Job Attraction–Selection–Attrition Model," *International Public Management Journal* 13, no. 2 (2010): 155–76.

39. J. Betts and R. Atkinson, "Better Research Needed on the Impact of Charter Schools," *Science* 335, no. 6065 (2012): 171–72.

40. Taylor, "At Success Academy School"; R. Whitmire, *On the Rocketship: How Top Charter Schools Are Pushing the Envelope* (New York: John Wiley & Sons, 2014).

41. Wohlstetter, Smith, and Farrell, *Choices and Challenges*, 159.

42. Ibid., 33–34.

43. See the appendix for a discussion of how the survey was administered.

44. Center for Education Reform, "Laws & Legislation: Charter School Law," Center for Education Reform, 2015, www.edreform.com/issues/choice-charter-schools/laws-legislation.

45. J. Buckley and M. Schneider, *Charter Schools: Hope or Hype?* (Princeton, NJ: Princeton University Press, 2007); C. Hoxby and S. Muraka, "Methods of Assessing the Achievement of Students in Charter Schools," in *Charter School Outcomes*, ed. M. Berends and H. Walberg (New York: Lawrence Erlbaum Associates, 2008), 7–37; J. Betts, "The Selection of Students into Charter Schools: A Critical Issue for Research and Policy," in *Taking Measure of Charter Schools: Better Assessments, Better Policymaking, Better Schools*, ed. J. Betts and P. Hill (New York: Rowman & Littlefield, 2010), 65–82.

46. M. Cannata and R. Penaloza, "Who Are Charter School Teachers? Comparing Teacher Characteristics, Job Choices, and Job Preferences," *Education Policy Analysis Archives* 20 (2012): 1–21.

47. Hoy, "Organizational Climate and Culture," 151.

48. In all the surveys examined here, teachers were told that their views would be recorded anonymously or confidentially, so there is at least a reasonable chance that respondents answered survey questions honestly.

49. R. Kelley, B. Thornton, and R. Daugherty, "Relationships Between Measures of Leadership and School Climate," *Education* 126 (2005): 17.

50. Berliner and Glass, *50 Myths and Lies*.

51. Simon, *Administrative Behavior*.

52. C. Anderson, "The Search for School Climate: A Review of the Research," *Review of Educational Research* 52, no. 3 (1982): 368–420; Cohen et al., "School Climate"; Thapa et al., "Review of School Climate Research."

53. N. Jacobs, "Understanding School Choice Location as a Determinant of Charter School Racial, Economic, and Linguistic Segregation," *Education and Urban Society* 45, no. 4 (2011): 459–82; Ravitch, *Reign of Error*.

54. J. Betts and Y. Tang, "The Effect of Charter Schools on Student Achievement."

55. J. Crawford, "Teacher Autonomy and Accountability in Charter Schools," *Education and Urban Society* 33, no. 2 (2001): 186–201; K. Finnigan, "Charter School Autonomy: The Mismatch Between Theory and Practice," *Educational Policy* 21, no. 3 (2007): 503–26; G. Garn and C. Cobb, "A Framework for Understanding Charter School Accountability," *Education and Urban Society* 33, no. 2 (2001): 113–28; P. Hill, R. Lake, and M. Celio, *Charter Schools and Accountability in Public Education* (Washington, DC: Brookings Institution Press, 2002); Miron and Nelson, *What's Public About Charter Schools?*; L. Renzulli, H. Parrott, and I. Beattie, "Racial Mismatch and School Type: Teacher Satisfaction and Retention in Charter and Traditional Public Schools," *Sociology of Education* 84, no. 1 (2011): 23–48; Wohlstetter et al., *Choices and Challenges*.

56. Buckley and Schneider, *Charter Schools: Hope or Hype?*

57. B. Fuller, introduction to *Inside Charter Schools: The Paradox of Radical Decentralization*, ed. B. Fuller (Cambridge, MA: Harvard University Press, 2000), 1–11.

CHAPTER 2

1. J. Stossel, "Let's Call Our Public Schools What They Really Are—'Government' Schools," *Fox News Opinion*, October 2, 2013, www.foxnews.com/opinion/2013/10/02/let-call-our-public-schools-what-really-are-government-schools.html.

2. J. Bryant, "The New Charter School Scheme: This Is How GOP and Privatizers Have Bled Pennsylvania Schools," *Salon*, September 8, 2015, www.salon.com/2015/09/08/the_new_charter_school_scheme_this_is_how_gop_and_privatizers_have_bled_pennsylvania_schools.

3. S. Skowronek, *Building a New American State: The Expansion of National Administrative Capacities, 1877–1920* (New York: Cambridge University Press, 1982).

4. D. Carpenter, *The Forging of Bureaucratic Autonomy: Reputations, Networks, and Policy Innovation in Executive Agencies, 1862–1928* (Princeton, NJ: Princeton University Press, 2001).

5. Rick Perlstein, *Nixonland: The Rise of a President and the Fracturing of America* (New York: Simon and Schuster, 2008); J. Quadagno, *The Color of Welfare. How Racism Undermined the War on Poverty* (New York: Oxford University Press, 1994).

6. M. Sanger, *The Welfare Marketplace: Privatization and Welfare Reform* (Washington, DC: Brookings Institution Press, 2003).

7. P. Pierson, *Dismantling the Welfare State? Reagan, Thatcher, and the Politics of Retrenchment* (New York: Cambridge University Press, 1994).

8. P. Light, "The New True Size of Government," Organizational Performance Initiative, research brief 2 (New York: New York University Wagner, 2006); US Office of Personnel Management, "Total Government Employment Since 1962," U.S. Office of Personnel Management, 2015, www.opm.gov/policy-data-oversight/data-analysis-documentation/federal-employment-reports/historical-tables/total-government-employment-since-1962.

9. D. Kettl, *Sharing Power: Public Governance and Private Markets* (Washington, DC: Brookings Institution Press, 1993); L. Salamon, *Partners in Public Service: Government-Nonprofit Relations in the Modern Welfare State* (Baltimore: Johns Hopkins University Press, 1995).

10. H. Feigenbaum, J. Henig, and C. Hamnett, *Shrinking the State: The Political Underpinnings of Privatization* (New York: Cambridge University Press, 1998); K. Morgan and A. Campbell, *The Delegated Welfare State: Medicare, Markets, and the Governance of Social Policy* (New York: Oxford University Press, 2011); A. Stanger, *One Nation Under Contract: The Outsourcing of American Power and the Future of Foreign Policy* (New Haven, CT: Yale University Press, 2009).

11. C. Goodsell, *The Case for Bureaucracy: A Public Administration Polemic* (Washington, DC: CQ Press, 2004).

12. R. Budde, "Education by Charter: Restructuring School Districts" (Andover, MA: Regional Laboratory for Educational Improvement of the Northeast and Islands, 1988); A. Shanker, "Restructuring Our Schools," *Peabody Journal of Education* 65, no. 3 (1988): 88–100.

13. D. Ravitch, *Reign of Error: The Hoax of the Privatization Movement and the Danger to America's Public Schools* (New York: Knopf, 2013).

14. B. Bozeman, *All Organizations Are Public: Bridging Public and Private Organizational Theories* (Washington, DC: Beard Books, 2004); H. Frederickson, *The Spirit of Public Administration* (New York: Wiley, 1997); L. Lynn, *Public Management as Art, Science, and Profession* (Chatham, N.J: Chatham House Publishers, 1996).

15. Frederickson, *The Spirit of Public Administration*, 1.

16. R. Davis and E. Stazyk, "Developing and Testing a New Goal Taxonomy: Accounting for the Complexity of Ambiguity and Political Support," *Journal of Public Administration Research and Theory* 25, no. 3 (2014): 751–75; K. Meier and L. O'Toole, "Comparing Public and Private Management: Theoretical Expectations," *Journal of Public Administration Research and Theory* 21, no. suppl. 3 (2011): i283–i299; J. Perry and H. Rainey, "The Public-Private Distinction in Organization Theory: A Critique and Research Strategy," *Academy of Management Review* (1988): 182–201; H. Rainey and Y. Chun, "Public and Private Management Compared," in *The Oxford Handbook of Public Management*, ed. E. Ferlie, L. Lynn Jr., and C. Pollitt (New York: Oxford University Press, 2005), 72–102.

17. D. Lewis, "Testing Pendleton's Premise: Do Political Appointees Make Worse Bureaucrats?," *Journal of Politics* 69, no. 4 (2007): 1073–88.

18. S. Pandey and P. Scott, "Red Tape: A Review and Assessment of Concepts and Measures," *Journal of Public Administration Research and Theory* 12, no. 4 (2002): 553–80.

19. M. Feeney and B. Bozeman, "Stakeholder Red Tape: Comparing Perceptions of Public Managers and Their Private Consultants," *Public Administration Review* 69, no. 4 (2009): 710–26.

20. J. Buchanan and R. Tollison, eds., *The Theory of Public Choice—II* (Ann Arbor: University of Michigan Press, 1984).

21. G. Boyne, *Public Choice Theory and Local Government: A Comparative Analysis of the UK and the USA* (New York: Macmillan Press, 1998).

22. J. Chubb and T. Moe, *Politics, Markets, and America's Schools* (Washington, D.C.: Brookings Institution Press, 1990).

23. Ibid., 32.

24. R. Hall, *Organizations: Structures, Processes, and Outcomes* (New York: Prentice Hall, 2002); M. Murray, "Comparing Public and Private Management: An Exploratory Essay," *Public Administration Review* 35, no. 4 (1975): 364–71; H. Simon, *Administrative Behavior: A Study of Decision-Making Processes in Administrative Organizations* (New York: Free Press, 1997); M. Weber, *Economy and Society* (Berkeley: University of California Press, 1968).

25. Goodsell, *The Case for Bureaucracy*.

26. Perry and Rainey, "The Public-Private Distinction in Organization Theory."

27. J. Alonso, J. Clifton, and D. Díaz-Fuentes, "Did New Public Management Matter? An Empirical Analysis of the Outsourcing and Decentralization Effects on Public Sector Size," *Public Management Review* 17, no. 5 (2013): 643–60; M. Barzelay, *The New Public Management: Improving Research and Policy Dialogue* (Berkeley: University of California Press, 2001); J. Soss, R. Fording, and S. Schram, *Disciplining the Poor: Neoliberal Paternalism and the Persistent Power of Race* (Chicago: University of Chicago Press, 2011).

28. B. Radin, *Challenging the Performance Movement: Accountability, Complexity, and Democratic Values* (Washington, DC: Georgetown University Press, 2006).

29. M. Poole, R. Mansfield, and J. Gould-Williams, "Public and Private Sector Managers Over 20 Years: A Test of the 'Convergence Thesis,'" *Public Administration* 84, no. 4 (2006): 1051–76; J. van Bockel and M. Noordegraaf, "Identifying Identities: Performance-Driven, but Professional Public Managers," *International Journal of Public Sector Management* 19, no. 6 (2006): 585–97.

30. P. Burch, *Hidden Markets: The New Education Privatization* (New York: Routledge, 2009).

31. M. Berends and H. Walberg, eds., *Charter School Outcomes* (New York: Lawrence Erlbaum Associates, 2008).

32. C. Boardman, B. Bozeman, and B. Ponomariov, "Private Sector Imprinting: An Examination of the Impacts of Private Sector Job Experience on Public Manager's Work Attitudes," *Public Administration Review* 70, no. 1 (2010): 50–59; J. Dias and S. Maynard-Moody, "For-Profit Welfare: Contracts, Conflicts, and the Performance Paradox," *Journal of Public Administration Research and Theory* 17, no. 2 (2007): 189–211; P. Light, *The New Public Service* (Washington, DC: Brookings Institution Press, 1999); M. Mazzetti, *The Way of the Knife: The CIA, a Secret Army, and a War at the Ends of the Earth* (New York: Penguin, 2013).

33. J. G. March and J. P. Olsen, "The Logic of Appropriateness," in *The Oxford Handbook of Public Policy*, ed. M. Moran, M. Rein, and R. Goodin (New York: Oxford University Press, 2006), 689–708.

34. Z. Oberfield, *Becoming Bureaucrats: Socialization at the Front Lines of Government Service* (Philadelphia: University of Pennsylvania Press, 2014).

35. Rainey and Chun, "Public and Private Management Compared."

36. S. Smith and M. Lipsky, *Nonprofits for Hire: The Welfare State in the Age of Contracting* (Cambridge, MA: Harvard University Press, 1993); Stanger, *One Nation Under Contract*.

37. L. Dickinson, *Outsourcing War and Peace: Preserving Public Values in a World of Privatized Foreign Affairs* (New Haven, CT: Yale University Press, 2011); Mazzetti, *The Way of the Knife*; P. Verkuil, *Outsourcing Sovereignty: Why Privatization of Government Functions Threatens Democracy and What We Can Do About It* (New York: Cambridge University Press, 2007).

38. Goodsell, *The Case for Bureaucracy*.

39. Ted Kolderie, "Beyond Choice to New Public Schools: Withdrawing the Exclusive Franchise in Public Education," policy report 8 (Washington, DC: Progressive Policy Institute, 1990); Joe Nathan, *Charter Schools: Creating Hope and Opportunity for American Education* (San Francisco: Jossey-Bass, 1996).

40. Nathan, *Charter Schools*, 8.

41. G. Miron and C. Gulosino, *Profiles of For-Profit and Nonprofit Education Management Organizations: Fourteenth Edition—2011–2012* (Boulder, CO: National Education Policy Center, 2013). EMOs provide a range of support to charter schools, from minor support, like running payroll services, to major efforts, like developing curricula, assessing teachers, and managing schools (K. Bulkley, "Balancing Act:

Educational Management Organizations and Charter School Autonomy," in *Taking Account of Charter Schools: What's Happened and What's Next,* ed. K. Bulkley and P. Wohlstetter [New York: Teachers College Press, 2004], 121–141). I am interested in this latter approach, which is likely to have the more significant impact on teachers and their schools' teaching climates. To make empirical sense of this range of EMO involvement, the book uses the language from the 2011–2012 SASS, which asks charter respondents to characterize the governance structure of their schools by choosing one of the following: "(1) An independent or stand-alone charter school, (2) Part of a non-profit charter management organization or network of schools that are managed by a central agency, (3) Part of a for-profit charter management organization or network of schools that are managed by a central agency, (4) Part of a traditional public school district, [or] (5) Other." Schools classified in groups 2 or 3 are referred to as "EMO-run," while all others are referred to as "non-EMO-run" though they may have some relatively minor services performed by EMOs.

42. H. Brown et al., "Scale of Operations and Locus of Control in Market- Versus Mission-Oriented Charter Schools," *Social Science Quarterly* 85, no. 5 (2004): 1035–51; Bulkley, "Balancing Act"; K. Finnigan, "Charter School Autonomy: The Mismatch Between Theory and Practice," *Educational Policy* 21, no. 3 (2007): 503–26; J. Goodman, "Charter Management Organizations and the Regulated Environment: Is It Worth the Price?," *Educational Researcher* 42, no. 2 (2013): 89–96.

43. C. Finn Jr., B. Manno, and B. Wright, *Charter Schools at the Crossroads: Predicaments, Paradoxes, Possibilities* (Cambridge, MA: Harvard Education Press, 2016).

44. W. Dobbie and R. Fryer Jr., *Are High-Quality Schools Enough to Close the Achievement Gap? Evidence from a Social Experiment in Harlem* (Washington, DC: NBER, 2009); R. Whitmire, *On the Rocketship: How Top Charter Schools Are Pushing the Envelope* (New York: John Wiley & Sons, 2014).

45. J. Stanworth and J. Curran, "Colas, Burgers, Shakes, and Shirkers: Towards a Sociological Model of Franchising in the Market Economy," *Journal of Business Venturing* 14, no. 4 (1999): 323–44.

46. I. Pizanti and M. Lerner, "Examining Control and Autonomy in the Franchisor-Franchisee Relationship," *International Small Business Journal* 21, no. 2 (2003): 131–59.

47. H. Rainey and B. Bozeman, "Comparing Public and Private Organizations: Empirical Research and the Power of the a Priori," *Journal of Public Administration Research and Theory* 10, no. 2 (2000): 447–69.

48. Pizanti and Lerner, "Franchisor-Franchisee Relationship."

49. J. Cox and C. Mason, "Standardisation Versus Adaptation: Geographical Pressures to Deviate from Franchise Formats," *Service Industries Journal* 27, no. 8 (2007): 1053–72.

50. Stanworth and Curran, "Colas, Burgers, Shakes, and Shirkers"; A. Watson et al., "Retail Franchising: An Intellectual Capital Perspective," *Journal of Retailing and Consumer Services* 12, no. 1 (2005): 25–34.

51. Simon, *Administrative Behavior.*

52. E. Conlon and J. Parks, "Effects of Monitoring and Tradition on Compensation Arrangements: An Experiment with Principal-Agent Dyads," *Academy of Management Journal* 33, no. 3 (1990): 603–22.

53. Finn et al., *Charter Schools at the Crossroads*; G. Miron and C. Nelson, *What's Public About Charter Schools? Lessons Learned About Choice and Accountability* (Thousand Oaks, CA: Corwin Press, 2002); National Alliance for Public Charter Schools, "FAQs," 2015, www.publiccharters.org/get-the-facts/public-charter-schools/faqs.

54. J. Donahue, *The Privatization Decision: Public Ends, Private Means* (New York: Basic Books, 1989). H. Simon, "Organizations and Markets," *The Journal of Economic Perspectives* 5, no. 2 (1991): 25–44.

55. Dias and Maynard-Moody, "For-Profit Welfare."

56. N. Gilbert, "Welfare for Profit: Moral, Empirical and Theoretical Perspectives," *Journal of Social Policy* 13, no. 1 (1984): 63–74; J. Soss, R. Fording, and S. Schram, "The Organization of Discipline: From Performance Management to Perversity and Punishment," *Journal of Public Administration Research and Theory* 21, no. suppl. 2 (2011): i203–i232; Wedel, "Federalist No. 70."

57. Ravitch, *Reign of Error*.

58. N. Zollers and A. Ramanathan, "For-Profit Charter Schools and Students with Disabilities: The Sordid Side of the Business of Schooling," *Phi Delta Kappan* 80, no. 4 (1998): 297–304.

59. C. Dykgraaf and S. Lewis, "For-Profit Charter Schools: What the Public Needs to Know," *Educational Leadership* 56, no. 2 (1998): 51–53.

60. E. Fierros and N. Blomberg, "Restrictiveness and Race in Special Education Placements in For-Profit and Non-Profit Charter Schools in California," *Learning Disabilities: A Contemporary Journal* 3, no. 1 (2005): 1–16.

61. W. Hoy, "Organizational Climate and Culture: A Conceptual Analysis of the School Workplace," *Journal of Educational and Psychological Consultation* 1, no. 2 (1990): 149–168.

62. The eight states without charter laws are Alabama, Kentucky, Montana, Nebraska, North Dakota, South Dakota, Vermont, and West Virginia (Center for Education Reform, "Laws & Legislation," Center for Education Reform, 2015, www.edreform.com/issues/choice-charter-schools/laws-legislation).

63. J. Buckley and M. Schneider, *Charter Schools: Hope or Hype?* (Princeton, NJ: Princeton University Press, 2007).

64. Center for Education Reform, "Teacher Quality," Center for Education Reform, 2015, www.edreform.com/issues/teacher-quality; Ravitch, *Reign of Error*.

65. K. Barghaus and E. Boe, "From Policy to Practice: Implementation of the Legislative Objectives of Charter Schools," *American Journal of Education* 118, no. 1 (2011): 57–86.

66. M. Lipsky, *Street-Level Bureaucracy: Dilemmas of the Individual in Public Service* (New York: Russell Sage Foundation, 1980); S. Maynard-Moody and M. Musheno, *Cops, Teachers, Counselors: Stories from the Front Lines of Public Service* (Ann Arbor: University of Michigan Press, 2003).

67. Oberfield, *Becoming Bureaucrats*.

68. C. Lubienski, *The Public School Advantage: Why Public Schools Outperform Private Schools* (Chicago: University of Chicago Press, 2013).

CHAPTER 3

1. D. Kirp, *Improbable Scholars: The Rebirth of a Great American School System and a Strategy for America's Schools* (New York: Oxford University Press, 2015).

2. D. Berliner and G. Glass, *50 Myths and Lies That Threaten America's Public Schools: The Real Crisis in Education* (New York: Teachers College Press, 2014).

3. D. Epple, R. Romano, and R. Zimmer, "Charter Schools: A Survey of Research on Their Characteristics and Effectiveness," working paper (National Bureau of Economic Research, 2015), www.nber.org/papers/w21256.

4. J. Buckley and M. Schneider, *Charter Schools: Hope or Hype?* (Princeton, NJ: Princeton University Press, 2007); D. Dreilinger, "How 3 Top New Orleans Public Schools Keep Students Out," *New Orleans Times Picayune*, May 26, 2016, www.nola.com/education/index.ssf/2016/05/exclusive_public_schools_nola.html.

5. Epple, Romano, and Zimmer, "Charter Schools"; J. Henig, "Charter Inroads in Affluent Communities: Hype or Turning Point?," in *Hopes, Fears, & Reality: A Balanced Look at American Charter Schools*, ed. R. Lake (Bothell, WA: National Charter School Resource Center, 2013); P. Wohlstetter, J. Smith, and C. Farrell, *Choices and Challenges: Charter School Performance in Perspective* (Cambridge, MA: Harvard Education Press, 2013), 156.

6. Henig, "Charter Inroads in Affluent Communities."

7. See the appendix for information about the model used in this and all other statistical analyses.

8. D. Brewer and J. Ahn, "What Do We Know About Teachers in Charter Schools?," in *Taking Measure of Charter Schools: Better Assessments, Better Policymaking, Better Schools*, ed. J. Betts and P. Hill (New York: Rowman & Littlefield, 2010), 129–52; A. Egalite and B. Kisida, "School Size and Student Achievement: A Longitudinal Analysis," *School Effectiveness and School Improvement* 27, no. 3 (2016): 406–417, doi:10.1080/09243453.2016.1190385.

9. J. Angrist and V. Lavy, "Using Maimonides' Rule to Estimate the Effect of Class Size on Student Achievement," working paper 5888 (Cambridge, MA: National Bureau of Economic Research, 1997), www.nber.org/papers/w5888; Berliner and Glass, *50 Myths and Lies*.

10. C. Finn Jr., B. Manno, and B. Wright, *Charter Schools at the Crossroads: Predicaments, Paradoxes, Possibilities* (Cambridge, MA: Harvard Education Press, 2016), suggests that the higher student-teacher ratio in charter schools may be driven by virtual schools. Although I could not examine this possibility, because the data do not indicate if schools were virtual, the differences noted in the figure date back to the early days of charter schools, a time when there were few (perhaps no) virtual charter schools.

11. Buckley and Schneider, *Charter Schools: Hope or Hype?*

12. RPP International, *The State of Charter Schools, 2000: National Study of Charter Schools, Fourth-Year Report* (Washington, DC: ERIC, 2000), http://eric.ed.gov/?id=ED437724.

13. Epple et al., "Charter Schools"; Henig, "Charter Inroads in Affluent Communities."

14. D. Ravitch, *Reign of Error: The Hoax of the Privatization Movement and the Danger to America's Public Schools* (New York: Knopf, 2013).

15. N. Lacireno-Paquet et al., "Creaming Versus Cropping: Charter School Enrollment Practices in Response to Market Incentives," *Educational Evaluation and Policy Analysis* 24, no. 2 (2002): 145–58.

16. Finn et al., *Charter Schools at the Crossroads.*

17. Though the percentage of IEP students in a school is a useful metric, it's not perfect: the severity of the disabilities experienced by students with IEPs varies. In fact, there has been some concern that charter schools attract or recruit IEP students with higher levels of functioning, while public school students retain most lower-functioning IEP students, K. Boccella, "Battle Brews over Charter School Compensation for Special Education Students," *Philadelphia Inquirer*, August 23, 2015, http://articles.philly.com/2015-08-24/news/65773715_1_public-charter-schools-robert-fayfich-pennsylvania-coalition. If this concern has merit and is a practice across the nation, a school's official IEP numbers wouldn't give us the most accurate possible picture of its student body or teachers' experiences. Without a breakdown of the types of disabilities reported by students in each school, it was not possible for me to determine how big or general of a problem this is nationally.

18. Brewer and Ahn, "What Do We Know About Teachers in Charter Schools?"; Finn et al., *Charter Schools at the Crossroads*; Wohlstetter et al., *Choices and Challenges.*

19. M. Burian-Fitzgerald, M. Luekens, and G. Strizek, "Less Red Tape or More Green Teachers: Charter School Autonomy and Teacher Qualifications," in *Taking Account of Charter Schools: What Happened and What's Next?*, ed. K. Bulkley and P. Vohlstetter (New York: Teachers College Press, 2004), 11–31; J. Christensen and R. Lake, "The National Charter School Landscape in 2007," in *Hopes, Fears, & Reality: A Balanced Look at American Charter Schools in 2007*, ed. R. Lake (Seattle: National Charter School Research Project, Center on Reinventing Public Education, 2007), 1–15; Epple et al., "Charter Schools"; M. Exstrom, "Teaching in Charter Schools" (Washington, DC: National Conference of State Legislatures, 2012); Wohlstetter et al., *Choices and Challenges.*

20. R. Kahlenberg and H. Potter, *A Smarter Charter: Finding What Works for Charter Schools and Public Education* (New York: Teachers College Press, 2014).

21. Epple et al., "Charter Schools."

22. L. Darling-Hammond, "Teacher Quality and Student Achievement," *Education Policy Analysis Archives* 8, no. 1 (2000): 1–44; E. Hanushek and S. Rivkin, "Teacher Quality," in *Handbook of the Economics of Education*, ed. E. Hanushek and F. Welch, vol. 2 (Amsterdam: North-Holland, 2006); A. Wayne and P. Youngs, "Teacher Characteristics and Student Achievement Gains: A Review," *Review of Educational Research* 73, no. 1 (2003): 89–122.

23. Kahlenberg and Potter, *A Smarter Charter.*

24. R. Cohen, "When Charters Go Union," *American Prospect*, June 18, 2015, http://prospect.org/article/when-charters-go-union.

25. J. Carpenter, D. Doverspike, and R. Miguel, "Public Service Motivation as a Predictor of Attraction to the Public Sector," *Journal of Vocational Behavior* 80, no. 2 (2012): 509–23; B. Schneider, "The People Make the Place," *Personnel Psychology* 40, no. 3 (1987): 437–53.

26. Z. Oberfield, *Becoming Bureaucrats: Socialization at the Front Lines of Government Service* (Philadelphia: University of Pennsylvania Press, 2014); A. Van Vianen and I. De Pater, "Content and Development of Newcomer Person-Organization Fit: An Agenda for Future Research," in *The Oxford Handbook of Organizational Socialization*, ed. C. Wanberg (New York: Oxford University Press, 2012), 139–57.

27. J. Donahue, *The Privatization Decision: Public Ends, Private Means* (New York: Basic Books, 1989); C. Guarino, L. Santibanez, and G. Daley, "Teacher Recruitment and Retention: A Review of the Recent Empirical Literature," *Review of Educational Research* 76, no. 2 (2006): 173–208; Z. van der Wal and L. Huberts, "Value Solidity in Government and Business Results of an Empirical Study on Public and Private Sector Organizational Values," *American Review of Public Administration* 38, no. 3 (2008): 264–85.

28. See chapters 1 and 2 for theoretical reasons underpinning this expectation.

29. B. Fuller, *Organizing Locally: How the New Decentralists Improve Education, Health Care, and Trade* (Chicago: University of Chicago Press, 2015), 132.

30. T. Smith et al., "General Social Surveys, 1972–2012" (Chicago: National Opinion Research Center, 2013).

31. J. Perry and W. Vandenabeele, "Behavioral Dynamics: Institutions, Identities, and Self-Regulation," in *Motivation in Public Management: The Call of Public Service*, ed. J. Perry and A. Hondeghem (New York: Oxford University Press, 2008), 3.

32. B. Wright, D. Moynihan, and S. Pandey, "Pulling the Levers: Transformational Leadership, Public Service Motivation, and Mission Valence," *Public Administration Review* 72, no. 2 (2012): 206–15.

33. Van der Wal and Huberts, "Value Solidity."

34. This section does not study the relationship between the operational flexibility of a state's charter school law (as graded by a charter school advocacy group), as there were few a priori reasons to expect differences between this variable and school, teacher, or student characteristics.

CHAPTER 4

1. R. Budde, "Education by Charter: Restructuring School Districts" (Andover, MA: Regional Laboratory for Educational Improvement of the Northeast and Islands, 1988); Ted Kolderie, "Beyond Choice to New Public Schools: Withdrawing the Exclusive Franchise in Public Education," policy report 8 (Washington, DC: Progressive Policy Institute, 1990); M. Millot, "Autonomy, Accountability, and the Values of Public Education: A Comparative Assessment of Charter School Statutes

Leading to Model Legislation" (Seattle: Institute for Public Policy and Management, 1996); G. Miron and C. Nelson, *What's Public About Charter Schools? Lessons Learned about Choice and Accountability* (Thousand Oaks, CA: Corwin Press, 2002); Joe Nathan, *Charter Schools: Creating Hope and Opportunity for American Education* (San Francisco: Jossey-Bass, 1996); A. Shanker, "Restructuring Our Schools," *Peabody Journal of Education* 65, no. 3 (1988): 88–100; A. Wells, "Why Public Policy Fails to Live Up to the Potential of Charter School Reform," in *Where Charter School Policy Fails: The Problems of Accountability and Equity*, ed. A. Wells (New York: Teachers College Press, 2002), 1–28; P. Wohlstetter, J. Smith, and C. Farrell, *Choices and Challenges: Charter School Performance in Perspective* (Cambridge, MA: Harvard Education Press, 2013).

2. Budde, "Education by Charter: Restructuring School Districts," 20.

3. Ibid., 13.

4. D. Kirp, "The Wrong Kind of Education Reform: Three New Books Decimate the Case for Charter Schools and Vouchers," *Slate*, September 4, 2013, www.slate.com/articles/news_and_politics/science/2013/09/charters_schools_ and_vouchers_decimating_the_case_for_privatizing_public.html; National Alliance for Public Charter Schools, "What Are Public Charter Schools?," *National Alliance for Public Charter Schools*, 2015, www.publiccharters.org/get-the-facts/ public-charter-schools.

5. V. Opfer, "Charter Schools and the Panoptic Effect of Accountability," *Education and Urban Society* 33, no. 2 (2001): 201–15.

6. P. Weitzel and C. Lubienski, "Grading Charter Schools," in *The Charter School Experiment: Expectations, Evidence, and Implications*, ed. C. Lubienski and P. Weitzel (Cambridge, MA: Harvard Education Press, 2010), 15–31.

7. G. Miron and C. Gulosino, *Profiles of For-Profit and Nonprofit Education Management Organizations: Fourteenth Edition—2011–2012* (Boulder, CO: National Education Policy Center, 2013); J. Scott and C. DiMartino, "Hybridized, Franchised, Duplicated, and Replicated: Charter Schools and Management Organizations," in *The Charter School Experiment: Expectations, Evidence, and Implications*, ed. C. Lubienski and P. Weitzel (Cambridge, MA: Harvard Education Press, 2010), 171–96.

8. M. Levenson, *Pathways to Teacher Leadership: Emerging Models, Changing Roles* (Cambridge, MA: Harvard Education Press, 2014), 34.

9. Wohlstetter et al., *Choices and Challenges*.

10. D. Brinson and J. Rosch, *Charter School Autonomy: A Half-Broken Promise* (Washington, DC: Thomas B. Fordham Institute, 2010).

11. J. Crawford, "Teacher Autonomy and Accountability in Charter Schools," *Education and Urban Society* 33, no. 2 (2001): 186–201, compares teacher autonomy in Michigan and Colorado and finds, in sum, few differences. J. Crawford and P. Forsyth, "Teacher Empowerment and Charter Schools," *Journal of School Leadership* 14, no. 1 (2004): 62–84, look at the same data from the standpoint of empowerment and find that teachers in public schools felt more empowered than teachers in charter schools did. However, their analysis suggests that these differences may be driven mostly by differences in teacher experience: in both types of schools, teachers who were more experienced felt more empowered. S. Bomotti, R.

Ginsberg, and B. Cobb, "Teachers in Charter and Traditional Schools," *Education Policy Analysis Archives* 7, no. 22 (1999): 1–22, examine teachers in charter and public schools in Colorado and find mixed results. In some respects, teachers in charter schools were less empowered; in other ways, they were more empowered or there was no difference. J. Powers, *Charter Schools: From Reform Imagery to Reform Reality* (New York: Palgrave Macmillan, 2009), uses national data from the 1999–2000 school year and—comparing the mean responses of charter and public school teachers—shows that charter school teachers reported greater autonomy in the classroom. J. Christensen and R. Lake, "The National Charter School Landscape in 2007," in *Hopes, Fears, & Reality: A Balanced Look at American Charter Schools in 2007*, ed. R. Lake (Seattle: National Charter School Research Project, Center on Reinventing Public Education, 2007), 1–15, uses national data from the 2003–2004 school year, and like the Powers comparison of differences in means, show that teachers in charter and public schools have comparable levels of classroom autonomy.

12. L. Renzulli, H. Parrott, and I. Beattie, "Racial Mismatch and School Type: Teacher Satisfaction and Retention in Charter and Traditional Public Schools," *Sociology of Education* 84, no. 1 (2011): 23–48.

13. To normalize, the original response was subtracted from the minimum possible response; this difference was then divided by the difference between the maximum and minimum responses for a scale in a particular year.

14. U. Boser and R. Hanna, "In the Quest to Improve Schools, Have Teachers Been Stripped of Their Autonomy?" Center for American Progress, January 21, 2014.

15. See the appendix for information about the model used in this and all other statistical analyses.

16. Wohlstetter et al., *Choices and Challenges*.

17. E. Goldring and X. Cravens, "Teachers' Academic Focus on Learning in Charter and Traditional Public Schools," in *Charter School Outcomes*, ed. M. Berends and H. Walberg (New York: Lawrence Erlbaum Associates, 2008), 39–59.

18. B. Bozeman, *Bureaucracy and Red Tape* (New York: Prentice Hall, 2000), 12.

19. Wohlstetter et al., *Choices and Challenges*, 17.

20. S. Pandey and P. Scott, "Red Tape: A Review and Assessment of Concepts and Measures," *Journal of Public Administration Research and Theory* 12, no. 4 (2002): 553–80.

21. The question asked in Tennessee differed slightly: "Efforts are made to minimize the amount of routine administrative paperwork teachers are required to do."

22. G. Garn and C. Cobb, "A Framework for Understanding Charter School Accountability," *Education and Urban Society* 33, no. 2 (2001): 113–28.

23. Wohlstetter et al., *Choices and Challenges*.

24. The job security question varied slightly over the four waves of the SASS. On the 1999–2000 SASS, the question read "I worry about the security of my job because of the performance of my students on state *or* local tests" (emphasis added). For the 2003–2004 and 2007–2008 surveys, the question was "I worry about the security of my job because of the performance of my students on state *and/*

or local tests" (emphasis added). For the 2011–2012 SASS, the text was changed to read "I worry about the security of my job because of the performance of my students *or my school* on state and/or local tests" (emphasis added). The biggest substantive change—the addition of "or my school"—may explain the increase in agreement with this question in the most recent SASS (see figure 4.5). However, because the increase was consistent across public and charter teachers, this difference doesn't harm inferences about differences in accountability between teachers at particular times.

25. See ibid. for more explanation.

26. The teacher performance and evaluation questions were not asked on the Colorado TELL survey.

27. Garn and Cobb, "A Framework for Understanding Charter School Accountability."

28. C. Finn, Jr., B. Manno, and B. Wright, *Charter Schools at the Crossroads: Predicaments, Paradoxes, Possibilities* (Cambridge, MA: Harvard Education Press, 2016).

29. Brinson and Rosch, *Charter School Autonomy.*

30. B. Hassel and S. Vergari, "Charter-Granting Agencies: The Challenges of Oversight in a Deregulated System.," *Education and Urban Society* 31, no. 4 (1999): 406–28.

31. A. Stanger, *One Nation Under Contract: The Outsourcing of American Power and the Future of Foreign Policy* (New Haven, CT: Yale University Press, 2009).

CHAPTER 5

1. R. Kahlenberg and H. Potter, *A Smarter Charter: Finding What Works for Charter Schools and Public Education* (New York: Teachers College Press, 2014), 34.

2. A. Shanker, "Restructuring Our Schools," *Peabody Journal of Education* 65, no. 3 (1988): 99.

3. P. Wohlstetter, J. Smith, and C. Farrell, *Choices and Challenges: Charter School Performance in Perspective* (Cambridge, MA: Harvard Education Press, 2013).

4. California Charter Schools Association, "Charter School Teaching Jobs: Working at a Charter School," 2016, www.ccsa.org/understanding/working.

5. National Alliance for Public Charter Schools, "What Are Public Charter Schools?," National Alliance for Public Charter Schools, Washington, DC, 2015, www.publiccharters.org/get-the-facts/public-charter-schools.

6. Kahlenberg and Potter, *A Smarter Charter,* 29.

7. M. Levenson, *Pathways to Teacher Leadership: Emerging Models, Changing Roles* (Cambridge, MA: Harvard Education Press, 2014).

8. J. Christensen and R. Lake, "The National Charter School Landscape in 2007," in *Hopes, Fears, & Reality: A Balanced Look at American Charter Schools in 2007,* ed. R. Lake (Seattle: National Charter School Research Project, Center on Reinventing Public Education, 2007), 1–15; J. Powers, *Charter Schools: From Reform Imagery to Reform Reality* (New York: Palgrave Macmillan, 2009).

9. Teacher leadership questions weren't asked on the 2007–2008 SASS.

10. In 1999–2000, the statement about performance standards read "Setting performance standards for students *of* this school"; in the 2003–2004 and 2011–2012 surveys, it said, "Setting performance standards for students *at* this school" (emphasis added).

11. To normalize, the original response was subtracted from the minimum possible response; this difference was then divided by the difference between the maximum and minimum responses for a scale in a particular year.

12. See the appendix for information about the model used in this and all other statistical analyses.

13. In Colorado, the opportunities question differed slightly: "Teachers are provided opportunities to take on formal leadership roles in the school (i.e., mentor, instructional coach, etc.)."

14. Respondents also had the choice to indicate "Don't know"; if they answered this way, they were dropped from the analysis.

15. The question about appropriate levels of influence over decision making wasn't asked in the Tennessee TELL survey.

16. D. Pounder, ed., *Teacher Teams: Redesigning Teachers' Work* (Albany, NY: State University of New York Press, 1998).

17. Shanker, "Restructuring Our Schools."

18. H. Simon, *Administrative Behavior: A Study of Decision-Making Processes in Administrative Organizations* (New York: Free Press, 1997).

19. Wohlstetter et al., *Choices and Challenges*, 33–34.

20. C. Goodsell, *Mission Mystique: Belief Systems in Public Agencies* (Washington, DC: CQ Press, 2011).

21. J. Wilson, *Bureaucracy: What Government Agencies Do and Why They Do It* (New York: Basic Books, 1989).

CHAPTER 6

1. C. Finn Jr., B. Manno, and B. Wright, *Charter Schools in Action: Renewing Public Education* (Princeton, NJ: Princeton University Press, 2000), 115.

2. M. Levenson, *Pathways to Teacher Leadership: Emerging Models, Changing Roles* (Cambridge, MA: Harvard Education Press, 2014), 33–34.

3. D. Goldstein, *The Teacher Wars: A History of America's Most Embattled Profession* (New York: Knopf, 2014), 224.

4. J. Christensen and R. Lake, "The National Charter School Landscape in 2007," in *Hopes, Fears, & Reality: A Balanced Look at American Charter Schools in 2007*, ed. R. Lake (Seattle: National Charter School Research Project, Center on Reinventing Public Education, 2007), 1–15.

5. In the 2003–2004 survey, the wording was the same, but the emphasis, capital letters, was only used for the words "full week."

6. The wording differed slightly in 2003–2004: "How many total hours do you spend on ALL teaching and other school-related activities during a typical FULL WEEK at this school?" (emphasis in original).

7. See the appendix for information about the model used in this and all other statistical analyses.

8. M. Jerkins, "Too Many Kids," *Atlantic*, July 1, 2015; W. Au, "Teaching Under the New Taylorism: High-Stakes Testing and the Standardization of the 21st Century Curriculum," *Journal of Curriculum Studies* 43, no. 1 (2011): 25–45.

9. The class size question for Colorado teachers differed slightly; they were asked how much they agreed with the statement "Teachers have reasonable class sizes." A supplementary analysis that excluded Colorado teachers from the pool revealed no substantive differences from the findings reported here.

10. Goldstein, *The Teacher Wars*.

11. C. Finn, Jr., B. Manno, and B. Wright, *Charter Schools at the Crossroads: Predicaments, Paradoxes, Possibilities* (Cambridge, MA: Harvard Education Press, 2016).

12. Ibid.

13. J. House et al., "Occupational Stress and Health Among Factory Workers," *Journal of Health and Social Behavior* 20, no. 2 (1979): 139–60; C. Maslach and S. Jackson, "The Measurement of Experienced Burnout," *Journal of Organizational Behavior* 2, no. 2 (1981): 99–113.

14. S. Kim, "Participative Management and Job Satisfaction: Lessons for Management Leadership," *Public Administration Review* 62, no. 2 (2002): 231–41; J. Zelenski, S. Murphy, and D. Jenkins, "The Happy-Productive Worker Thesis Revisited," *Journal of Happiness Studies* 9, no. 4 (2008): 521–37.

15. H. Rainey, *Understanding and Managing Public Organizations*, 3rd ed. (San Francisco: Jossey-Bass, 2003); B. Wright and B. Davis, "Job Satisfaction in the Public Sector," *American Review of Public Administration* 33, no. 1 (2003): 70–90.

16. D. Organ and A. Lingl, "Personality, Satisfaction, and Organizational Citizenship Behavior," *Journal of Social Psychology* 135, no. 3 (1995): 339–50.

17. S. Dinham and C. Scott, "Moving into the Third, Outer Domain of Teacher Satisfaction," *Journal of Educational Administration* 38, no. 4 (2000): 379–96; J. Grissom and L. Keiser, "A Supervisor Like Me: Race, Representation, and the Satisfaction and Turnover Decisions of Public Sector Employees," *Journal of Policy Analysis and Management* 30, no. 3 (2011): 557–80; L. Renzulli, H. Parrott, and I. Beattie, "Racial Mismatch and School Type: Teacher Satisfaction and Retention in Charter and Traditional Public Schools," *Sociology of Education* 84, no. 1 (2011): 23–48; C. Rhodes, A. Nevill, and J. Allan, "Valuing and Supporting Teachers: A Survey of Teacher Satisfaction, Dissatisfaction, Morale and Retention in an English Local Education Authority," *Research in Education* 71, no. 1 (2004): 67–80.

18. D. Ravitch, "Eva's Success Academy Raises $9.3 Million in One Night," *Diane Ravitch's Blog*, April 21, 2015, http://dianeravitch.net/2015/04/21/evas-success-academy-raises-9-3-million-in-one-night; P. Tough, *Whatever It Takes: Geoffrey Canada's Quest to Change Harlem and America* (New York: Houghton Mifflin Harcourt, 2009).

19. M. Batdorff et al., *Charter School Funding: Inequity Persists* (Muncie, IN: Ball State University, 2010); M. Batdorff et al., *Charter School Funding: Inequity Expands* (Fayetteville: School Choice Demonstration Project, University of Arkansas, 2014); M. Batdorff et al., *Buckets of Water into the Ocean: Non-Public Revenue in Public*

Charter and Traditional Public Schools (Fayetteville: School Choice Demonstration Project, University of Arkansas, 2015).

20. Batdorff et al., *Charter School Funding*.

21. Finn et al., *Charter Schools at the Crossroads*.

22. Carnegie Foundation for the Advancement of Teaching, *The Condition of Teaching: A State-by-State Analysis, 1990–A Technical Report* (New York: Carnegie Foundation, 1990).

23. In the Colorado survey, the Internet access question was not asked, and three other questions differed slightly. The communication technology statement to be rated by teachers was "Teachers have sufficient access to reliable communication technology, including phones, faxes, and email." The professional support statement was "Teachers have sufficient access to a broad range of professional personnel." The instructional materials statement was "Teachers have sufficient access to appropriate instructional materials and resources." A supplementary analysis that excluded Colorado teachers from the pool revealed no substantive differences from the findings reported here.

24. D. Epple, R. Romano, and R. Zimmer, "Charter Schools: A Survey of Research on Their Characteristics and Effectiveness," working paper (National Bureau of Economic Research, 2015), www.nber.org/papers/w21256.

25. M. Exstrom, "Teaching in Charter Schools" (Washington, DC: National Conference of State Legislatures, 2012); B. Gross and M. DeArmond, "Parallel Patterns: Teacher Attrition in Charter vs. District Schools" (Seattle: Center on Reinventing Public Education, 2010); G. Miron and B. Applegate, "Teacher Attrition in Charter Schools" (Boulder: Education and the Public Interest Center, 2007); Renzulli et al., "Racial Mismatch and School Type"; D. Stuit and T. Smith, "Explaining the Gap in Charter and Traditional Public School Teacher Turnover Rates," *Economics of Education Review* 31, no. 2 (2012): 268–79.

26. Stuit and Smith, "Explaining the Gap."

27. Gross and DeArmond, "Parallel Patterns"; Renzulli et al., "Racial Mismatch and School Type."

28. Although we saw that the rating given to a state by a procharter organization—based on an assessment of operational flexibility—can be related to teacher characteristics like autonomy and accountability, the rating probably has little bearing on aspects like pay and burnout. As such, it is not considered here.

CHAPTER 7

1. J. Buckley and M. Schneider, *Charter Schools: Hope or Hype?* (Princeton, NJ: Princeton University Press, 2007); US Department of Education, *Strong Families, Strong Schools: Building Community Partnerships for Learning* (Washington, DC: US Department of Education, 1994); J. Epstein, *School, Family, and Community Partnerships: Preparing Educators and Improving Schools* (Boulder, CO: Westview Press, 2010).

2. A. Henderson and K. Mapp, *A New Wave of Evidence: The Impact of School, Family, and Community Connections on Student Achievement—Annual Synthesis*

2002 (Austin, TX: National Center for Family and Community Connections with Schools, 2002), 24.

3. W. Jeynes, "A Meta-Analysis of the Efficacy of Different Types of Parental Involvement Programs for Urban Students," *Urban Education* 47, no. 4 (2012): 706–42.

4. K. Taylor, "A Door-to-Door Push to Get Parents Involved at Struggling Schools," *New York Times*, September 8, 2015, www.nytimes.com/2015/09/09/nyregion/a-door-to-door-push-to-get-parents-involved-at-struggling-schools.html.

5. P. Wohlstetter, J. Smith, and C. Farrell, *Choices and Challenges: Charter School Performance in Perspective* (Cambridge, MA: Harvard Education Press, 2013), 15.

6. National Alliance for Public Charter Schools, "What Are Public Charter Schools?," National Alliance for Public Charter Schools, 2015, www.publiccharters .org/get-the-facts/public-charter-schools.

7. Buckley and Schneider, *Charter Schools: Hope or Hype?*

8. Decisions about school choice are often presented in this way—charter school enrollment represents an affirmative choice, whereas public school enrollment does not (J. Betts and Y. Tang, "The Effect of Charter Schools on Student Achievement: A Meta-Analysis of the Literature" [Seattle: Center on Reinventing Public Education, 2014]; Buckley and Schneider, *Charter Schools: Hope or Hype?*). However, many parents who choose public schools have made a choice. For example, the strength of a public school district, even if it is assessed informally, often plays an important role in shaping parents' decisions about where to live (J. Holme, "Buying Homes, Buying Schools: School Choice and the Social Construction of School Quality," *Harvard Educational Review* 72, no. 2 [2002]: 177–206). In this way, parents of students in public schools—if the family has the resources—may have made a meaningful choice about their children's education (choosing among public schools). Nonetheless, within a location that offers charter and public schools, there may be important differences between parents who choose a charter school and those who do not (G. Miron and C. Nelson, *What's Public About Charter Schools? Lessons Learned About Choice and Accountability* [Thousand Oaks, CA: Corwin Press, 2002]).

9. T. Deal and K. Peterson, *Shaping School Culture: The Heart of Leadership* (San Francisco: Jossey-Bass, 1999); W. Hoy, "Organizational Climate and Culture: A Conceptual Analysis of the School Workplace," *Journal of Educational and Psychological Consultation* 1, no. 2 (1990): 149–68.

10. A. Lopez, A. Wells, and J. Holme, "Creating Charter School Communities: Identity Building, Diversity, and Selectivity," in *Where Charter School Policy Fails: The Problems of Accountability and Equity*, ed. A. Wells (New York: Teachers College Press, 2002), 129–58; National Alliance for Public Charter Schools, "Facts About Charter Schools," National Alliance for Public Charter Schools, 2015, www .publiccharters.org/get-the-facts/public-charter-schools/faqs; Wohlstetter et al., *Choices and Challenges.*

11. In the 1999–2000 survey, this prompt was followed by the following direction: "Indicate whether it is a serious problem, a moderate problem, a minor problem, or not a problem in this school." Subsequent surveys did not include this direction, but the answer choices were the same.

12. The 1999–2000 item differed by asking about "parent involvement" rather than "parental involvement."

13. See the appendix for information about the model used in this and all other statistical analyses.

14. The specific prompt asked, "In an average week, how much time do you devote to the following activities during the school day (i.e., time for which you are under contract to be at the school)?"

15. Henderson and Mapp, *A New Wave of Evidence.*

16. S. Olson, *From Neurons to Neighborhoods : An Update—Workshop Summary* (Washington, DC: National Academies Press, 2012).

17. Joe Nathan, *Charter Schools: Creating Hope and Opportunity for American Education* (San Francisco: Jossey-Bass, 1996).

18. Because the community communication question differed significantly in Tennessee and Maryland, teachers from those states were excluded from the analysis of that question.

CHAPTER 8

1. J. Blase and G. Anderson, *The Micropolitics of Educational Leadership: From Control to Empowerment* (New York: Teachers College Press, 1995); T. Deal and K. Peterson, *Shaping School Culture: The Heart of Leadership* (San Francisco: Jossey-Bass, 1999); M. Tschannen-Moran and C. Gareis, "Faculty Trust in the Principal: An Essential Ingredient in High-Performing Schools," *Journal of Educational Administration* 53, no. 1 (2015): 66–92; G. Shannon and P. Bylsma, *Nine Characteristics of High-Performing Schools: A Research-Based Resource for Schools and Districts to Assist with Improving Student Learning*, 2nd ed. (Olympia, WA: OSPI, 2007).

2. R. Kelley et al., "Relationships Between Measures of Leadership and School Climate," *Education* 126 (2005): 17.

3. National Alliance for Public Charter Schools, "About Charter Schools," National Alliance for Public Charter Schools, 2016, www.publiccharters.org/get-the-facts/public-charter-schools.

4. K. Barghaus and E. Boe, "From Policy to Practice: Implementation of the Legislative Objectives of Charter Schools," *American Journal of Education* 118, no. 1 (2011): 57–86.

5. M. Gawlik, "Breaking Loose Principal Autonomy in Charter and Public Schools," *Educational Policy* 22, no. 6 (2008): 784.

6. D. Moynihan, *The Dynamics of Performance Management: Constructing Information and Reform* (Washington, DC: Georgetown University Press, 2008).

7. See the appendix for information about the model used in this and all other statistical analyses.

8. The Colorado survey asked a question about feedback, but the question was not comparable to this feedback question. For this reason, Colorado teachers were not included in the analysis of that question. The North Carolina survey phrased the shared vision question differently: "The faculty and staff have a shared vision." The results from the analysis were the same when teachers from North Carolina were included or excluded from the pool.

9. C. Heinrich, "Third-Party Governance Under No Child Left Behind: Account-ability and Performance Management Challenges," *Journal of Public Administration Research and Theory* 20, no. supp. 1 (2010): i59–i80; Moynihan, *The Dynamics of Performance Management*.

10. R. Walker, F. Damanpour, and C. Devece, "Management Innovation and Organizational Performance: The Mediating Effect of Performance Management," *Journal of Public Administration Research and Theory* 21, no. 2 (2011): 367–86.

11. E. Hanushek and S. Rivkin, "Generalizations About Using Value-Added Mea-sures of Teacher Quality," *American Economic Review* 100, no. 2 (2010): 267–71; D. Ravitch, *Reign of Error: The Hoax of the Privatization Movement and the Danger to America's Public Schools* (New York: Knopf, 2013).

12. Wohlstetter et al., *Choices and Challenges*.

13. M. Crocco and A. Costigan, "The Narrowing of Curriculum and Pedagogy in the Age of Accountability: Urban Educators Speak out," *Urban Education* 42, no. 6 (2007): 512–35.

14. The questions about local assessment data and teacher use of assessment data were not included on the Colorado TELL survey; in Tennessee, the question about teacher use of assessment data was phrased slightly differently: "Teach-ers in this school use assessment data to inform their instruction." The results from the analysis were the same when teachers from Tennessee were included or excluded from the pool.

15. B. Bass, "Is There Universality in the Full Range Model of Leadership?," *International Journal of Public Administration* 19, no. 6 (1996): 731–61; K. Leithwood and D. Jantzi, "The Effects of Transformational Leadership on Organizational Con-ditions and Student Engagement with School," *Journal of Educational Administra-tion* 38, no. 2 (2000): 112–29; T. Trottier, M. Van Wart, and X. Wang, "Examining the Nature and Significance of Leadership in Government Organizations," *Public Administration Review* 68, no. 2 (2008): 319–33.

16. Trottier et al., "Leadership in Government Organizations."

17. T. Kirshtein, *Charter School Principals' and Teachers' Leadership Perception Scores on the Five Dimensions of the Leadership Practices Inventory Instrument* (South Orange, NJ: Seton Hall University Dissertations and Theses, 2012).

CHAPTER 9

1. In drawing summative conclusions, I give most weight to the findings that emerged from the SASS, which is nationally representative and has the most robust set of control variables.

2. M. Berends, "Sociology and School Choice: What We Know After Two Decades of Charter Schools," *Annual Review of Sociology* 41 (2015): 159–80.

3. R. Ferguson and E. Hirsch, "How Working Conditions Predict Teaching Qual-ity and Student Outcomes," in *Designing Teacher Evaluation Systems: New Guid-ance from the Measures of Effective Teaching Project*, ed. T. Kane, K. Kerr, and R. Pianta (New York: Wiley, 2014), 332–80; H. Ladd, "Teachers' Perceptions of Their Working Conditions: How Predictive of Policy Relevant Outcomes?" working paper 33 (Washington, DC: Urban Institute, 2009); New Teacher Center, "Research Brief:

TELL Maryland Student Achievement and Teacher Retention Analyses" (Durham, NC: New Teacher Center, 2014).

4. New Teacher Center, "Research Brief: TELL," 13.

5. B. Gill, "The Effect of Charter Schools on Students in Traditional Public Schools: A Review of the Evidence," *Education Next*, 2016, http://educationnext.org/the-effect-of-charter-schools-on-students-in-traditional-public-schools-a-review-of-the-evidence; P. Wohlstetter, J. Smith, and C. Farrell, *Choices and Challenges: Charter School Performance in Perspective* (Cambridge, MA: Harvard Education Press, 2013).

6. NAACP, "Statement Regarding the NAACP's Resolution on a Moratorium on Charter Schools," NAACP, 2016, www.naacp.org/latest/statement-regarding-naacps-resolution-moratorium-charter-schools.

7. "A Misguided Attack on Charter Schools," op-ed, *New York Times*, October 13, 2016, www.nytimes.com/2016/10/13/opinion/a-misguided-attack-on-charter-schools.html?ref=todayspaper&_r=0; "The NAACP's Disgrace," op-ed, *Wall Street Journal*, October 16, 2016, www.wsj.com/articles/the-naacps-disgrace-1476653537; "The NAACP Opposes Charter Schools. Maybe It Should Do Its Homework," op-ed, *Washington Post*, October 11, 2016, www.washingtonpost.com/opinions/the-naacp-opposes-charter-schools-maybe-it-should-do-its-homework/2016/10/11/473bbb36-8d75-11e6-bf8a-3d26847eeed4_story.html?utm_term=.dc6e9c4ac336.

8. B. Bozeman, "A Theory of Government 'Red Tape,'" *Journal of Public Administration Research and Theory* 3, no. 3 (1993): 273–303; B. Bozeman, *All Organizations Are Public: Bridging Public and Private Organizational Theories* (Washington, DC: Beard Books, 2004); J. Donahue, *The Privatization Decision: Public Ends, Private Means* (New York: Basic Books, 1989); J. Wilson, *Bureaucracy: What Government Agencies Do and Why They Do It* (New York: Basic Books, 1989).

9. K. Meier and J. Bohte, *Politics and the Bureaucracy: Policymaking in the Fourth Branch of Government* (New York: Thomson/Wadsworth, 2007); Wilson, *Bureaucracy*.

10. K. Meier and L. O'Toole, "Comparing Public and Private Management: Theoretical Expectations," *Journal of Public Administration Research and Theory* 21, no. suppl. 3 (2011): i283–i299; M. Murray, "Comparing Public and Private Management: An Exploratory Essay," *Public Administration Review* 35, no. 4 (1975): 364–71; M. Poole, R. Mansfield, and J. Gould-Williams, "Public and Private Sector Managers Over 20 Years: A Test of the 'Convergence Thesis,'" *Public Administration* 84, no. 4 (2006): 1051–76; Y. H. Chun and H. Rainey, "Goal Ambiguity and Organizational Performance in US Federal Agencies," *Journal of Public Administration Research and Theory* 15, no. 4 (2005): 529.

11. J. Soss, R. Fording, and S. Schram, "The Organization of Discipline: From Performance Management to Perversity and Punishment," *Journal of Public Administration Research and Theory* 21, no. suppl. 2 (2011): i203–i232.

12. H. Kaufman, *The Forest Ranger: A Study in Administrative Behavior* (Washington, DC: Resources for the Future, 1960); Wilson, *Bureaucracy*.

13. Z. Oberfield, *Becoming Bureaucrats: Socialization at the Front Lines of Government Service* (Philadelphia: University of Pennsylvania Press, 2014).

14. H. Simon, "Organizations and Markets," *Journal of Economic Perspectives* 5, no. 2 (1991): 25–44.

15. Donahue, *The Privatization Decision.*

16. A. Stanger, *One Nation Under Contract: The Outsourcing of American Power and the Future of Foreign Policy* (New Haven, CT: Yale University Press, 2009).

17. J. Cox and C. Mason, "Standardisation Versus Adaptation: Geographical Pressures to Deviate from Franchise Formats," *Service Industries Journal* 27, no. 8 (2007): 1053–72.

18. Wohlstetter et al., *Choices and Challenges.*

19. E. Bardach, *The Implementation Game: What Happens When a Bill Becomes Law* (Cambridge, MA: MIT Press, 1977); M. Lipsky, *Street-Level Bureaucracy: Dilemmas of the Individual in Public Service* (New York: Russell Sage Foundation, 1980); J. Pressman and A. Wildavsky, *Implementation: How Great Expectations in Washington Are Dashed in Oakland* (Berkeley: University of California Press, 1973).

20. D. Ravitch, *Reign of Error: The Hoax of the Privatization Movement and the Danger to America's Public Schools* (New York: Knopf, 2013).

21. B. Farmer, "Teachers Go Door-Knocking in Nashville," *NPR.org*, December 4, 2014, www.npr.org/sections/ed/2014/12/04/365692610/teachers-go-door-knocking-in-nashville.

22. C. Finn, B. Manno, and G. Vanourek, *Charter Schools in Action: Renewing Public Education* (Princeton, NJ: Princeton University Press, 2000).

23. Ibid., 93–94; National Charter School Resource Center, "Effective Community Engagement Aids Charter School Development," *NCSRC Newsletter*, June 30, 2012, www.charterschoolcenter.org/newsletter/june-2012-effective-community-engagement-aids-charter-school-development; Wohlstetter et al., *Choices and Challenges.*

24. B. Fuller, *Organizing Locally: How the New Decentralists Improve Education, Health Care, and Trade* (Chicago: University of Chicago Press, 2015).

25. J. Cohen et al., "School Climate: Research, Policy, Practice, and Teacher Education," *Teachers College Record* 111, no. 1 (2009): 180–213; A. Thapa et al., "A Review of School Climate Research," *Review of Educational Research* 83, no. 3 (2013): 357–85.

26. National School Climate Center, "Measuring School Climate (CSCI)," 2016, www.schoolclimate.org/programs/csci.php.

27. C. Payne, *So Much Reform, So Little Change: The Persistence of Failure in Urban Schools* (Cambridge, MA: Harvard Education Press, 2008).

28. L. Cuban and D. Tyack, *Tinkering Toward Utopia: A Century of Public School Reform* (Cambridge, MA: Harvard University Press, 1995).

29. Ravitch, *Reign of Error: The Hoax of the Privatization Movement and the Danger to America's Public Schools.* A recent article by Carol Burris argues that charter schools are so opaque and unaccountable that they shouldn't be thought of as public schools: "Why Charter Schools Get Public Education Advocates So Angry," *Washington Post*, July 24, 2016, www.washingtonpost.com/news/answer-sheet/wp/2016/07/24/why-charter-schools-get-public-education-advocates-so-angry.

30. J. Madison, "Federalist No. 10: The Utility of the Union as a Safeguard Against Domestic Faction and Insurrection," *Daily Advertiser*, 1787.

APPENDIX

1. C. Maslach and S. Jackson, "The Measurement of Experienced Burnout," *Journal of Organizational Behavior* 2, no. 2 (1981): 99–113; Z. van der Wal and L. Huberts, "Value Solidity in Government and Business Results of an Empirical Study on Public and Private Sector Organizational Values," *American Review of Public Administration* 38, no. 3 (2008): 264–85; T. Smith et al., "General Social Surveys, 1972–2012" (Chicago: National Opinion Research Center, 2013); J. Perry, "Measuring Public Service Motivation: An Assessment of Construct Reliability and Validity," *Journal of Public Administration Research and Theory* 6, no. 1 (1996): 5–22; B. Wright, D. Moynihan, and S. Pandey, "Pulling the Levers: Transformational Leadership, Public Service Motivation, and Mission Valence," *Public Administration Review* 72, no. 2 (2012): 206–15.

ACKNOWLEDGMENTS

MANY YEARS AGO, my parents chose for their children a primary school that remains an exemplar to me: Media Providence Friends School was at once intellectually challenging and deeply caring; it was accepting of who students were, while trying to get them to think critically about who they wanted to be. In short, MPFS was (and still is) committed to the development of the whole child. I am grateful to have had this model in the back of my head as I wrote this book and thought about what makes for a good school.

More recently, when this book was just a germ of an idea, I had terrific student research assistants to huddle with and make sense of the vast literatures on privatization and school choice. Along the way, they helped me gather and organize data and make sense of the findings presented here. For this help, my sincere thanks to Linus Marco, Daniel Salem, David Cookmeyer, Ryan Baxter-King, Matt Novak, and Rachael Garnick. Also, thank you to Kimberly Benston and Fran Blase, and Haverford College in general, for funding these assistants and supporting this project in numerous ways.

As I designed the Delaware Teacher Survey, I benefited from the advice and experience of several excellent teachers: David Banister, Sophie Oberfield, Josh Oberfield, Lizbie Porter, Becky Porter, and Sally Tallmadge. When I turned from data collection to writing, I received considerable help and guidance, in the form of phone calls, meetings, or comments on draft chapters, from Jeff Henig, Chris Lubienski, Michael Ford, Jack Schneider, Tamar Hoffman, Heather Curl, Jack Buckley, Katy Bulkley, Robin Lake, Jonathan Cohen, Amrit Thapa, Michael Lipsky, and Hal Rainey. I am also grateful to my colleague Bret Mulligan—and our fuzzy friends Wilson and Pippa—for reminding me to periodically step away from the book and take a walk outside.

I presented parts of this work at Haverford College, American University's School of Public Affairs, the International Conference on Public Policy, the conference of the International Research Society for Public Management, and the Association for Public Policy and Management. Thanks to my colleagues in these venues for the many helpful comments and criticisms. I would also like to thank the *American Educational Research Journal* for permission to reprint parts of an article that I published there: "A Bargain Half Fulfilled: Teacher Autonomy and Accountability in Traditional Public Schools and Public Charter Schools," 53(2): 296–323, © 2016 Sage Publications.

This book would not have been possible without access to the School and Staffing Survey, conducted by the National Center for Education Statistics in the Department of Education and the Teaching, Empowering, Leading and Learning surveys, conducted by the New Teacher Center. I thank these organizations and the various officials who approved my request to use these data. In particular, thanks to Chelsea Owens, Amy Ho, and Jesse Rine, at the National Center for Education Statistics, and Keri Feibelman, at the New Teacher Center. Also, I am grateful to the many teachers in Delaware who took the time to complete the Delaware Teacher Survey and talk about their work in in-depth interviews. And thank you to Ben Jann for creating the Stata programs that helped me present the findings from this analysis more clearly.

Caroline Chauncey, the editor in chief at Harvard Education Press, has been a pleasure to work with from the beginning. She helped translate a work written by a political scientist, who typically writes for scholars of public management, to a book that is (I hope) accessible for teachers, education scholars, and policy makers. But more than that, I've appreciated her enthusiasm for the idea of the book and her warmth as we've interacted over email and the phone.

Finally, I thank my family. My parents, Lynn and Bill Oberfield, have a refrigerator magnet with a quote attributed to Cicero: "If you have a garden and a library, you have everything." When I think back to the home that my parents created, I think he's only partly right: you also need love. Luckily for me, our home had all three. I also thank them—and my Aunt Sally—for their help with raising our children. Seeing the connections forged across these generations fills me with hope and gratitude. Thanks also to my wife, Felicia Lin, for being so marvelously Fifi in so many ways. I love sharing a life with you and walking alongside our dear little ones, Theo and Charlie, as they navigate this world. I dedicate this book to you three.

ABOUT THE AUTHOR

ZACHARY W. OBERFIELD is an Associate Professor of Political Science at Haverford College. His research interests include schools, leadership, and street-level bureaucracy. He is the author of *Becoming Bureaucrats: Socialization at the Front Lines of Government Service*, which studies the development of police officers and welfare caseworkers during the first two years of their careers. It won the 2015 Best Book Award from the Public and Nonprofit Division of the Academy of Management.

INDEX